OBSESSIVE

DISORDER

OBSESSIVE COMPULSIVE DISORDER

Frederick Toates D. Phil., D.Sc.

Foreword by Hans J. Eysenck Ph.D., D.Sc.

Thorsons
An Imprint of HarperCollins*Publishers*

Thorsons
An Imprint of HarperCollins*Publishers*
77–85 Fulham Palace Road,
Hammersmith, London W6 8JB
1160 Battery Street,
San Francisco, California 94111-1213

First published by Thorsons as
Obsessional Thoughts and Behaviour 1990
This edition 1992

3 5 7 9 10 8 6 4 2

© Frederick Toates 1990

Frederick Toates asserts the moral right to
be identified as the author of this work

A catalogue record for this book
is available from the British Library

ISBN 0 7225 2912 0

Printed in Great Britain by
Mackays of Chatham, Kent

Contents

Foreword

A few years ago, Stuart Sutherland wrote a book entitled *Breakdown* about the psychiatric troubles which all but put an end to his academic career as an experimental psychologist. In this book, Frederick Toates, another well-known experimental psychologist, describes graphically his own troubles with obsessive-compulsive thoughts and ruminations, and gives the reader an opportunity to discover just how debilitating such thoughts can be, and just what they mean in the life of a busy professional man. Both authors clearly needed a lot of courage to disclose their troubles in public, and we owe a debt of gratitude to both for making it much easier for other sufferers to realize that they are not alone with their troubles, and to gain access to professional advice as to what can be done, and what cannot be done, in order to lessen their burden.

One might have thought that psychologists should know enough about the mind not to fall prey to such disorders, but this is not a realistic way of approaching the topic. Just as physicians often fall ill, or have physical diseases, so psychologists and psychiatrists quite frequently fall prey to psychiatric ones – indeed, unkind critics have often suggested that psychiatrists and psychologists frequently take up the study of their subject because they hope to find therein some help for their neuroses! As the ancients used to say: 'Physician – heal thyself!', and the attempts of these two authors to run the gamut of therapies offered on all sides is one of the most interesting aspects of their work. It will certainly be of considerable interest to all those who are suffering from obsessive-compulsive thought disorders, because usually the advice given to them is one-sided, and often based on ignorance rather than on thorough knowledge of what is available. What indeed can psychology do for the sufferer? It would be idle to pretend that we have foolproof methods of treatment which guarantee success, but equally it would be wrong to imagine that nothing can be done. This book discusses in considerable detail the methods used, and what is known about their success, as well as the author's own experiences with them. Anyone suffering from obsessive-compulsive thought disorders, and the attending anxieties and depressions, would be hard put to find a better survey to guide him in this labyrinth. It seems likely that Stuart Sutherland and Frederick Toates are shaping the beginnings of a new tradition in psychological writings, for the benefit of their colleagues as well as of fellow sufferers. Let us hope that this tradition will establish itself quickly, and that other sufferers from psychiatric disorders will come forward to write equally courageous accounts of their sufferings!

H. J. EYSENCK, Ph.D., D.Sc.
Emeritus Professor of Psychology,
University of London

Preface

This book describes unwanted, intrusive thoughts and associated compulsive behaviour. The thought that one's hands are contaminated, that one might have done a murder, that 2 and 2 might make five, are of this kind. They are irrational in the sense that they are at odds with the rest of the person's lifestyle and purpose in living. I have a peculiar dual interest in this subject, as both a psychologist and as a sufferer.

As a sufferer from obsessional neurosis over a long period, I have tried a large number of therapeutic techniques. I can't say that any method offers an absolutely reliable cure; one person's cure might only be a source of more suffering to another person. This is therefore specifically not a DIY book on how to cure obsessions in 12 easy lessons. If it were claimed to be so, the reader would rightly ask why I am not able to cure myself. It is perhaps more a *User's Guide* to the obsessional personality and disorder. All that I can offer is the view of an 'expert witness', with some leads that *might* help both the sufferer and those with whom they come into contact. I am saying to the sufferer 'You are not alone. In all probability, you are not on the first step towards insanity.' Even that message can be of considerable help to some people. In some cases, medical help proves to be of enormous benefit.

Admitting to mental disorder is rarely easy. Old prejudices die hard, even in the progressive circles of academia. Thus, for no entirely convincing or well thought-out reason, I have always had a strong reluctance about going public on this subject. However, in 1986, I read a book by a distinguished researcher in this area, Professor Graham Reed, of York University, Canada. So much of what Professor Reed had to say rang true for me, so I wrote to him to report my own observations. Professor Reed replied immediately, describing me as an 'expert witness' and urging me to go public with my story. At first I resisted. I did not look forward to the prospect of walking down the street mentally naked; neither did I want to provoke the ruminations. However, on reflection, I felt convinced that I had a useful contribution to make, and hence wrote the present book. The first version of it almost succeeded in omitting from the autobiographical section any reference to sex, thereby possibly implying that I had led a life of celibacy. It was soon pointed out that this was intellectually somewhat dishonest and from this criticism arose the somewhat more frank version.

By all estimates, literally millions of people in the UK and USA are suffering from this condition, yet many think they are quite alone in their bizarre disorder. Countless people are spending their days washing their hands, checking gas-taps and wondering why 2 and 2 make 4. Now is the time to come out of the closet! (no pun intended). I hope that my going public will assist this.

I would like to thank a number of people who have greatly helped in various direct and indirect ways in the production of this book. Julia Adams, Margaret Adolphus, Hans Eysenck, Graham Reed, Padmal de Silva and Madeline Watson read one or more versions, and their comments were of great assistance. An Open University student of mine, Maureen Blandy, pointed me towards the work of George Borrow.

Sometimes, as I ruminated endlessly over the exact choice of words, the music of Fauré, Mozart and Vivaldi, as well as Smokey Robinson, The Beach Boys and The Lettermen, not only helped to maintain my spirits but also gave me a standard of perfectionism to emulate. Finally, my students gave me much inspiration.

Note: The superscript numbers indicate references, and where the argument is taken further.

PART 1
Autobiographical sketch

1

Home in Histon

'It is by studying little things that we attain the great art of having as little misery and as much happiness as possible.' Samuel Johnson

At the time I am talking about, Histon was a small village, four miles from Cambridge. Living there were 'true villagers' and a few 'outsiders': a Pole and people from the surrounding villages. All the true villagers knew one another. The village sat between two very different cultures: on one side the dreaming spires of Cambridge University and, on the other side, the wild open fens. The academic tradition of Newton and Russell was far removed from the fen life of Willingham and Over.

I was born in Histon on October 23rd 1943. My parents reflected, to some extent, the two cultures. Though not a bad pupil, my father had left school at 14 to work for the Chivers family, whereas my mother had been brilliant at school in Cambridge, and earned a mention in *The Times*. The young Minnie Jean Maxim, as she was then called, came to work as a research chemist at Chivers, where my parents met. Intellectually and culturally they were very different, but much in love, with my father having dashing good looks.

In terms of income, we were working class, but we had a middle-class streak on my mother's side. My mother appreciated Handel's *Messiah*; my father had preferred motorbikes and amateur boxing. I had one sibling, a sister, Mary, 6 years older than me.

I had a number of fears as a child. Burglary was rare in 1949, but the prospect still bothered me. I tried to estimate what the chances were of our home being broken into. Suppose that intruders started at one end of the village, and worked their way house by house. How long would it be until they got to us? I was frightened of the dark, making shapes out of shadows on the wall and hiding my face under the sheets. In spite of all the love and security at home, here were the possible signs of trouble. However, it is known that fears and rituals are common in many children, so one cannot afford to place too much weight upon such evidence. Some relief from the fear of the dark was afforded by fantasy; night after night I imagined the bed to be the cockpit of an aircraft and I was the pilot, accompanied by an ever-faithful co-pilot named Doedie. We flew for miles over the fens of East Anglia, never crashing once; our control was perfect.

There was some neuroticism in the family. My paternal grandmother could be described as 'highly strung', as could my father, who suffered from spells of depression. These were never serious enough to be incapacitating or to merit seeking medical help. My impression is that we have more than the average share of fears and mild phobias in the family. My father is asthmatic, and hay fever is well represented. I recall my mother 'coming over funny' at the sight of liver in the larder, and my sister being petrified by a spider. The house in which I grew up was cold in winter, but the atmosphere was one of unambiguous security. Only twice did I see angry words exchanged between my parents and they seemed to be over matters of triviality. I was encouraged, and received devotion from them. I was fortunate to grow up in a secure matrix of wider family relationships; aunts, uncles and grandparents were all nearby and there was much contact.

School exposed me further to the two cultures: children from the fens spoke one way and those whose parents were associated with the University spoke a rather different English. A rich variety of expressions was acquired at school and taken home; not all of them were either fully understood by me or approved of by my parents. In spite of his own Cambridgeshire accent, my father made it clear that I was expected to speak correctly, using my friend Robert as an example. He added that in later life I would be laughed at if I spoke fen-English. This was all said in a fairly kind, or at least unintimidating, manner. There was the implicit assumption that good speaking was associated with good and morally desirable behaviour. So I was gently cultivated into some of the more easily acquired habits of the middle class. I was sent to piano lessons, but the teacher soon discovered that such talents as I might have possessed were not of a musical kind.

Life was somewhat straight, even Victorian and Calvinist. One was discouraged from displaying strong emotion. On one occasion we were on our way to Heathrow to watch the planes and, to my delight, a Lockheed Constellation coming in to land skimmed low over the bus. I was told not to get overexcited in public. Social respectability, hard work, impeccable manners and correctness of behaviour were emphasized. Taste in clothes was distinctly conservative. The model of behaviour that I acquired from my father was predominantly one of respectability and integrity, with a tendency towards conformity and deference to authority. There was a *they* out there who generally knew best. On the rare occasions when we visited a café, there was some pressure for all of us to order the same dish, in order not to be difficult. However, my father had a threshold of intolerance, albeit a high one; he could be stubborn when on rare occasions someone was perceived to be trying to get the better of him.

Honesty in dealing with money was especially firmly emphasized, as was the undesirability of asking what things cost or mentioning a person's income. My father was generous with money, but parsimonious with natural resources: we were always being instructed to switch lights off wherever possible. He was a 'green', years before the term came into vogue. When making tea for two, he would measure out exactly two cupfuls of water and boil just that amount.

On visiting my father in hospital, my mother issued instructions on correct behaviour: always to stand up when a doctor or nurse came over. At all times, the restrained use of the personal pronouns 'he' or 'she' in the presence of the person concerned was emphasized, the logic of which I had some difficulty understanding.

Not perhaps showing great originality, but certainly sincerity, I informed my parents of a burning ambition to become an engine driver. If I couldn't achieve that, then I wanted some other job on the railways – 'any job, even Swank's, when he retires.' 'Swank', a well-known village character, was the level crossing keeper.

Hard work, though seen as a virtue by the family, was not always to be viewed as an unqualified pleasure. One day, my father and I were walking through the main street and passed the time of day with some men digging a trench to lay sewage pipes. They were sweating profusely. Looking back, my father pointed to them and said quietly '. . . that is the fate that awaits people who don't try hard at school. But if you do well, then nice clean office jobs are available.' All this had the effect of giving me an awareness of social class, but certainly put no pressure on me. It was not said in a way likely to intimidate. In any case, we were part of the class that mattered most in a rural community, and cut across all other categories: the respectable.

The children of the village discussed their summer holidays and these were used as the index of our parents' status. Our own family's highest aspirations, of a week at Hunstanton or with relatives in London, did not place us towards the upper end of the village social scale.

Histon was then dominated by the Chivers family, who were devoutly Christian. The pub, The Railway Vue, was felt to be out of bounds to Chivers employees at lunch time. The family were held in high esteem in the village. It was with great respect that my father would greet 'Mr Stanley', 'Mr Oswald', 'Miss Hope' and 'Mr William'. They were a kindly and paternalistic family on good terms with their employees. The Chivers' orchards provided a means of earning pocket money for the children of the village, myself included, in the fruit-picking season.

Life in Histon was highly predictable. What to our social class was 'dinner' appeared at 1.05pm and tea at 6.05pm. Tea was invariably bread and Chivers jam, with the added luxury of spam at weekends. Each Saturday we caught the bus into Cambridge to do the shopping and visit my grandmother. During the week, the Chivers buzzer was sounded to announce the start or end of work. On hearing the 6pm buzzer, I would race to the end of the road in order to cycle home with my father.

It seemed that we had no enemies. The village behaved like an organic whole, everything ticked smoothly. I was never warned about the dangers of talking to strangers, possibly because there were no strangers in Histon. Everyone seemed to know their role in life, and there was no one to distrust, though there was an abundance of trivial gossip. I was made to feel that harm didn't come to someone growing up in that kind of environment. I acquired a naive and global trust in the goodness and integrity of my fellow humans, which I have found very difficult to refine in the light of experience.

In spite of the security, there was paradoxically also an insecurity instilled in us, in so far as the physical world was concerned. We tried not to sneeze within earshot of my father, since he was sure to ask whether we had caught a cold. We were regularly instructed never to go out with damp hair or without a raincoat, since you can 'so easily catch your death of cold'. On saying something like 'we will go to London in August', my father would invariably reply 'D.V. – God willing. Don't forget.' The world of people might well have been a safe one in Histon, but outside this shelter, life was dangerous.

I was oversensitive, wanted to be liked and make a good impression. If I thought I had caused offence then I would ruminate on the issue inordinately. As a joke, I told Frank, our neighbour, that I no longer liked the plums he gave us each year. My father later pointed out that, unlike his brother Jack, a noted village comedian, Frank didn't have a sense of humour, and one should avoid remarks that might offend. I was shocked. Too shy to go back and explain what I meant, I kept debating in my mind whether he had taken it in good humour, but couldn't convince myself. On being invited to Robert's house when I was about 12 years old, apart from finding his mother very attractive, I was conscious of attempting to do what was socially acceptable. Later I kept trying to recall exactly what words I had used. It worried me that there might be someone in the world who held me in a less-than-good light.

Histon Baptist chapel had been built by the Chivers family and my paternal grandparents were unquestioningly devoted to the

Lord. My own parents were not quite so devout, but nonetheless I was sent to Sunday school each week and taken to the evening service. Sometimes, I was allowed to take a book with me in the evening in case the lengthy sermon bored me. I was fascinated by, even awed by, my Aunt Winnie's copy of Bunyan's *Pilgrim's Progress*.

When a distant relative died it was explained that the body might be dead but the soul departs from it and goes to heaven. This intrigued me and stimulated much thought. Later, when my goldfish died, I gave it a Christian burial in the garden, marking the spot with a cross made from twigs and 'composing' a short requiem, 'This little fish is dead', to the amusement of the grown-ups.

Each summer the Sunday school went on an outing to Hunstanton. This was a major event in the life of the village; the sandcastles, the hard-boiled eggs dropped onto the sand, the deck-chairs and their incumbents wearing knotted handkerchiefs, were immortalized on film for the benefit of future years. I was taken for a ride on a donkey and my father ended up supporting me and, it seemed, the donkey, for most of the way.

There was much humour in the village, including the occasional practical joke, which I much enjoyed. In this and other contexts, like my father, I was blessed with a sense of humour. We were sitting one day on my grandfather's lawn and someone walking past stared at us. My grandfather turned to me and in a strong accent said 'Wha's 'e lookin' at?' 'E can go and sit on 'isn grass if he wants.' My emerging awareness of social class was such that, in school for some weeks after this, the memory of my grandfather's expression and accent would come into my mind, and it was very difficult to stop laughing out loud.

Sometimes I looked at my picture-books in church, but much of the time I listened to the service, learning the general notions of sin and goodness, heaven and hell. The prospect of hell-fire was to cause me some very real fear both then and in the future; it would doubtless have helped keep me on the straight-and-narrow for the next few years, had my social life been such as to permit anything to pull me off.

Then one Sunday – I guess when I was about 11 years of age – something the minister said made me wonder for the first time about where we all came from. If God created the world, who created God? When did time begin? I was of course not the first to wonder along these lines. What was perhaps odd was my intense fear. This was my first experience of something that in adults would be termed 'existential terror' and it made me very uncomfortable. For ages, I ruminated about this issue, of course getting nowhere. I was fascinated by the supernatural; ghost stories both intrigued and terrified me, sometimes literally bringing me to tears. I wondered whether I would suffer damnation if I mistreated one of my pet newts.

School was a mixture of pleasure and pain. I soon showed some of the makings of an intellectual, but, being a loner and non-conformist, didn't devote myself sufficiently to the formal curriculum. My mother helped me with French. I loved biology and collected various amphibians and reptiles at home, to the guarded horror of my parents, who were somewhat phobic towards them. I was put in charge of a museum at school, and made myself busy labelling owl pellets. Another great love was chemistry, and my uncle Ron (Maxim) who was a chemist in Cambridge provided me with some surplus equipment. He was a notable East Anglian photographer and had strong connections with the University, unambiguously a model uncle to me for intellectual development. My solitary pursuit of science grew into a devotion. One concession to normal boyhood was a fascination with model aircraft. I loved putting transfers of insignia on my models, and reflecting upon their historical significance.

Our annual holiday in London gave immense pleasure; the city was so full of stimulation. We were very much country folk coming to the big city. Once, shortly after arriving at Liverpool Street, we stepped into the road without looking carefully. A passing taxi driver called out to my father 'Watch it, dad! You're not in the country now.'

At school a sense of politics was awakened in me. My parents were Labour voters, though not with great conviction, and I identified with Labour. Once, when I eavesdropped on a conversation, I heard my mother inform my father that she had just been told about the headmaster's support for Labour. This made me happy. Other children in class were also identified by their politics, and we had lively discussions. By this time my ambition had got elevated from engine driver to Prime Minister. I would later settle for either working for the Labour Party or, very much as a third choice, at 'Butlins' in Cambridge, the local pejorative term for the civil service offices.

Life seemed simple; there was injustice in the world and only through socialism could riches be directed to those who needed them. I prayed to God for Socialist victories in various elections throughout the world, though I have no reason to suppose that this influenced their outcome. I wrote to the Labour Party for literature and read it avidly. This was where my heart was. I hated football and cricket, being rather hopeless at all sports; I couldn't stand getting dirty.

My thoughts, which were often of a morbid and egocentric nature, were recorded at length in a special book. I was subject to mood swings, my father sometimes asking why I looked so unhappy. Yet the prospect of a political discussion on the radio in the evening would bring great joy – pleasures in Histon for this 12-year-old were nothing if not simple. Friday evening was particularly exciting, since it was then that Freddy Grisewood presented the political discussion programme *Any Questions?* Innocent situation comedy appealed to me. In those days, my favourite was *Take it from here*, perhaps partly because it reminded me of neighbours.

I felt intolerance towards my father when he disagreed with me, and in retrospect he was so often right. At times, I felt the need to be different, to stand out from the crowd, by for example trying to persuade my classmates that I had psychic powers. My grand-mother's repeated praise of my red hair might have helped cement the notion that I was in some important regard different.

I started to read avidly paperback books about the war, something that my father tried in vain to discourage, regarding this as being psychologically unhealthy. 'Why not do the same things that other children do?' My morbid fascination with the war was often brought into discussions with classmates.

At the age of about 13, I decided to write a book on the case for nationalization. On the front was pasted a picture of a Western Region express train. Here was the perfect synthesis: the politics of Utopia and railways, a fusion so meaningful to me. With such credentials, why did destiny not lead me into becoming a vicar? I lent the work to my schoolmate Christopher, who in turn showed it to his father, a Conservative. It evoked the comment 'Not bad. At least he is not a communist.' I then wrote a short book about a traveller in the Soviet Union, much to the amusement of a gathering of our family in London.

At this early stage there were some clear signs of obsessionality. I was concerned as to where I would ultimately be laid to rest, feeling for some inexplicable reason that this should be in the USA. Rumour was that when the daughter of a certain atheistic professor at Cambridge died, she was simply buried in the professor's garden. This image caused me much distress. There was a perfectionist craving for peace and unity, and an intolerance of ambiguity. Ideas needed to be fitted into a whole, a world view, but this was inevitably frustrated time after time. One day a ticket collector at Waterloo was impatient in giving me directions, and for about two days this caused me to ruminate on the wisdom of nationalization.

During our holidays with my aunt and uncle in London, I spent much time on my own watching trains at Clapham Junction. Southern Region expresses in beautiful green livery rushing past the platform and destined for such exotic-sounding places as

Bournemouth put me on a 'high'. The names of their locomotives, *Biggin Hill* and *Howard of Effingham*, the smoke that they belched and the eerie whistles served to enhance the effect. But even in the midst of such excitement there was little escape from chronic worries about the Labour Party; indeed, the positive emotion seemed to trigger the associated doubts. Things wouldn't fit into a happy whole. Would the Gaitskellite right of centre, where I placed myself, be dominated by the left, with their policy of unilateral nuclear disarmament? Gaitskell seemed to represent a secure future, but how secure? I worried a lot that automatic, driverless trains would one day be introduced, since the train would lose its romance in the absence of a living being at the controls. Was it worth all this investment of time and emotion in a system that might be so dehumanized?

A somewhat eccentric and insatiable curiosity led me to visit various fringe political and religious organizations in London, the political aspect being much to the disapproval of my father. 'We will go back to Histon at the weekend if you can't behave like other people.' Though deviations from the norms of society were not welcomed, adherence to respectable middle-class behaviour, such as devotion to homework, was met with lavish and sincere praise. I attended a couple of seances at a spiritualist church in London, where I was offered messages, it was said, from a friend of the family who had been killed in World War II. Later, I compared notes with some others present at the seance. For some time after this I was even more than normally afraid to be in the house alone, though I had been somewhat encouraged by a medium telling me that one day I would make a significant contribution to science. Birdwatching was a passion of mine, and my father encouraged this. Each Sunday morning he would take me to the Histon sewage farm, equipped with binoculars and an identification book. I would avidly tick off those that we had seen. Occasionally, Mrs Schicher, a Quaker, took me to a sewage farm at Milton to look for greenshanks and other fascinating species. My parents regarded establishing contact with adults in Cambridge as evidence of great social confidence, but to me it was just normal. School discovered that I had a talent for public speaking and I was invited to address the parent-teacher association on the subject of spotting birds; I loved the limelight.

Aircraft held great fascination for me. I would cycle to Waterbeach to watch the Hunters. The annual Battle of Britain celebrations were a time of great excitement. On one such open day, my father took me for my first flight, a quick 10 shillings' worth, a thrilling 15-minute trip over Cambridge in a Dragon Rapide.

Usually I spotted trains alone at Cambridge, but sometimes on a Saturday, my father would take me to the main Cambridge to

London railway line. As a special treat, I was taken to Huntingdon to see expresses go through at high speed, an awe-inspiring afternoon. Then came the climax of my train-spotting career, a trip to Kings Cross as a special birthday present. The loudspeaker announced '*The Flying Scotsman* from Edinburgh will shortly be arriving.' My father and I raced to platform 5, just in time. The haunting sound of the A4 cow-whistle was echoing through the tunnel and one could see the light on the front of the engine. I was trembling with excitement. Here was the perfect synthesis, power, beauty, efficiency, patriotism and public enterprise. I looked with awe at the driver and fireman as they brought this fantastic beast to rest.

I was fascinated by the constituencies of Labour MPs, as listed in the Party diary; I learned ('collected in memory') most of these. Again in terms of collecting, I loved the *I Spy* books; one had to spot such things as a Dutch barn and a round church. Through the *Daily Herald,* my parents had purchased the *Odham's Encyclopaedia,* in 12 handsome maroon volumes. I spent hours poring over their pages, looking up foreign countries, reading about their imports and exports, learning their capital cities.

On reflection, it is easy to identify possible signs of problems to come – developmental precursors of unwanted thoughts. For instance, I became a devoted collector of stamps, London trolley-bus tickets and cheese labels, acquiring a large number of the latter from various countries. However, my pleasure in the hobby of fromology was contaminated by the fear that the cheese labels would fade in colour. I wrote to an expert to seek advice and he seemed surprised that this should be a matter of concern. 'Maybe they will fade in time, but that will be ages yet.' The dilemma that something worth having was also mortal, even a cheese label, was unresolvable. Its mortality detracted from its value.

I felt a fear of the 'ships that pass in the night' phenomenon. My parents had taken me on holiday to London to stay with my aunt Olive and uncle David. One evening we were walking in the King George Vth park in Wandsworth, and, as he so often did, my father struck up conversation with a stranger out taking his dog for a walk. The man related to us that he had been recently made a widower and asked about Histon and our holiday. After about 20 minutes, by its persistent tugging, the dog persuaded him to continue the walk. I experienced a deep sympathy for this old chap, a feeling of regret that he would probably never again cross my path. How might I be sure of meeting him again? I arrived at a plan, vowing that five minutes each subsequent day would be devoted to reviving and exercising his memory in my mind. This exercise had no compulsive quality about it; it was a voluntary plan of action. In this way, when we returned to London next year, I would be able to wander about the park, go up to him and say hello. I kept up the memory exercise for some weeks, but never met him again.

I showed excessive fear and sensibility as a child. Sad movies easily brought me to tears. After hearing the news that Arthur, a neighbour, had died while eating an orange, I later came over nervous after picking one up and recalling this. I caused headaches by acquiring food fads, regarding meat eating as being disgusting. Even when persuaded to toy with a small portion of meat, it was vital that the gravy should not be allowed to contaminate the vegetables. I felt the need to be able to categorize and demarcate foods. For example, if I had eaten cracker biscuits from a plate, I did not like fruit to come into contact with the crumbs.

The opposite sex evoked an uncomfortable mixture of desire, tension and confusion. Sex was not discussed at home, so I was left to learn from kids in the street, some of whom were anything but morally respectable. Fantasy played an inordinate role in forming my ideas. I was socially inept and didn't establish normal relationships with members of the opposite sex. Over time, I had crushes on various girls in the village, particularly Margaret, but never dared do much about it. I admired from afar. At best I would ask a good friend to have a word with her and convey my feelings. I felt strong frustration and speculated whether I would ever find a partner.

I had a crush on Barbara, a girl from Girton. In my fantasy, holding and kissing her drove me wild. Her uncle worked in a Post Office in Cambridge, and I would go in with the excuse of asking the price of sending a letter to somewhere like Canada. One day, we were on the sports field in Histon, and the wind lifted Barbara's skirt. That was awe-inspiring, such an erotic impact; the breathtaking image with its frustrating connotation of unavailability was to trouble me much.

I gave the advice to a friend that one should not acquire a girlfriend whose parents were in the forces (there were several airbases nearby). The logic was simple: the father could be transferred to Hong Kong and thereby take away the loved one.

A thought pattern seemed clearly to be emerging: life was frightening because of its transient aspect and one should try to protect against this in every way. Security and certainty needed to be built into life.

2
Leaving school

'Happiness must be something solid and permanent, without fear and without uncertainty' Samuel Johnson, Rasselas

After taking my O-levels, I left school to pursue a career in engineering science. I entered a traineeship programme with a scientific firm in Cambridge. One day and three evenings per week and in my spare time, I studied for the exams to allow entry to university. Two years after joining them, the firm were to support me at university.

The factory at first came as a shock to a naive and formally prudish school leaver. Well-worn and finger-printed sets of pornographic postcards were available on the shop floor, to help relieve the monotony. They evoked in me a mixture of self-righteous horror and erotic fascination.

I found some of my tasks quite intellectually fascinating. I recall devising a new method for inspecting the lamps that were destined for a scientific instrument and being warmly praised for my initiative by the foreman.

As a hobby I learned French and German. I had obtained the rudiments of French in school but this was not taught as a living language. So I bought some books and records, and in my spare time buried my head in the two languages. As I cycled to Cambridge, I would imagine everyday scenes in France and Germany, and speak the actors' roles to myself. This consolidated my learning. I guess that I must have shown the obsessional trait of persistence, since later in life I was able to lecture to university students in both languages, as well as Danish.

Sex was, as always, a problem. Still socially inept, I found the establishing of relationships an unsurmountable burden. My passions were ignited constantly but to no avail. I was concerned lest those girls I desired should fall into habits of impurity with someone else. That they might fall into impurity with me was a prospect that evoked considerably less dread. I was told that Pauline, whom I had long admired from afar, had been seen on King's Parade one night with an undergraduate. I solved some of my discomfort by reasoning that he might have been a theology student and therefore of impeccable morality.

One day I was taken ill with influenza and confined to bed. Thoughts of eternal damnation occupied my fever-ridden mind, and I was torn by conflict. Whatever it was that went on behind the cowsheds would have to be incredibly good to run a risk like that. Life without female contact might be frustrating for me but at least I was not risking damnation.

Each Saturday evening I would take the bus into Cambridge to join some of the workers from the factory for a pub crawl. My friends were older than me, and from them I learned the ways of the world; in exchange I offered gems of wisdom on subjects I had studied. I probably bored them with philosophy and the Labour Party. On one such evening, Len, a compulsive womanizer, introduced me to a friend, Jane, in the bar of The Still and Sugarloaf. Jane was considerably older than me, said to know a thing or two, and I soon learned that she lived in a caravan. She asked me to go to her home, so we said goodbye to Len and took a taxi. Although my morals were still in one respect prudish, such prudery concerned the behaviour of other people rather than myself, so I was not unduly disturbed at the prospect before me. It was there in a caravan, with a parrot looking on, that I lost my innocence, never to regain it. I can't say it was fantastic; in fact, I wondered whether that was really what it could be all about. I was terrified afterwards, spending a sleepless night thinking I might have caught some awful disease.

Life at home in Histon was not all cerebral, though most of it was. I avidly collected popular music discs, falling for the group The Lettermen. I bought everything they made, importing it from the USA if necessary. People told me that they sounded morbid. Now, 37 albums and 25 years on, I am still collecting them. Brand loyalty is surely a trait of the obsessional.

The firm wanted me to spend time in Germany to study engineering techniques and write a report for them. In my fantasy world, occasionally a Heidi or Ursula had entered the compartment of my train, and I had been able to play the naive foreigner role to advantage. Germany might provide a good foraging ground. However, on reflection, since I was on the lookout for a girlfriend here, I thought that Germany might disrupt my plans. It wasn't that Cambridge was bad territory; I was just an awfully incompetent forager.

Thoughts of going to university now aroused mixed feelings. I longed for the intellectual stimulation and big-city life, yet the prospect of being away from home created anxiety. I took David, a socialist working in the electronics assembly shop, into my confidence. 'Suppose', I said, 'that I meet a girl at university who lives far away, in Edinburgh or somewhere. What do we do when the university term ends? Would such a relationship be viable?' He had long been used to my posing what doubtless seemed eccentric and paranoid questions. He gave me a sympathetic hearing and answer. 'Cross that bridge when you come to it. There will be a solution.' But my inability to wait until reaching the bridge before planning the crossing was becoming very apparent. Every important crossing demanded meticulous planning. Each contingency needed debating; something of such monumental importance as finding a girlfriend could not be left to chance. Nothing must cause me to miss out on life.

3
Student life

'. . . the obsessive may gravitate toward endeavours that affirm an illusory acquisition of control, and shun "fuzzier" ones. He believes that he can someday solve, via intellectual effort and ultimate understanding, the governing laws of the universe.' Dr Allan Mallinger, The obsessive's myth of control

I went to the City University, London, to study systems science, which meant a broad introduction to science and engineering. I felt lonely in the big city but soon settled down. Some good friendships were established with fellow students in my lodgings in Muswell Hill. On learning that I had gained a place at university, Mr Chivers came to see my parents and offered financial help if this were needed. My father told Mr Chivers 'He takes after his mother, you know. Not after me!'

Each Wednesday afternoon was free from lectures and tutorials. This was so that students could play sport but I preferred to join the curious and morbid in the public gallery at the Old Bailey. I attended the trial of the Kray brothers and, after a four-hour queue, that of Dr Stephen Ward, involved in the Profumo scandal. It was exciting to hear the evidence and brush shoulders with the star witnesses, Christine Keeler and Mandy Rice-Davies – a new source of fantasy.

I went home some weekends to Histon. Once I was waiting at Cambridge for the train to Histon and a railwayman asked if he could help me. 'Do you know what has happened to the Histon train?' I asked. 'You don't know? They closed the line last month.' I was shocked and angry. How could a country perform such an act of stupidity and vandalism as to close its railways? The cost to the public purse in terms of the damage to the environment, extra load on police, ambulance and fire services, involved in a switch to road transport would be certain to exceed the so-called subsidy to the railways. I couldn't see the logic of it then and still can't today.

Within about 4 months of starting at university my mother was taken into hospital. One Friday morning, I received a letter from her, telling me that she was going home that day and looked forward to seeing me. At the end of the day's lectures, I went to

Histon. I was in good spirits, uplifted by the contents of the letter. However, Mrs Eden, a neighbour, saw me walking from the bus stop, stopped to offer a lift and reported that my mother was very ill. Surely this couldn't be right: her letter said that she was going home and wanted to see me. I should have read between the lines and judged by the handwriting, but I have never been good at that, tending to see only what I want to see. The neighbour dropped me at the house, and I entered to find my father in the kitchen in a distressed state. 'She is very ill,' he told me.

I went into the living room and spoke to my mother. She was clearly near to death and I couldn't be sure that she even recognized me, though I prefer to think that she did. I came out of the living room and fainted onto the kitchen floor. My father panicked, thinking I had died. I soon got up and he requested that I should go to bed and leave things to him. The next morning Peggy, a neighbour, came into my bedroom to tell me that Mum had died. I cannot recall any further details until that evening, when the vicar came round to comfort us.

My father was shattered by his wife's death. Any faith in God that he had, seemed to be lost. 'Why me?' was a natural reaction. Mum was cremated in Cambridge on the Tuesday, and I left for London that evening. I was given a sympathetic reception back at the university and did well in my end-of-term exams.

This was now the time for finding a serious girlfriend, and so I set my mind to the task. I met various nurses, always of high moral standards, who invariably told me disapprovingly of their associates of lower moral standards. Any disapproval I might earlier have shared was now overshadowed by a feeling of immense regret that I hadn't met the associate. This would keep me awake at night sometimes. On one occasion I did sleep with a girl from Wanstead. This was better than the experience in Cambridge, but the relationship did not survive.

Then I found myself a girlfriend and this made me even more attached to the big city, and the fun of being a student. However, I soon felt a compulsive need to ring up regularly to find out if she was OK. Then, sometimes after finding out that she was well and feeling happy, my memory would play tricks with me; I would need to ring back to make sure she was really all right. I told myself that there was something strange in her voice. The compulsive feeling that I should phone was at its worst when it was viable to phone. After midnight, when it would have been too late to phone, the feeling was somewhat less strong. I was very happy in her presence, but as soon as we parted I had awful withdrawal symptoms. There was no momentum in my psychological make-up, no resources to carry me over. We parted after a year.

After my final exams, I flew to America for a long holiday. I stayed most of the time in a YMCA hostel in New York City, and travelled around from this base.

One day I literally bumped into a girl crossing Times Square. I apologized, and she replied 'That's OK – I like your jacket.' This was wonderful: the excitement of a novel city and a new girl. We got closer and closer as the evening drew on, and she explained that she would be leaving NYC the next day by Greyhound bus. We could hardly retire to my room at the YMCA, so we found a cheap hotel, and I signed in as Mr and Mrs Stanford. My new-found friend rang her parents to explain that she wouldn't be home that night. The next morning when we got up I was thrilled on turning on the TV by chance to see The Lettermen. We parted after having lunch together, and exchanging addresses. I was then overcome with grief; I couldn't just leave a soul like that, and, in tears, something pulled me irresistibly to the bus station. I asked for help in finding her coach, but without success. It had just left.

I was sorry to leave America; I had enjoyed my month and had experienced so much. The Bristol Britannia flew me together with my withdrawal symptoms back to Heathrow. Life was a particular agony exactly one week after my chance encounter in Times Square: the passage of a unit of time since a particular event has always assumed a great significance to me. I couldn't play The Lettermen LP that I had been given, since it evoked nostalgia.

I had been accepted on an M.Sc. course at the City University, as a logical extension of the B.Sc., and started back at university in October 1966. It was suggested that I might do a project on the application of systems theory to biology, on the control mechanisms of the eye. A combination of systems theory and biology provided a very satisfying level of intellectual stimulation. I read avidly all the available literature and thought laterally about the results. In the end a novel theory of the eye's accommodation emerged and has subsequently been widely assimilated into the literature. I loved this work and knew that I wanted the future to be connected with biology or psychology.

As a student of City, I lived in a hall of residence, Northampton Hall, just off Moorgate. It was here that I met Ljiljana, who was from Yugoslavia and working temporarily in Britain. We married in 1967. I didn't think very much about whether I was making the right decision in getting married, which is perhaps odd given the normal obsessional tendency to ruminate interminably over choices. I bought *Teach Yourself Serbo-Croat* and used every spare moment to learn words and phrases.

One Sunday the newspaper carried an article by Stuart Sutherland, professor of psychology at Sussex. Amongst other things, Sutherland suggested that it would be useful for engineers to come into experimental psychology, bringing their systems understanding to behavioural research. This seemed to be just the cue for which I had been waiting. I wrote to him, was given an interview by Keith Oatley and Professor Sutherland, and accepted to do research towards the degree of doctor of philosophy.

None of us could have supposed just how cruelly the peace of that enthusiastic group was to be shattered in the near future. Stuart Sutherland was to suffer a crippling mental breakdown, recorded in detail in his autobiographical book. I was to suffer obsessional illness combined with depression.

The research topic suggested to me for my doctorate was motivation theory, with particular reference to the biological bases of thirst and drinking. I contacted the firm where I had been employed in Cambridge, explaining the situation and my wish to move out of engineering. They generously wished me well in the new career, saying that, if it didn't work out, to let them know. A holiday was now called for.

Ljiljana and I flew to the Croatian capital, Zagreb. Even with an awareness of the danger of clichés, I can say that I fell in love with Yugoslavia. A romantic streak in me felt empathy for the simple peasant lifestyle, though whether I would ever elect to live it remains a moot point. Provided that the people spoke slowly, I could follow a lot of what they were saying. They sometimes laughed at me when I spoke to them, and not seeing that the content was particularly funny, I assumed that this was a reaction either to my accent or to mistakes. Croatian with its three genders and seven cases presents a rich scope for errors. However, they insisted that it was for neither reason, but just that it sounded funny for a foreigner to speak their language.

On returning to Brighton, I started as a postgraduate student at Sussex. In London, university had been rather straight and conservative. Sussex was to be neither. I was struck by the sheer volume of hair in the university, hair everywhere and growing in various places and directions. The revolutionary left was much in evidence in student affairs: Maoism, Trotskyism and Stalinism. This was a very different socialism to the safety of Attlee and Gaitskell. I staged my own revolt by moving much further to the right, an aberration that would be corrected in time.

I was kept extremely busy at Sussex, working strange and unsocial hours to fit in with the nocturnal habits of rats. It made for a rich source of intellectual stimulation but hardly promoted marital harmony. I loved the work. I could not imagine any pursuit in life that could give me as much pleasure as this. I would sometimes have pleasant dreams of rats.

I read avidly and was most impressed with the writings of B. F. Skinner. His optimistic vision of a utopian society that eschewed punitive measures and was run along positive reinforcement lines was attractive to me. It fitted my own belief that there had to be one right solution to the world's problems. Our task consisted in slowly moving towards this solution.

The delight of being at Sussex was occasionally tempered by obsessional thinking. I used to dread my birthday, since it reminded me of the fact that I was getting older all the time. One day I heard a radio broadcast in which an obsessional was describing her inability to accept the finite nature of existence. I felt that I was a bit like that too. Things were however very safely within bounds.

I had always suffered from the occasional nightmare and had even been found sleepwalking outside the house in Histon. Now nightmares were more frequent than before. Their content was of a bizarre nature, consisting of such regular themes as torture and reptiles entering the bedroom. Very occasionally, both then and since, a grief theme has been present. A Freudian would have a field day with such events, but I would be more cautious.

At the end of my doctorate, Keith Oatley applied for 2 years' money, so that I could stay as a research fellow in the area of motivation. Sussex was a stimulating environment in which to do research in psychology. Almost everyone of significance in the subject paid a visit, including B. F. Skinner. Brighton was a delightful town. I regarded myself as a most fortunate person to be doing exactly what I wanted in life in such surroundings.

Each summer, Ljiljana and I spent about a month in Yugoslavia and our relatives came over to stay with us. In 1971 two strange things happened to me. We ascended a tower at Zagreb in order to get a view over the whole city. Up till then I had experienced no fear of heights. Indeed, only 5 years earlier, I had positively enjoyed looking at New York City from the top of the Empire State Building. Now I was really frightened and wanted to come down as soon as possible. A few days later, we were flying back to London, a perfectly normal and regular flight, just like one of the many I had experienced. But suddenly I was terrified. My terror was of one thing only – death – the prospect of a crash. I came out in a cold sweat and shook with fear. On getting to Heathrow, I felt that I would never again be able to get into an aircraft.

Unfortunately, after 5 years, our marriage was near to an end. I found myself unable to resist the temptations of the swinging sixties and we parted. I met Gill, who announced she was in an open marriage and was a 'swinger type'. This helped to complete my education. Alas, my wife did not share my newly-found 'progressive' ideas. I regretted our parting but accepted that it was probably the best solution. It was a divorce not just from a person, but from a whole culture, and a vacuum was left. Ljiljana returned to Yugoslavia, and though this time was not easy, I was not left shattered by it. My mind was soon to be occupied with Denmark.

4
Denmark – almost heaven

'Look round and tell me which of your wants is without supply: if you want nothing, how are you unhappy?' Samuel Johnson, Rasselas

I felt the wish to travel and experience a new culture. My attention was drawn to a job as assistant professor at Odense University. Feeling myself to be suitable, I wrote off, and with eager anticipation awaited a reply. Academic jobs were easier to find then than now. Nonetheless, career prospects were a serious consideration. After 2 months, I had given up all hope of hearing from Denmark, and started to negotiate a job in West Germany. Then a letter arrived, with an invitation to attend for an interview the next week. I took the ferry, and arrived at the flat of Inga, a former colleague from Sussex, in Copenhagen, ready to go the following day to Odense.

Excitement at the prospect of living in this country filled me as I travelled to Odense. I was interviewed and asked to give a lecture, in English, to a student class. Shortly afterwards the professor informed me that the lecture had been well received and that I was offered the job, subject to the formality of senate approval. Words fail me to convey my feeling of total and unqualified euphoria.

Having the chance to sit alone and reflect on the decision, in the train from Odense back to Copenhagen, the euphoria grew. It was a beautiful evening and the scent of the breeze through the window could only confirm the mood of pure pleasure. This was truly a 'peak experience'; I felt that I had come a long way from humble beginnings. Now I could exploit singular and selfish ecstacy. There might have been wars and famine in the world but, right now, the fact that these didn't fit into an acceptable overall perspective need not bother me. The world of my primary concerns simply looked and felt good, and for just a little while that was all that mattered.

At Nyborg two Danish men got into the compartment, the one somewhat more drunk than the other. They carried on drinking in the train but this seemed not to affect their ability to speak good English. When the train crossed the Kattegat on the ferry, they invited me to join them in the bar. What a delight was the sea breeze blowing gently across the ferry, and surely no expensive wine had ever tasted quite so good as the cheap label on offer in that bar. On arriving at Copenhagen, the less-drunk asked if I would take care of the more-drunk, while he went to seek help. We propped him up and I stabilized him against a wall until help arrived. A policeman asked if all was well, and I assured him that it was. This was a great introduction to Denmark. That evening, Inga and I celebrated the good news by going out for a meal.

In the remaining two days of the stay, there was much for me to see in Copenhagen, the zoo, the Tivoli Gardens and, of course, the mermaid in the harbour, intact with head again. The rough and lively harbour bars were a joy to visit, as was Istergade, then the world's pornography centre. This was an erotic eye-opener; the clandestine black-and-white loan-service in the factory at Cambridge had nothing to compare with this technicolour.

I returned to England in a good mood; withdrawal symptoms were cancelled by the eager anticipation of a new way of life and the practical tasks involved in moving abroad. Odense University telephoned to announce senate approval of my filling the post. My thoughts turned to learning to speak Danish, and so I acquired a 'Teach Yourself Danish' course. Over the next few weeks, the record player relayed a set of phrases and stories in Danish; while shaving, cooking and eating, I was incessantly bombarded at each possible moment. I enjoyed these sessions of language absorption, in the company of Linguaphone's Copenhagen family, the Hansens. I soon made good progress in my fifth language. That wonderful feeling of being able to monitor one's progress exactly was with me, as I gained in confidence.

As the date for my departure drew near I worried that something might go wrong. Keith Oatley, my supervisor, gave me advice, as best he could, probably feeling that these conversations were taking creative worrying to ridiculous lengths. Would I get my work permit? Would the Danes decline EEC membership, and not want foreigners in the country? The work permit arrived safely, just as Keith said it would. I had not been taken ill at the last minute.

September 1972 saw my departure from England by boat, with all my worldly possessions in three large suitcases. I stopped off briefly in Odense to organize myself, and then left for a week's holiday in Sweden. The holiday was a delight, but at the end I was glad to board the Stockholm–Copenhagen sleeper to take up residence in Denmark.

The weather was excellent and the suburbs of Copenhagen, their houses flying the red and white Danish flag, and the stirring of activity on a new day, provided a welcome sight in the early morning sun. This country was growing on me fast.

The professor at Odense showed me my office and then we went to the university flat that had been allocated to me. Just a few minutes' walk from the university, it was ample for all requirements. The first day brought an invitation from a lecturer to have an early dinner with him that evening. Before going out, I took a shower in my new-found home, and felt simply ecstatic. How could life have so much to offer? But it was to have still more. Søren W. asked me in and opened a bottle of wine. 'Let's drink to your promotion', he said. – 'But, what promotion?' – 'They didn't tell you? You have just been made into a full lektor of the university.' Reflecting on Histon and on the university here, I glowed inwardly and raised my glass. Were there no limits to how good life could be?

Søren had an evening engagement and I decided to spend the remainder of the evening wandering around the town centre. On entering a bar, I was recognized by some students who had been at my interview lecture. They invited me to join them for a drink and then took me on to a disco. Whenever I hear Don McLean's 'American Pie', memories of that lovely evening are revived. The taxi taking me home got hopelessly lost in the fog and I was most impressed when, finally arriving at my flat, the driver refused to take any money for the fare. Here was a reminder of the moral scruples of my upbringing. The following night I went out for a meal with Winnie whom I had met on the ferry and who taught in Odense.

I began work very diligently, by starting to prepare lecture notes. When finally convinced that the teaching plans were in order, I turned to research and working on my first book, which had been started at Sussex. The first lecture series was to be given in English, while I was busy working at Danish. The university ran a course 'Danish for foreigners' which I attended, together with twelve others, including a Yugoslav, a German and a Nigerian. Our only common tongue was Danish, and like foreigners everywhere, in our conversations we sought a bond by tending to exaggerate the eccentricities of our host country.

Television helped a lot with the language since half of the programmes were in English with Danish subtitles. Of the rest, a significant number were German, French or Swedish, so watching TV served as a congenial language laboratory. My German and French improved, as well as Danish. The staff–student liaison body was told by their student representative that my lectures were much appreciated, a tit-bit of nice news relayed to me by Søren A. There were occasionally language problems, but for the most part the students understood English well.

Denmark seemed such a small country, almost having the feel of a village about it. I was regularly able to swoon over its glamorous Minister of Education and MP for Odense, Ritt Bjaergaard, shopping in the local supermarket. On writing a letter one day to the Minister of Transport, Jens Kampmann, concerning a traffic scheme, I asked a friend where to obtain the address. 'In the phone-book, under Kampmann' was the answer. So I sent it to his private address and got a handwritten reply.

Within about a month of arriving, I was introduced to a research assistant in physiology, named Mette. The following evening, Mette and I visited a disco, where 'good vibes' echoed between us. In the next few weeks I spent little time in my own flat, preferring to be with Mette in her house in Fruens Bøge, a suburb of Odense.

Christmas 1972 brought an invitation to Mette's parents' home in Valby. They lived in a large old house. This was a time for visiting relations, drinking and eating plenty. This is what Danes call *hyggeligt*, a word having no obvious English equivalent but is epitomized by a group of Danes sitting around a fire in a comfortable flat and eating chocolates. By now I was fairly competent at Danish and could participate in the conversation. In Mette's family, meals were a grand affair, with different glasses for red and white wine.

After Christmas, the family were invited for a big get-together by Mette's grandparents. Drink was flowing freely and the conversation was good. Switching between Danish and English meant that everyone had a turn at exercising their foreign tongue. However, at the time of taking coffee, something was wrong; I was feeling sad. I had started to think about the killings in Northern Ireland and to compare my lot with that of the rest of the human race. I was not feeling any sort of guilt; hard work had got me to the University. I had no frustration in life, by any flight of the imagination. I had everything that I could have dreamed of. I had no suppressed anger or, if I did, then I had suppressed it so well that I knew nothing of it. As an undergraduate, I had read about the ancient philosophers who warned of the perils of pleasure being turned into pain. Samuel Johnson had waxed eloquent on the same theme, in his classic *Rasselas*, but now all of this was happening to me and it was awful. It was agony.

This was a strange variety of sadness. I excused myself from the table and went into the study. The walls were covered with old family photographs, handsome blond Danes, and as I glanced at them I was feeling a distinct emotion, perhaps best described by the word 'grief'. But why? I was not grieving for anyone, not even missing anyone. No one had died or gone away. But this did not seem to matter; the object of my grief was the fragility of life, that life is uncertain, that the human condition is a precarious one. How long could the good life last? What had led me to this luxury, while others were being bombed and shot? I was not responsible for their suffering and I was not guilty over it, but I was being powerfully reminded that nothing is certain. These thoughts passed through my mind but words cannot capture the existential terror that I felt, the fear that one day *what is* will be no more. Mette was alive and well in the next room but things could be otherwise. She came into the study to see how I was and I burst into tears. 'What's wrong? Have I done something? Has someone offended you?' I tried to explain that it was because life was so good that I felt so sad, but this inverse logic made little sense to her. How can one explain disembodied grief? What sense does anticipatory grief make? What was happening to me?, I asked myself. I had everything that I could possibly dream of. Why was I sad? The paradise of Denmark seemed to be showing its first sign of turning sour.

5
Signs of trouble ahead

'Thus, a dead fly was in my phial, poisoning all the pleasure which I could otherwise have derived from the result of my brain sweat.' George Borrow, Lavengro

After the new year, we took the train back to Odense. I was sorry to leave Mette's family but looked forward to getting back to the students. The holiday had been mixed; it was mainly good fun and relaxation but had been contaminated by the episode of sadness. I wondered about what had set off this negative reaction, but in general life felt very positive.

I was getting better at Danish all the time and took evening classes in sociology where I was able to participate fully in discussions. Being a Copenhagener, Mette occasionally spoke about our moving from small-town Odense but I resisted. Life had just become so good to us, and I didn't want any better, at least not yet. I would move to Copenhagen, yes, but not to another country, except perhaps Sweden. She accepted this and stopped talking about moving overseas.

In February 1973, Mette went with her family on a long-arranged skiing trip to Norway. Although it was only for one week, the thought of her going evoked dread in me. I saw her off on the Copenhagen train, with a lump in my throat. This was like being at a funeral. I felt shattered, scared and alone, but couldn't say exactly why. I had some good friends in the university and in the evening classes. There was nothing concrete to fear or feel sad over. Mette would soon be back. I was not worried that she would leave me for someone else. She was unlikely to come to harm on the gentle slopes of Norway. The job at the University was going brilliantly. But it was like the morbid experience in Valby: the same feeling of grief all over again, as if Mette had died.

Using emotional blackmail, I had tried for some time to persuade Mette to give up smoking, showing the trait well known amongst obsessionals of trying to reform their loved ones. Mette promised that while in Norway she would make a special effort to give up.

After seeing the train off, I went straight back to work, but was unable to concentrate. Proofreading with the secretary, the task assigned for the afternoon, proved impossible. I was desperately fighting back the tears and she could see it. So I went home to weep. On Saturday evening I was invited to dinner with some friends and, not yet having a phone of our own, used theirs to call Norway. Speaking to Mette cheered me up. I felt quite good for the remainder of the week.

Mette returned from Norway, still smoking but looking beautifully brown. We took a taxi from Odense station to our home in Fruens Bøge and it felt so good to be together. Life went on very well for some months, with no abnormal behavioural reactions or mental events.

A year in Denmark passed, and all-in-all it had been an excellent period. The lectures were well received. The book was with the publishers. I had been back to England to see my father. In a confident mood, I announced that in future all my lectures were to be in Danish. The University agreed that this would be desirable. There was so much to think about and so much to do.

At about this time, I perceived that something strange was starting to happen. While engaged in, say, reading a book or looking out of a train window, unpleasant thoughts were appearing in my consciousness. They concerned tragedy, illness and death, and always had the common theme 'The good life will not last'. At first seldom in their appearance, but getting more and more frequent, these thoughts both depressed and scared me. They detracted from the pleasure of life, contaminating the experience that otherwise was on offer.

There was some continuity from the past in that I had always been a chronic worrier, often seeing particular disasters ahead. Somewhat similar themes had occasionally arisen before but these thoughts were now rather different in form. They were gratuitous and exaggerated, alien and irrelevant to my activity and plans. They were frequent and insistent. The unwelcome intrusions would have their frightening effect and then go away, to leave me with the thought patterns that I wanted. Some of the intrusions concerned my own vulnerability and mortality, and others concerned Mette, but the generic theme was always 'This heaven of Denmark will not last for ever'. 'Doesn't that detract from its current value?'

Typically, thoughts about my current academic pursuit would switch out and my own death would take over for about 30 seconds, sometimes for much longer. Then about 10 minutes later, Mette's death would be presented to my consciousness. The obsessional nature of the thoughts was characterized by their taking over, their blocking of my voluntary course of mental activity. The thoughts intruded and threw me off course; I needed to get back into the logical flow of the scientific discourse.

To try quantifying the unquantifiable, I would say that these intrusions both frightened and depressed me in about equal proportions. Sometimes their fear-evoking power was dominant and at other times I would describe them as more depressing or frustrating than frightening.

At times it seemed that specific and appropriate cues triggered the thoughts, such as reading an obituary or seeing a news report on the Vietnam war. More often, they appeared just to be spontaneous or 'free-floating'. My intrusions have never been associated with a standard automatic 'neutralizing' thought or ritual (see page 83 for a discussion of neutralizing thoughts). The only time that counter-thoughts (i.e. a thought which attempts to 'cancel out' the original intrusive thought) have been present is when I have tried as a conscious strategy to devise them, and no given counter-thought has ever remained in use by me for any substantial length of time.

Sometimes the thoughts suggested no obvious course of action. In such cases, the intrusion of death would take a passively-associated form; simply the certainty and unavoidability of death would occupy me. At other times the thoughts concerned the prospect of a particular mode of death in the near future and urged a course of action to avoid it. Typically I would read about the numbers killed on the road from Copenhagen to Odense, and this would form the principal theme of the spontaneous obsessions for some days. It might lead me to take the train and decline the lift that had already been accepted. Not wishing to talk about the ruminations, I always found a rational excuse to present to others, such as that there was a paper I had to read, and 3 hours on the train to Copenhagen would allow this.

I experienced inordinate difficulty in arriving at certain decisions, for example buying things in a supermarket. I would select some Israeli oranges, and then imagine that they might have been poisoned, so I would return them to the shelf and select some Chilean grapes. I would then imagine these to have been contaminated by either the CIA or the KGB, according to the current political climate in Chile, and would return my preference to the oranges, and so on. I was scanning for potential disaster. Ironically, I would gladly have eaten Israeli oranges, or Chilean, or any other sort of grapes, there and then in the supermarket; the worry concerned only the future prospects, the *anticipation* involved in taking them home with me.

My intrusive thoughts stimulated much reasoning that seemed motivated by the need to make them less painful, but which was invariably fruitless. I would go around the same loops time after time, and always the logic that was presented as the best solution had the same total lack of conviction. You are now 30 years old . . . That's a lot of years . . . You will be only 60 years old when another

30 years elapse . . . It's ages yet. Don't worry. It's so long until you die that, in effect, it's an eternity. But then the inevitable reply would seem to come from another part of my brain: no – it isn't! The last 5 years appear to have gone quicker than ever. Four times 5 is 20 and in 20 years' time you will be 50. That's nearer to death than now, by a significant amount. And so it went on; the same fruitless calculations and estimations, the unwanted retort, making the situation worse rather than better.

Statistics of accidents were ruminated on at length, as follows. The figures show that so many people are killed each year on the roads. The population of Denmark is around four and a half million. Divide one by the other and then divide by 365 and your chances for today can be calculated. A small chance. Yes, but someone has got to be the one, so why not you? So it went on and on. No matter what calculation I did the conclusion was always the same: that life is a risk and perfect security cannot be obtained. There was always room for fear, intense fear.

My death-related intrusions didn't conflict with any moral principle; I was not offended by them in any meaningful sense. I didn't consider myself a bad person or a weak one for having them. However, they clearly went against my goals in life – to attain pleasure, to have a wide range of experiences. They were tormenting, interfering with my work; they caused me to cancel journeys. They contaminated the experience of pleasure. In the 17th century, John Bunyan compared his intrusions to 'a clog on the leg of a Bird to hinder her from flying', and I could put it no better than that. Life would have been bliss for me without these thoughts – everything else was right about my existence. I regarded them simply as an intrusion, like interference on a television screen. I didn't try to interpret any hidden message behind them.

Generally, my intrusions followed a hierarchy; one object of fear would be more or less replaced when a more frightening candidate came along. For example, ferry boats across the Kattegat can suddenly seem much less frightening when someone invites you to fly to New York. In general, I found the arousal of a fear by, for example, a natural reminder, to be much less painful after the fear was no longer the dominant one. Suppose one particular frightening thought were to be toppled from top place by another. It might then feel as if the loser were trying to wrest control back. This was not usually successful, unless new information was obtained to boost the strength of the loser. Such a hierarchy of obsessions, with one being dominant and an apparent competition, is also often seen in subjects where there are multiple distinct obsessions (e.g. cleanliness and checking) rather than one central theme (e.g. death) that comes up in different forms.

I found that when a dominant intrusive theme had been resolved, as very occasionally happened, a glow of euphoria would be experienced and the world would be beautiful and trouble-free. Predictably, the effect was invariably short-lived. A visit to the doctor and reassurance would typify such a situation. This experience is vividly portrayed in the Woody Allen film *Hannah and her Sisters*, where Mr Sachs, played by Allen, leaves the hospital jumping with joy after learning that he does not have a brain tumour. However, he is all too soon stopped in his tracks by the intrusion of the thought that this represents only a temporary stay of execution and death will find him one day.

I must have irritated my doctor with my imaginary illnesses, each of which seemed convincing to me. Sometimes what is good and beautiful in life would be turned into bad. For example, I would touch Mette and this would arouse fear in me of what could happen to her in the future: imagining that wonderful form as no longer a wonderful form was tormenting.

Despite the intrusions, life went on as usual. I didn't tell anyone about them and thought that in time they might go away. The professor was delighted at my teaching in Danish, having attended the first lecture. My ego was increased by his comments. It went up still more when a Bulgarian student stopped me to announce that mine were the first lectures he could understand. 'The way the Danes speak is impossible for a foreigner to understand,' he informed me.

Strange as it might sound, I was still happy most of the time. Even though intrusions came often, then still 90 per cent of my time was spent with thoughts other than the intrusion. No one at work thought I looked ill, or, as far as I know, perceived that anything was particularly odd about my behaviour. Obsessionals are often inveterate experts at covering their tracks even where overt rituals are concerned. Denmark suited me well. I put a lot of effort into developing a computer model of feeding, working in collaboration with David Booth at Birmingham. This work showed great promise and it was very rewarding for me.

I started to feel homesick for England, a sentiment that was unknown to me during the first year. I would look forward to watching trash on TV just because it was British trash, material that I wouldn't have dreamed of watching in England.

6
Decline

'I finished dressing and left the room, feeling compelled, however, as I left it, to touch the lintel of the door. Is it possible, thought I, that from what I have lately heard the long-forgotten influence should have possessed me again? but I will not give way to it . . .' George Borrow, Lavengro

By November 1973 when I had just turned 30, the ruminations were getting much worse in both intensity and frequency, and I decided to seek help. So bad were they that the term 'intrusion' would be something of a misnomer, since they were rapidly forming the major content of my consciousness. My GP gave a receptive and sympathetic hearing. I was referred to a local psychiatrist, who asked a large number of questions about my life, my background and ambition.

I made several further visits and was told that the problem arose from a subconscious fear of losing Mette to another man. The logic seemed odd and somewhat arbitrary to me. I had never once considered the prospect. How did he know it was that? I was told to write down the content of my worry, then tear up the piece of paper so as to exorcise the thought symbolically. Some medicine was prescribed. The psychiatrist's attitude was polite but strictly formal. He was the only person in Denmark to whom I spoke for any length of time using the formal *De* (you) rathen than the informal *du*. The tablets worked at first, in that my mood improved, but this was a small mercy since their effect soon wore off. The dose was increased, thereby causing the symptoms of Parkinsonism, an excruciating combination of muscular rigidity and fidgeting. It felt like I imagined a Chinese torture to be. Further tablets were prescribed to take away the symptoms of the first lot. I was getting more and more worried about the future but was still able to function. The country that had offered so much was now turning sour. The intrusions were to become more intense and frequent, and there was no defence. The jolt of the alarm clock in the morning was the most painful event of the day and the evenings were perhaps the least painful.

I then sought help outside conventional medicine. A well-known hypnotist lived in Odense and a meeting with him was arranged. He gave me a demonstration on a willing young subject and I was impressed. I was convinced that he had something to offer when I observed him performing therapy over the telephone to a Swedish air force officer, in danger of sliding into alcoholism. However, when he tried the technique on me, it was clear to both of us that I was immune to his words. He didn't charge me anything, saying that he felt the failure was because I was analysing the situation. 'If only you were able to switch off the scientist in you, and give yourself to it.'

One night, in desperation, I turned to the Danish equivalent of the Samaritans and was made very welcome in a local church. The pastor put the Christian argument on pain, suffering and death to me, but I remained unconvinced. On leaving him, I was told that, despite everything, I still had a warm smile and asked 'please – try not to lose it'.

Out of the chaos and complexity of mental illness, one certainty emerges: human sympathy and empathy are such that most people want to help. Also, most, irrespective of their expertise or lack of it, irrespective of school or technique, will claim that they can help. I have found very few indeed (possibly only one) who say that they have little or nothing to offer. This does not mean that people are making false claims in order to boost your morale or make money. Some might do just that but I don't think I have met any. The feeling of wanting to help is overwhelming and tends to colour everything. In the case of obsessional neurosis, there is often the feeling that one can treat it by the use of common-sense rationality, or by logical extension of what would be appropriate in treating, say, depression or marital disharmony. Alas, such good intentions might unwittingly make the condition worse.

In addition to the conventional, you are likely to meet the fringe or even crank elements. If my experiences are anything to go by, even a hard-nosed scientist will try almost anything on offer when times are desperate. There lurks the suspicion that even a method that appears nonsensical and scientifically unsound might just work for reasons that we don't yet understand. Even meeting total strangers while travelling, I would at first feel naively that they might hold some secret key to understanding life and would be anxious to strike up conversation with them. They seemed to have a mastery over existence that I was lacking; if only they could teach me.

I answered an advertisement in the local newspaper for a new form of therapy. The therapist turned out to be a Russian immigrant who, on learning where I was from, spoke excellent English. 'My method is that you send me a sample of your blood. Prick your finger with a needle, let some blood drip into a small container. Send it to me, I will feel the vibes and transmit a healing signal to match them'. I didn't pursue it.

The transcendental meditation movement was holding a series of lectures in Odense, so I subscribed and was taught meditation. At first an almost drug-like euphoria was obtained, but over a period of daily sessions, the effect wore off. I now suspect that it might (and only *might*) have been worth persisting for longer.

I was sometimes able to reduce very significantly the frequency and particularly the intensity and quality of the intrusions by drinking alcohol, but this of course brought only temporary relief and the after-effects were most unpleasant. Under alcohol, even if the content of the thought was the same, its cutting edge of fear was blunted somewhat. I could have slid into alcoholism, but mercifully I did not rate the chances very highly, and I was spared it. How I was able to resist when the temporary positive effects were so evident, I do not know.

My compulsive behaviour developed at around this time. Sitting on a bus, I would fix on a passenger who had just alighted, and try to hold him in my gaze for as long as possible. If I couldn't hold him until the bus turned the corner, I was worried that this was an omen that tragedy might shortly befall me. Crazy? Irrational? Yes, particularly for a scientist who had hitherto prided himself on the disinterested and objective pursuit of knowledge, but it was compelling. It lasted for some months and then slowly went away.

I found that I had to go to the toilet immediately before a meal; otherwise, I felt the pressure in my bladder would spoil the experience. Whether I had a full bladder or not, had recently been to the toilet or not, I felt compelled to urinate before the meal. I had to be certain that I had fully emptied my bladder, so the visit to the toilet was longer than might be expected. The logic was odd. 'A full bladder would clearly detract from the meal. But you don't have a full bladder. You know you don't. But if you did it would detract. I can't eat the meal on the basis of the information that I believe, but I must test the information that I don't believe in case it is true.' Discomfort would be dissonant with a pleasant experience like eating in a Chinese restaurant. It would not be so dissonant with a somewhat less desirable activity like marking exam papers, and so then there would be little or no urge to urinate.

I also found myself checking and double-checking that I had switched off electric equipment, locked doors, etc. I could not resist going back for yet one more 'final' check. This behaviour was about to add to the discomfort of what was to be the worst day of my life up till then, as I slipped deeper into depression.

I took the morning train to Svendborg to meet someone who was a friend of a friend. Being into alternative medicine, he might just have something to offer. In fact he couldn't do much but I was well received in his room in a home for retired clergy. Later in the day, he ran (!) with me back to Svendborg station and wished me well. I felt at an all-time low in the train, made worse by a group of lively young students, who served as a painful reminder of when times were so infinitely better, at London and Sussex. Could all that pleasure in living really be over for good? How long would this hell last and would I get even worse? I couldn't imagine what it would be like to be in a mood even worse than this. I was now in a state of panic, feeling, I guess, something like the proverbial rat trapped in a corner.

Getting back to Odense at about 5pm, I went to the university to make sure that everything was in order. On leaving, I carefully checked that the laboratory equipment had all been switched off, but then went back for another confirmatory inspection. Indeed, all was well. I caught the bus to Odense town hall, where I would change to a second bus for Fruens Bøge. On arriving at the town hall, I was overcome with the feeling that something had been left switched on. There was nothing for it, but to wait for a bus to take me the 3km or so back to university. Sure enough, all was well in the laboratory, just as a more rational bit of my brain seemed to be saying all along. Arriving by bus a second time at the town hall, the same insecurity prevailed. It was now getting late and I was torn as to what to do. A taxi was the only way to have one last look at the laboratory. The driver waited for me while I checked and then drove me to Fruens Bøge. That did finally settle the issue for that day.

What was I afraid of during this checking? What pulled me to do it? I can't say, but using my conscious thoughts as evidence would suggest that it was the need to avoid a catastrophe, such as the university going up in flames. On the one level I knew all was well; on another level, I just doubted it.

Did I *remember* switching the apparatus off? Maybe. It seemed to me that the essence was in terms of the *utilization* of the memory. On the one hand, intellectually, I knew that the apparatus was switched off. Had I been asked by a bookie to estimate the chances, I would have given 1000 to 1 in favour. But, on the other hand, I couldn't use that same memory to move on to another activity. It was as if the decision mechanism would scan for problems before allowing me to start a new activity. The memory got corrupted in this decision process.

The fear was that I would be responsible if a disaster were to happen, because I had left something switched on. I thought – maybe the switch I thought was down was really up. Could it be that my attention had wandered while at the crucial stage in the check? I might remember well enough touching the switch, but maybe I actually pushed the switch *up* while pressing it to make 100 per cent sure it was down. Perhaps I was deceiving myself and the memory I was then reviewing was that from yesterday's check rather than today's. One last check will do it, and so on ... The motivational basis of checking is attributed by some investigators to a concern to prevent guilt or criticism.

Apart from wasting time on checking doors and electric switches, I spent time checking the contents of letters. I would write several letters, seal them and take them to the post, only to feel insecure that I had put the right letter in the right envelope. I would then open them up to read their contents. Of course, my friend, David Booth, could never have realized just how many envelopes addressed to him ended up in the rubbish-bin for every one sent.

Where does the motivation for checking come from? For checking gas taps, it could be argued that there is an exaggeration of a perfectly rational fear of a fire. It is difficult to see what awful consequence could follow mixing up letters, at least of the sort I was writing that concerned motivation in rats! I guess that in some cases the obsessional's craving for personal perfection has a lot to do with it. Things have to be *exactly* right, there must be no room for doubt. One's standing in life might fall if a curious letter were to arrive on the desk of an associate. Like a child, the obsessional craves assurance and comfort and is locked in a fruitless search for security. Nothing must be left to chance. Even harmless errors must be avoided in the relentless pursuit of perfection. However, in some cases it is difficult to see by any stretch of logic that a negative state is being avoided. For example, an obsessional might spend hours checking that books on a shelf are aligned correctly. To attempt to explain this in terms of a search for perfection is tautological.

For me, things were now going from bad to worse; serious depression was setting in. Depression in the past, present or future is often associated with obsessional-compulsive disorders. Some writers characterize the phase of depression following a period of obsessional rumination as being one in which the subject has no more fight left to oppose the obsession. Graham Reed describes this by military analogy as a surrender to the intrusion instead of the previous combat. I certainly felt now that I had exhausted all of the fight that had been in me. I had no intellectual tricks up my sleeve, no new modes of living, no way of looking at the world that was able even to begin to fight hard enough against the curse.

Associated with the depression, my sleep was very badly affected. I awoke early in the morning, unable to get back to sleep (a well-recognized symptom of depression). On the other hand, by day, I was so tired that I had difficulty in concentrating. Several times people came to my office, to find me in an exhausted state, slumped over my typewriter. Something was pulling me downhill fast and there appeared to be no brake. I looked half-dead and it was apparent to all that things were seriously wrong. My associates in the department asked me what was happening.

The world is perceived so differently through the eyes and ears of a depressive. The Danish language, which had brought such a thrilling challenge and later allowed assimilation into a new culture, now sounded unpleasant. It irritated me and was alien, ugly and threatening. I switched to the security of English whenever I could.

I told the psychiatrist of my utter despair. He said that the only solution left was for me to be hospitalized and to receive electroconvulsive therapy. He would however be reluctant to prescribe this, because I needed my brain for academic work, and he couldn't rule out memory impairment. I left his office and took a shortcut through the H. C. Andersen gardens to get back to the city centre. I had taken a similar route some 20 months earlier, on leaving the restaurant with Winnie. Then I had just arrived in Denmark and was full of enthusiasm for life; now I was a broken man. The memory from 20 months earlier came back and tortured me.

On travelling around Odense, I would look out of the bus window at car drivers and pedestrians and think to myself – 'I bet you are well. You are not suffering as I am. Why me? Why not you? You've never had this cross to bear.' By a curious logic, I also felt cheated, because this was all unexpected. So often in England and after arriving in Denmark, I had predicted and planned for potential disasters that would take my new-found paradise away from me. The Danish *Fremskrits* Party might be elected and close Odense University, but I had done all in my power to become assimilated into this land. If that were to happen, Copenhagen University would surely offer something. Nothing could surely go wrong that hadn't been anticipated and ruminated about, but now it had.

One of the symptoms of depression is a tendency for the sufferer to distort what, by popular consensus, is reality. Amongst other things, this distortion consists of self-devaluation, sometimes done to a gross extent. Later, and with the benefit of hindsight, I was able to see that I was massively devaluing my abilities and potential. Of course, one gets into a vicious circle, where the devaluation can become a self-fulfilling prophesy. That apart, devaluation can also be applied to things for which there are more objective indices. By any criterion our study on the computer simulation of feeding was coming along very well. In only 4 years' time David Booth was to publish an influential book of readings, inspired by our work. Objectively speaking, I just had to get well and I would have interesting challenges. But I couldn't see it that way. To me, the future would be such that, whether healthy or not, there would exist nothing more for me to do as a scientist. I felt guilty accepting my salary cheque from the university. I was finished. There were no more avenues of challenge to go down. There were no more books that I could write, since I had nothing more to say. The truth is, and would have been obvious to anyone else, that the potential was enormous. Fifteen years and seven books later, I feel that I have only scratched the surface of motivation theory. My professor tried to give me guidance but I was not receptive. I never once doubted my moral worth as an individual. I didn't feel guilty about anything, except my salary cheque. I saw myself unambiguously as a victim and felt no personal responsibility in how I had led my life up till then.

There was now a real danger that Mette, who was voicing fears for her own mental health, would be dragged down with me. She had just got a place at university to read for a law degree. She tried to help for a while but simply could not cope with this nightmare. Her helplessness was total, for what could she possibly do? She felt that everything was right in our relationship, as did I. It was not so long ago that we had discussed buying a new house in Odense. What could we do? Suppose I went into a mental hospital in Denmark. Then I thought of the unthinkable: suppose psychiatric care were better in Britain. Maybe I needed to leave Denmark, return home, and find out. Mette and I discussed this endlessly, concluding that psychiatric care might be better in the UK.

Could all this really be happening to me? When one feels like a helpless child, is there no one to appeal to, a kind of psychiatric policeman or ombudsman who will somehow sort one's life out? This country seemed so sweet a little while ago. I felt certain that it was now a matter of life and death, and so I got compassionate leave from the university.

The next three days were spent in a state of endless rumination about death, my health and future. Should I leave or should I stay? My mind was made up and then unmade again, time after agonizing time. Schemes and plans were entertained and then the dread of their implications turned me against them. When things seemed utterly insoluble, thoughts of climbing the highest building in Odense, the hospital, came into my consciousness. No – I couldn't take that way out of it. I ate almost nothing. My weight, already low (well below 10 stone for a height of 1m 83), now slipped down still further. Night merged into day, and nightmares were muddled with reality. The only mercy was a period of sleep from about 12pm to 3am. Something radical had to be done and at last the strength came to me to make the decision to go.

I sneaked away from university, without properly saying goodbye to anyone, not even Mette. It was all too painful, feeling that for better or worse, I would not be coming back. Mette would only discover that I had gone when she got home and read my desperate note. I would write to Lars, my professor, from England. A taxi took me to Fruens Bøge, I picked up all of my essential worldly possessions, and we were quickly at Odense station. Now there really must be no turning back, even if things were temporarily to get worse.

The boat-train *Englaenderin* had left Copenhagen that morning and now it pulled into Odense. This was the same type of mauve train that had often taken me to the capital, for work or for relaxation at Mette's home, always in pleasure. But now the screech of its brakes evoked no awe in me, no revival of happy memories from childhood train-spotting days in Cambridge; that noise like any other now served only to accentuate the terror that I was already feeling. This was the terror of the helpless and hopeless, those who feel they can no longer exert any control over destiny.

A group of carefree Danes were in my compartment laughing and drinking. I found a window seat, and soon we were under way to the port of Esbjerg. A blonde and blue-eyed Scandinavian woman was on the platform waving goodbye to a friend. In one respect, my sexual drive was zero if not actually negative right then, but at another level, almost sadistically, the memories were still intact and their awful tantalizing significance was not lost on me. Could I be making a gigantic mistake in leaving? Maybe I had not yet exhausted all the possibilities. Perhaps there existed a new drug, if only I could find the right expert. My eyes followed the marvellous form of the woman on the platform as she, and then the town of Odense, receded into the distance. I asked myself 'how could life be so cruel? How can such beauty exist in the midst of suffering? What might England offer me?'

My family were pleased to welcome me back home in Histon. My father had been worried sick when he knew that I was in trouble, offering to fly out to the rescue. He showed obvious signs of delight at getting me back in one piece. I visited friends in the village and relatives came to see me. I cycled around Cambridgeshire, preoccupied with what to do. I ruminated about future possibilities. Should I go to see the village GP? Have I any useful contacts here? Then in the midst of these ruminations it occurred to me – I was having fewer intrusions about death. Come to think of it, even in the last few days in Denmark, the other problems that I was debating, to stay or go, were causing so much anguish that they pushed death into second place. Things might be bad now, but at least they were less bad and differently bad. Thank God for small mercies, or rather in this case big mercies. I had something to ruminate over that was, at least in principle, within my control.

Should I stay or risk moving away from Histon to return to academia? I applied for a job at Hatfield Polytechnic, which was not too far away, was offered an interview, but declined it out of cowardice. I felt I was not up to it, which, on reflection, was patently nonsensical.

I spent a weekend in Brighton with some friends. Passionate political debate, laughter and a party were good for my spirit. Yes, death was slowly losing some of its potency, but why? Was it simply being usurped by the demands of choosing a future? That weekend in Brighton, I wrote my letter of resignation from Odense, but couldn't find the courage to post it. What could the future hold for me if I did post it? Unemployment? On returning to Cambridge via London, I stopped for a bite to eat in the Charing Cross Road. A young couple were sitting in the restaurant and my attention was drawn to the attractiveness and style of the woman. I looked at her for as long as would be decent for an Englishman. Then I heard the sound that I wanted least of any in the world to hear: they started speaking Danish. That experience made dropping the resignation letter in the postbox at Leicester Square all the more agonizing, but at last I found the courage to do so.

7
Getting back to normal

'Reader, amidst the difficulties and dangers of this life, should you ever be tempted to despair, call to mind these latter chapters of the life of Lavengro. There are few positions, however difficult, from which dogged resolution and perseverance may not liberate you.' George Borrow, Lavengro

A vacancy had arisen in the Psychology Department at Preston (now 'Lancashire') Polytechnic. I applied and was given the date for an interview. Cowardice shortly took over: I declined the interview. Then I became worried about not finding another job, so I rang Mike Stone, the head of department, and asked him to negate my cancellation, which he very kindly did.

The people conducting my interview were a nice group. When they offered me the post I accepted. I returned to Histon but again got scared of the unknown, so after some weeks I wrote to Preston to decline the offer. I then thought that this was an awful mistake. Having to make a decision was a terrible experience; I tried to put it off as long as possible. I would make a provisional decision, accept it and then search for disadvantages associated with the choice. I would switch to the alternative but immediately interrogate the new choice for flaws. As I read the *Guardian* in bed each morning, I told myself 'just one more page, and you must get up and face it'. I was always able to find a new excuse to put off making each decision.

Three days after posting my second resignation to Preston, I visited David Booth in Birmingham, feeling very low. My emotions were combined fear and depression but watching David at work in the University was a vivid reminder of just how attractive this profession is.

I looked at David's phone, and thought 'perhaps the letter has not arrived yet in Preston. I might preempt it. They might still want me.' David was talking about the motivational significance of the rate at which food leaves a rat's stomach, a subject having a particular appeal for him and me too when times were better. My mind was not with him: my thoughts were hovering between Preston and Histon. Perhaps if I were to ring, they will confirm that I no longer have the job and that could resolve it. But the first term's teaching load was not heavy. Surely I could do it. Do I want the job or not? Could David help? Should I seek his advice? No. *I* must decide.

That afternoon I used David's phone to ring the head of department, quite expecting to be told where to go. Yes, he had received the letter. The computer had been told and had deleted me. He did understand my problem. But could I change my mind one last time? Yes!!

It started to rain as my train pulled into Wigan. Somehow arriving there in the grey of evening didn't have quite the romantic appeal of seeing Copenhagen in the morning sun, but I was prepared to settle for a life without glamour now. At Preston station, Maurice McCullough, senior lecturer in psychology, was waiting with his dog. He took me to his house where I had been invited to stay, adding 'I wondered whether you would really be on the train!' It was good being with Maurice and his wife Camille, and I was made so welcome. Irish hospitality was just what I needed to complete my recovery. I soon found a flat, in an attractive part of town, overlooking Avenham Park. The students were a friendly and lively bunch and life was good.

I phoned Mette to tell her the good news that stability prevailed and she visited me shortly afterwards. The experience in Preston felt like being snatched from the jaws of death, and in a strange way I was convinced that it would not be necessary to go through such suffering again. Just walking around Preston doing the shopping took on a delight.

Amongst other things, the department put me in charge of entertainment. A local disco was hired and my flat was used for student parties. Some memorable jokes were told and got passed on to future generations of Preston students. Every day I thought back to Denmark and sighed inwardly at the relief of having escaped from the torture of mental illness.

At Christmas 1974, I met Helen at a party put on by a psychology student. I had earlier ogled her from afar at an election meeting, but was not able to talk to her. I liked what she had to say to me and it matched her stunning good looks. We soon formed a partnership.

After about 6 months in Preston, there were just a few signs that all was not going entirely as it should. However, seen in the context of earlier, it did not amount to a package of symptoms that caused me worry. Nightmares came back. To be precise, they were now more often *night terrors*.[1] Sometimes the generic term 'nightmare' is used to cover both the true nightmare and the very much rarer and more serious condition of night terror (also termed *pavor nocturnus*). I would wake up screaming in the night or crying out for help. The terror was indescribable. Sometimes I would simply scream and sit up or jump out of bed, never being able to articulate any associated thought process. Usually, I could easily return to sleep afterwards, a somewhat surprising aspect of this condition. Very occasionally, I didn't remember anything about the nocturnal activity, until Helen told me the next day. More commonly the same simple theme would reappear regularly; my breathing was being arrested, or I had poison placed in my mouth and I had to expel it. This would prompt a rush to the bathroom as I desperately tried to rid my mouth of the substance. An attacker might appear and I would leap from the bed to evade his knife. At times the threat was one I would be unable to define, of the kind 'this is it – you are going to die now, this second'. The theme was always a single image corresponding to a single event in the outside world, like one or two frames frozen and cut from a horror movie. Sometimes I would be falling and would awake gaining my balance. The falling theme was particularly likely to occur very soon after passing into sleep. The themes had one important feature in common: they were always ones involving me as the victim; I was never the violent party.

In addition to night terrors, a compulsive checking ritual reappeared. On leaving my flat I would check again and again that the door really was secured. In fact, if anything, this threatened rather than increased my security, since the lock was positively weakened by the strain of testing. I was also cautious about possible disasters ahead, predicting accidents of various kinds, but in spite of all this, my mood could be described as very happy and 'well', and I was working efficiently.

Paradoxically, I noticed that the intensity of the fear of a disaster declined as the event in question got nearer in time. The intrusive thoughts themselves seemed to be much worse than performing the action that they concerned. For example, a planned journey down the motorway would evoke considerable fear, until the day of departure. The journey itself would present little or no problem. Anticipated fear as measured by the frequency of intrusions would be all the greater if there were no unambiguous reason for engaging in the activity. A motorway journey would evoke more anticipatory fear if there were a railway connection that presented a possible alternative means of travel. A journey would also present more fear if I had no way out of the commitment. A casual invitation would evoke little fear even if I knew that in all probability I would take it up, provided I could always feel that it was possible to get out of it.

In 1976 I was asked by David McFarland to serve as external D.Phil. examiner for a candidate at Oxford. Richard Dawkins was the internal examiner. On the way to the Zoology/Psychology building, I purchased a copy of *Breakdown*, an account of a nervous breakdown written by my professor at Sussex, Stuart Sutherland. The *viva voce* was followed that evening by a celebratory party, a wonderful occasion, rich in fun and intellectual stimulation.

David McFarland later escorted me back to his home where I was to spend the weekend. I stayed up late that night reading *Breakdown*, and was distressed to read of Stuart's suffering. So much of it rang true after my experiences. It was rather cold in the bedroom and I kept a pullover on while I was reading. I got up to where Stuart was lying in the street in Naples screaming from mental torment and then I put the book down. I put out the light and dropped off to sleep. Suddenly, in my dream, I was being sucked into a building by my poloneck sweater, which had got caught in the ventilation propeller. I fought to resist, but all I could do was to tear off the collar, let that be sucked in, and thereby try to escape. On awakening the next morning I found to my horror that in reality I had indeed torn the neck off my pullover and it was lying on the bed.

In the following months, the intrusions were still there at low frequency. It was like the days in Denmark before things got bad. However, I felt myself to be master of fate and captain of my soul. For a physical analogy, the intrusions at that time were like having a medium-to-bad cold, whereas the latter stages in Denmark had been like a kidney stone. Anyone unfortunate enough to have experienced the latter will know what I mean. I didn't think that I would sink again, but I would rather have been without the intrusions. Life between 1974 and 1978 was good. I still basked in the joy of escaping from permanent mental torment.

8
Misplaced complacency

'He may even believe, at an unconscious level, that he can avoid death altogether, if only he gives the problem enough time, thought and effort.' Dr Allan Mallinger, The obsessive's myth of control

In 1978, I got a job at the Open University and Helen and I moved down to Milton Keynes in September. At the stage where I was getting used to the Open University, the intrusions were still there, but at a relatively low frequency and intensity, still analogous to a cold rather than a kidney stone. However, after 5 years of being in Milton Keynes, I did feel that it might be worth seeing whether British medicine and psychiatry had anything to offer.

I felt odd talking to my GP about this, wishing that I had come with a 'proper illness', like tonsillitis or an ingrowing toenail. He gave me a sympathetic hearing, saying 'This fascinates me. I wish I had time to devote myself to it. I sometimes look at the stars at night, and wonder what it's all about. It's occasionally uncomfortable.' He referred me to a local clinical psychologist.

The clinical psychologist tried two techniques to counter the intrusive thoughts. One consisted of getting me to place a rubber band around my wrist, and to ping it whenever an unwanted thought intruded. At the same time, I was to give myself a silent message of the kind 'Go away' or 'You are not wanted'. If I were able to anticipate the intrusion by getting in with the ping first, so much the better. That is to say, I should try to identify the cues that trigger the thought and react to them with corrective action. To this end, it was necessary to record a sample of situations in which intrusions occurred. I found this no easy task. Imagine how easy it is to disturb a psychological process by monitoring it, particularly when observer and observed are one and the same concerned individual. There are few better stimuli to ruminate than a notebook of ruminations but therapists are well aware of this problem.

The observations were started while on a visit to Holland and West Germany; time, content of the thought, intensity (on a scale from 0 to 8, the worst possible) and duration were recorded. Typical observations were (1) arrival in Hagen → feeling: how nice to be here → nice now, but will not last (intensity 5, duration 10 minutes), (2) at breakfast a waiter congratulates me on my German → good feeling → my forthcoming stay here → but it can't last (intensity 3, duration 5 minutes), (3) train passes cemetery → my own death (intensity 4, duration 5 minutes), (4) two Turkish *Gastarbeiter* pass me in the street → immigration → recent neo-Nazi activity → a recent arson attack on some Turks → my own death (intensity 2, duration 10 minutes).

A pattern was emerging: as an approximation, one could divide the intrusions into three classes: (a) those triggered by a positive cue, such as receiving congratulations, reflecting upon good in the future or being reminded of one's worth; (b) those triggered by a negative cue, such as reading about a plane crash, an obituary or being reminded of the passage of time; and (c) no obvious cue present, 'spontaneous intrusions'. Consider where the waiter told me that I speak good German – 'Hoch Deutsch'. This was an example of type (a), something to make one feel good. Contrast this with passing a cemetery, a typical type (b), a rather obvious one linked to the morbid. Somewhat more subtle, but still I would place in class (b), is someone saying 'it's your birthday next month', and thereby reminding me of the passage of time. The division was roughly one-third falling into each of the three categories.

There was also a time factor involved. The time most free of intrusions was upon waking, particularly if I could afford the luxury of lying in bed for a while with no particular immediate purpose. Paradoxically, at other times, the best situation would be one of hard work in which there was little or no scope for free-flowing thoughts.

The thoughts invariably concerned either the future in its own right or the past as an index of the passage of time. 'The last year seemed to fly past.' 'It can't be a year since then.' Thus ruminations were never over past events themselves or how the past might have been. Even nostalgia for the past, for the music of the sixties or for my schooldays, did not have a negatively-toned quality to it. Such thoughts have always been pleasant.

The technique of thought-stopping seemed not to work. I then attempted to convert thought-stopping into a schedule of punishment. In response to an intruding thought, I would pull the elastic band rather far and then let it go, which certainly felt like punishment. I would also pinch my skin hard for the thought to be really punished, but this didn't seem to work either.

Back in Milton Keynes, the clinical psychologist was very interested in these results and tried a second technique. He invited me to think about a morbid theme, to deliberately excite the intrusion. Then, having told me to close my eyes, he would slam a book down on the table, shouting 'STOP', I think that the STOP instruction might have had some slight effect, but it was weak at best.

On my own initiative, I then tried visiting a hypnotist in London. He produced a tape of the session, which contained the following messages amongst others.

'You are going now into a peaceful and calm world. There is nothing to bother you. Now relax. It is a beautiful day and you are lying on a sandy warm beach.

Looking back on the time when you used to be anxious you can now put that out of your mind. Now see yourself as the person you want to be. Not allowing pessimism and worry to dog you.'

Unlike in Denmark, this time I was very receptive to hypnotism. I also tried the Alexander technique, being taught by Alexander's nephew, which certainly helped my posture, if not my mind! I suffered no more backaches. His first question to me was 'Have you ever been in the army?' 'No, why?' 'Because your posture is so stiff, as if you were on a parade ground. Try to lower your shoulders. You don't need to clench your fists!'

Yoga, which I tried at about the same time, had an immediate and dramatic effect on reducing the frequency and intensity of ruminations, but the unambiguous effect was short-lived. I think that there remained a residual small benefit from regular practice. Hard physical exercise, jogging and particularly aerobics had a good effect, as did listening to the hypnosis tape. It seemed that there was no magic cure but one could hold the enemy at bay with passive resistance or 'hand-to-hand fighting'.

Helen and I took a holiday in Ireland, mainly in the South, but visiting Londonderry briefly. Later, in the south, we stared hard at the statue of the Virgin Mary in Ballinspittle, Co. Cork, which was said to move. It failed to do so for us, but the visit was fascinating. One day we were wandering around Dublin, and Helen remarked:

'I think that it was here last year where the coach driver told us not to walk around. It's a tough part of town.'

We didn't think too much about this; after all, unlike in New York, the people in Ireland looked just like us. A few seconds later someone pounced and grabbed me round the neck from behind. I immediately thought of Canice, an Irish student at Preston. At a flash, in my mind, he had spotted his former tutor, and wanted to surprise us. Obsessionals can sometimes be hopelessly naive optimists. Being somewhat less of a naive optimist, Helen quickly let out a piercing scream and I felt a hand tugging violently at my money. No; it wasn't Canice. On failing to destabilize me and get my money, he fled.

In 1984 and 1985, I spent two periods abroad, at the Ruhr University in Bochum, West Germany and Claude Bernard University in Lyon, France. Each of these visits was a spectacular success and I loved my time there. On my first Saturday in Bochum I took the tram down to the market to do the week's shopping and felt that warm glow of my first year in Odense once again. I had great fun in the town's bars and memories of an evening spent at *Trauminsel* will be with me forever.

The next year in France the sun also shone brightly on my life and the food was better than in Germany. By request, in the lunch hours, I taught conversational English informally to the staff who needed it, secretaries, technicians and even the occasional academic. I was many times invited to their homes for meals, the wine was good and flowed freely; this was truly a great period in my life. I would sometimes take the high-speed train (*Le TGV*) to Paris at the weekend, and get a thrill out of the big-city life. I felt the cares of the world disappear in the bustle of the Métro, with the help of a glass or two of wine. The smell of the Métro always evokes a wonderful emotion in me.

The ruminations were at a relatively low level in France, but I was curious to see whether anything might be available to help. One day I was having an intimate tête-à-tête with Jacques Mouret in Lyon, and he described his electrical brain stimulation technique for helping depressives and heroin addicts. I went to the hospital on several occasions, and had current passed through my brain for an hour or so. Whether it changed the state of my central nervous system, I am not sure, but certainly the sight of the nurse in charge of the apparatus did.

Back in Britain, I missed Lyon very much, but managed to readapt to Milton Keynes.

9
Never get complacent

'And as time went on the thought of death began to haunt him till it became a constant obsession. In the daytime, fascinated by it, he would lay down his pen and sit brooding on it; at night, he would lie tossing feverishly from side to side, with the blackness that was awaiting ever before him. And with the sickly light of the early morning, there met him the early relief of having dragged on one day nearer the end.' 'A conflict of egoisms' in Wreckage *by Hubert Crackanthorpe, 1893*

The thoughts were still at a low frequency. However, trying to eliminate them, I wrote to Professor Jeffrey Gray, at the Institute of Psychiatry in London, whom I had met on a couple of occasions. I was in the process of writing a book for a series of which he was general editor. His predecessor as professor of psychology, Hans Eysenck, had pioneered behaviour therapy for phobias and compulsive behaviour. I would have taken this course of action much earlier had my problem been essentially behavioural. Jeffrey suggested that I contact an associate of his, Padmal de Silva. By coincidence, I had just read an article by him, comparing Buddhist and behaviourist techniques of controlling unwanted thoughts.

Padmal talked at length to me and was most sympathetic. I took an immediate liking to him. He suggested that I write out the content of the intrusions and record them on tape; I should then play them back to myself. When patients are told that treatment consists of exposure to the very stimulus that they most dread, they sometimes decline it out of fear. However, this technique appealed to me; it fitted my preference for methods close to behaviourist psychology. The logic behind it is simple: if something is repeated enough times with no significant consequence, it tends to lose its attention value. The ticking of a clock is an obvious example. In my case, I would flood myself with intrusions and hope to *habituate* to them.

Padmal admitted that nothing in this area is certain: the technique works for some people but not others. As a psychologist, I was in a good position to appreciate this. I should come back in three weeks' time to report progress. Padmal then announced that we were both invited to Hans Eysenck's 70th birthday party. It was a jolly and pleasant occasion. The lively conversation made me realize that I still had my sense of humour, in spite of the ordeal before me, and I left as always in an optimistic mood. Such optimism in a treatment might be expected to have the effect, if any, of increasing its success, the so-called 'placebo effect'. Also, it is often argued that the establishment of a trusting rapport with the therapist is a major factor in the success of any therapy. Padmal gave me some scientific papers to read, suggested I get hold of *Living with Fear* by Isaac Marks and wished me well. These papers were to lead ultimately to the present book.

I employed free association to generate as many intrusions as possible. It was not difficult to fill a few sides of A4. My recording, involving names of psychologists most meaningful to me, went like this 'J. Watson is dead. Edward Tolman is dead. Like them, you too will one day be dead. There is nothing that you can do to avoid it. Try as hard as you like, it will catch you. Who knows when? Ten years, 20 years, 50 years? One thing is certain; it will find you wherever you may try to hide. Who knows how you will die? You can't say.

What will happen to your body after death? No one can say. Only one thing is certain: it will find you and everyone close to you. Your father and sister will go just like you.' I guess that this sample is enough to give you a feel for the general theme! I made a 20-minute tape like that, and played it with the same enthusiasm that I had earlier shown for learning foreign languages. Shaving, eating and dressing were accompanied by this macabre message, rather than a day in the life of a Yugoslavian family.

Much to my regret both as client and psychologist, after 3 weeks I was unable to report any success. I discussed this at length with Padmal, and he suggested a variation on the theme. Rather than develop the full richness of the thoughts, it might be better to record one single thought 'You will die'. I should put aside up to 2 hours each day just listening to this message. I should not try to economize on time by shaving or eating while the tape is playing, it needed to be my sole concern. Furthermore, it would be better to listen to the message through earphones, by means of which it would appear to originate in my head. After some thousands of exposures, any decrease could be compared with a thought that had not been habituated ('control condition'), for example, the death of someone close to me. He expressed sympathy and understanding at the prospect of a not very pleasant experiment. Again though, following exposure, I felt no diminution in the power of the thought to evoke a negative reaction. Death was as bad at the end of each session as at the beginning, and I could perceive no decline between sessions.

I then 'invented' a technique which was a variation on an

experiment of Pavlov's and used in behavioural therapy subsequently. Pavlov had shown that if an unpleasant event is
immediately followed by a pleasant one, the unpleasant one
sometimes loses its negative effect and can even appear to acquire a
positive aspect. For example, a dog will even come to salivate rather
than jump to a mild electric shock, if the shock heralds food. So
how could an unpleasant intrusion be followed by something
positive? A pleasant thought – sex? I discussed this with Padmal.
We both realized that there is a danger that the inverse can happen:
rather than death becoming less negative, one might become
frightened by sex. What would be a pleasant thought, but one not
quite so fundamental? We arrived at Indonesian food. Even if I
were to develop an aversion to this, though unfortunate for my visits
to Holland, it would not be catastrophic; I could always eat Indian
food. To every morbid thought, I answered with thoughts of a plate
of *gado gado* or *tahu goreng*. It appeared not to work, but was worth
the try.

Padmal questioned me closely on the exact nature of the
intruding thoughts, with a view to gaining control over them. What
sensory form did they take? Were they represented visually or
semantically? Was there consistency in their form?

A fundamental property of humans as well as other animals is the
desirability of having *control* over a situation. Take control away and
something vital is lost. One can try to gain some control over even
intrusive thoughts, which might lower their intensity. For example,
suppose someone's intrusive thought is always of a coffin in a
particular position. The subject can try to rotate this image in her
mind, or change its distance from 'the observer'. I tried to recall the
exact form that the intrusions took but this was surprisingly
difficult. I had not been required before to consider the problem in
this way – I had just lived with it on and off for 13 years. My recall,
confirmed by subsequent introspection, was that in general no one
single image or form was involved. The exact content varied. For
periods of a month or so, a distinct visual form would tend to
dominate. I would see myself in a coffin in church. That would be
followed the next month by seeing myself six feet underground.
Sometimes I would visualize the flames of the crematorium. At
other times, death would take a more abstract form. I would see
(yes, I think 'see' is right) a dimension marker like those used by
draughtsmen extending from now to about 40 years into the future,
with a clear end point indicated. The marker would nudge me with
'It's limited, it will not last forever'.

At times the intrusions were abstract, almost cryptic. A joyful
anticipation would trigger 'it' – it being, as best I can describe it, a
feeling of 'negative emotion' that had no immediate sensory
thought content. 'It' was almost independent of the death thought –

one might imagine this feeling as serving as a messenger that all is not well. Unity was not there. Anticipation was a risky business since the good will be tainted with the bad. Were I to probe what was going on, to ask myself immediately after feeling the wave of negative emotion what it was about, then the associated thought content was clear enough: death.

After extensive discussion with Padmal concerning the richness of content of my intrusions, represented in both visual and semantic forms, we felt that they did not lend themselves to the approach of trying to gain control over the exact form of their content.

The methods of behavioural psychology not having worked, I turned again to my GP for help, suggesting medication. Knowing me to be a psychologist, he asked what I thought. I said that anxiety was the most obvious feature, any depression was secondary to anxiety. Therefore, it would suggest anti-anxiety agents. The choice was between anti-anxiety or anti-depressant tablets, though the distinction is not always a clear one. We settled for anti-anxiety agents, though he wasn't entirely convinced that this was right. These tablets did not appear to help. I then tried beta-blockers but they didn't help either.

Now in 1986, the ruminations were getting worse again and they were taking a somewhat different character, towards the philosophical. Hitherto their intellectual content had hardly been profound, consisting of repetitions of a few uncomplicated black thoughts. Now I was being tormented by associated existential dilemmas and theological ideas that might have been fascinating, had I been strong enough to take them. But they were bringing me much bother for very little insight; I simply wanted to be rid of them.

Up till then on being asked if I were a Christian, I would reply rather light-heartedly 'if I wake up one day in heaven, I'll believe. Until then I am a card-carrying agnostic.' The question didn't really trouble me, though it was a matter of some detached intellectual fascination. The fear of death was certainly not a fear of divine retribution or theological uncertainty, but simply one of losing my earthly identity. Now the thoughts concerned the insignificance of a mortal existence. This moved me to read a great deal to try to come to terms with the problem. Donald Mackay's views on the after-life, Russell Stannard's on the relation between science and religion and the work *The Intelligent Universe* by Sir Fred Hoyle, amongst many others, provided a rich source of stimulation, but no answers to reduce the discomfort. Helen and I parted under the strain.

Nothing seemed to add up; it just wouldn't work any way. Being raised on a belief in Darwinian evolution, it was difficult to see why or how a system should need to go through the tortuous stages of evolution to get to us, if it were in some meaningful sense instigated by an omniscient and omnipotent source. On the other hand, purpose is an intrinsic feature of how biological systems work, and so by logical extension one might feel it necessary to impute a purposive quality to the whole evolutionary process. Could God be the end point rather than the start? The discussions I was hearing from my associates in physics, with time running backwards and subatomic particles seeming to exist for a microsecond only in the eye of the beholder, would permit almost anything to be believed.

To ask how long the physical universe has existed used to be described as being philosophically naive. Now such a question was again respectable. I ruminated endlessly on these issues, torturing myself with them. The possibility of, the hope of, life after death assumed an inordinate significance for someone who previously would have described the issue as naive and a waste of time. The distinguished neuroscientist Professor Donald Mackay made the prospect of a transformation from a physical body to a non-physical one sound almost easy, by comparison with a translation of computer software from one computer to another, but this helped not at all. Indeed, it only fuelled further pointless speculation. Suppose the transformation to the after-life went wrong; by analogy with my experience of computers, an unexpected bug in the translation program could cause havoc. Suppose the transformation yielded only a pale imitation of a conscious being. Suppose there is something about the real biological nerve cells, flesh and blood that yields consciousness, something that could not be captured by a computer program. Suppose. Suppose. Suppose . . . Just let me get out of this madhouse!

Hard-nosed mechanistic science and analogies between humans and rats, in which I had placed so much faith, were now just another source of fear. Something essential was missing, if not in any rational or scientific sense then certainly as far as my psychological needs were concerned. Was I craving for the impossible? But this was a real need, a need for security that my science could not provide.

Now the obsessions were accurately characterized not so much as an image or a spoken word, but as a series of related intellectual puzzles, ones that I only wanted to be rid of. Life after death triggered the speculation 'why couldn't the world be a secure place where death never intruded?' How could anyone be expected to cope with the vagaries of mortal existence? If only things had been different in the beginning, we might have had an immortal consciousness. If only . . . If only . . . The philosophical dilemma of it all, or 'pathological dilemma' if one prefers the expression, tortured me. It was as if I had been programmed to search out the incongruous, the fearful in everything that impinged upon me. The world can be a terrifying place if viewed through such a mental processor, and this one seemed brilliant at finding anxiety- and depression-evoking dilemmas.

I understand how the obsessional, John Bunyan, felt:

> *'But yet all the things of God were kept out of my sight, and still the tempter followed me with,* But whither must you go when you die? what will become of you? where will you be found in another world? what evidence have you for heaven and glory, and an inheritance among them that are sanctified? *Thus was I tossed for manie weeks, and knew not what to do . . .'*

Doubtless Woody Allen could have put some of the content of my more absurd thoughts to productive artistic use, but I could see no humour in any of it.

When the intrusive thought did have a clear visual character, this was now most often of the earth spinning on somewhere in the vast expanse of the universe. How little and insignificant we seemed in all this space. How terrifying was the lack of control over fate implied by this image.

Fear alternated with frustration and jealousy, a kind of egotism and narcissism that one would be ashamed to make public. I didn't even want to contemplate the universe going on without me. I wanted to be 'where it is all at'; I couldn't possibly delegate this to anyone else. No; posterity earned through writing books didn't even begin to answer the need. The possibility of some form of survival in the consciousness of my friends and students was just a mockery of my basic need; there was only one variety of posterity that mattered, the survival of personal consciousness. All else was nonsense. Nothing appeared to be of any value, since nothing would be permanent. Why bother to achieve anything? Every task before me seemed meaningless since none of them would survive. Every goal was measured against the potential mortality of the end point, and every task of course failed the test.

A paradox was becoming more and more evident. As bad as the intrusive thoughts were, and as strenuous and unambiguous as my efforts to fight them were, when I reflected upon the possibility of life without them, this prospect held its own peculiar anxiety. Imagine facing death unexpectedly. At least the way things are at present, it can never catch you unawares. I might even resolve the issue, provided I worked hard enough at it. But if I don't reflect on the issue, there is no chance of resolving it. Could there be a bizarre mechanism at work that was sustaining these thoughts because on the one level they were a protection mechanism? Maybe, but what did that lead to? Never for a moment in my actions did I detract from the battle to eliminate the enemy.

In November 1986, my mental state moved worryingly downwards. I noticed that my startle reaction, always sensitive, was now hypersensitive. I walked into my office one day, expecting to find no one there, and was met by my secretary. My reaction was one of intense fear. Things that went even mildly bang in the night put me into a state of immediate panic. My fear level as indexed by the pounding of my heart was sensitive to such normally innocuous sounds as the refrigerator going on and off in a distant room.

The anxiety was bad but perhaps depression was now the most dominant emotion. Feeling desperate, I looked into the possibility of private medical care, but was advised against it. I lost both my appetite and my interest for work, and started waking each morning at about 4am. Getting up was such a struggle. I couldn't face the day and I kept telling myself that if only I could have stayed in bed, things might have been better. Sleeping pills were prescribed for me. I was told to take no more than two in a week, in order to avoid dependence. I stretched it to three. At first, those two or three nights were a great relief, but even the pills could not spare me from the ruminations. The most trivial of tasks seemed utterly daunting; I would find reasons to put off composing even a 'thank-you' letter since I couldn't face the effort involved in writing it.

People looked unattractive to me, and yet paradoxically they all looked so well-adjusted and successful. Their behaviour annoyed me and evoked covert hostility and impatience. Whether shopping or waiting for a bus, the crowd had one thing in common: they were in my way. Then, in a queue, experiencing such a feeling, I might feel guilty when an old lady would turn to me and say 'Sorry I'm slow'. This was a useful reminder that so much of what we perceive depends upon our own interpretation. In spite of my intolerance, I was frightened to be alone. I tried to engineer the week ahead to make sure that I always had someone around me. People at work said that I looked ill.

A few weeks before this decline I had obtained a new book on obsessions by Professor Graham Reed[1] and read it with interest. Reed argued for anti-depressants as a treatment for obsessions. Knowing that British GPs do not always appreciate being told what to prescribe by their patients, it was with some reservation that I took Reed's book with me to the next appointment. However, my own GP has a rather progressive approach and has said that he always appreciated having an 'expert witness' as patient. He agreed that it would be wise to try anti-depressants, and prescribed Flupenthixol *(Fluanxol)* for me. Unfortunately, it had little desirable effect, and induced tiredness and an inability to concentrate, a zombie-like state.

I visited some GP friends of mine, Barbara and Richard, in

Coventry, and they recommended the powerful anti-depressant Clomipramine (*Anafranil*). The next day, I had an appointment with a local psychiatrist and I mentioned their advice. He also felt that this would be a wise choice and prescribed it. I told him that I might be sinking, but at least I will go down with a fight. 'That's the spirit. Fight it,' he replied, 'You won't sink.'

A low dosage of 10mg of Anafranil per day was to be increased progressively to 75mg per day. These tablets appeared to work well for me. My appetite came back. Healthy workaholic tendencies reemerged and sleep was much improved. The intrusions were less frequent and certainly less frightening. I was back in control again. The only undesirable side-effects were the relatively minor ones of mid-day tiredness, excessive yawning at times and a dry mouth, particularly in the morning. Some of these problems can be answered to some extent by taking a glass of water to bed with you and trying to steal a 10-minute nap at lunchtime. I put on a significant and unwelcome amount of weight.

Both the psychiatrist and my GP were very pleased with the results but the psychiatrist said he saw Anafranil as only being a kind of first aid. In the longer term, the answer would probably lie in some form of psychotherapy. I have the usual behaviourist suspicion of psychoanalysis but do not feel so antagonistic towards other forms of therapy. The psychiatrist announced that a clinical psychologist, Hilary Edwards, trained in *cognitive* therapy had just joined the Milton Keynes practice, and recommended that I see her.

An example of part of our conversation went something like this.

'What bothers you about death? Is it a fear of what might happen to you after death or a fear of the process of dying?'

'Well . . . er . . . it is a fear, true, but sometimes perhaps not so much a fear as such but more a disappointment, a frustration, it messes things up to know that they won't last . . . it is a fear and a regret in one . . . er . . . it's difficult to explain really.'

'Yes, I know that it is difficult, but are you saying that things that must end are intrinsically of little value? Do only eternal things have value?'

'Yes . . . I guess so, . . . sort of . . .'

'Have you ever had a really good holiday?'

'Yes.'

'But that had to end. Because it had to end, and you knew that it had to end, did that make it not valuable?'

'No' . . .

In this way, the therapist tries to give the client some tools to reconstruct the way he or she sees the world. It is more subtle than pinging elastic bands or repeated exposure. It tries to reshape thought processes that have become automatic and self-reinforcing.

The cognitive therapist invited me to try to find some constructive answers to the obsessional thoughts. For example, in response to the intrusion 'death will come', one might find that its impact can be neutralized to some extent by thinking 'Yes, it will, but that is something beyond my power to worry about. I must concentrate on what I can do at this moment, and leave such matters to others. It will probably be all right on the night.' I tried that counter-cognition repeatedly but I didn't manage to convince myself. The technique did not work for me.

In response to 'all will end' one might try 'We can't be sure that all will end. We simply don't know what will happen. Let's wait and see.'

Another technique that we tried was role reversal. The therapist argues for the motion, in this case death is something to fear and dread, and the client attempts to marshal arguments against it. The exchange went something like this.

'It's just not worth it. I might as well die.'

'But surely it is worth it. Your husband and child need you.'

'But since it will end it all makes no sense now to bother about anything. I really couldn't care less about life unless it is eternal life.'

'But you don't act that way. Your actions are those of someone who does value even a mortal existence.' . . .

This is something that the obsessive can try out with a partner or friend.

But does any of this work? I don't think it helped me much to explore my cognitions, but it might help some people. I concluded that there is no magic solution. Each of these techniques can possibly help in a little way to undermine the power of the intrusions.

I had now established a correspondence with Graham Reed, in which we exchanged ideas about intrusive thoughts. Professor Reed urged me to go public, arguing that I would have a valuable contribution to make. I resisted but soon saw the wisdom of putting my thoughts together.

Clomipramine having rescued 'me, life proceeded smoothly and got better. The intrusions were still there, but at a low frequency and intensity and I felt resigned to them. They were able to be lived with. A person might have a wooden leg and wish that they had one made of flesh and bone, but they can live life nearly to the full. That was how I felt.

Padmal had earlier directed me to the book *Living with Fear*, by Isaac Marks. After reading this excellent work, I decided to try a slightly different technique of confronting the intrusions. It is one also described by Viktor Frankl, as *paradoxical intention*. Rather than lengthy sessions of saturation bombing with thoughts of the kind 'it will happen, it's hopeless,' I specifically answered each intrusive thought with a silent thought that was even more negative than the intrusion. Only in *response to* an unwanted mental event did I present myself with this counter-thought. I confronted myself in my imagination with the worst possible situation that could prevail. For example 'death will come,' I answered with 'of course it will and it will be terrible when it does'. I felt that this worked better than sessions of exposure that were conducted regardless of ongoing mental activity. For me, paradoxical intention was effective.

Now a big event was looming; in June 1987, I was to give the opening talk at an international symposium in Italy on emotion, and I devoted myself to this task. I needed to do a lot of prior reading.

I travelled by train to Pisa. The conference was a wonderful success but during the week my thoughts turned to transport for getting back to England. The journey out by train had been fine, allowing me to visit Paris. But I needed to get back to England soon after the conference. I hadn't flown for 16 years since coming back from Ljubljana, when I was terrified. In the meantime I had been forced to decline invitations to give lectures in, amongst other places, Moscow and Atlanta. Now was my chance to attempt overcoming the fear. I could try flying on impulse and thereby relatively little anticipation need be involved. Just go to the airport and try to get on the next flight to England.

One of the benefits of being at such a conference is that amongst the delegates are some of the leading figures on the subject of emotion, with little else to do in the evenings but to drink wine and talk about emotion. I approached Professor Albert Bandura of Stanford University, who emphasized the vital role of trying to gain mastery in any situation of fear. But how at this late stage does one get to master an aircraft, unless you happen to be the pilot? It seemed though that I had some minimal potential mastery. I had to go to the airport and buy my ticket. Even at that late stage, I could always opt out and go by train. I could learn something about aircraft. I could try talking to the steward. The wisdom of drinking alcohol was mentioned by my associates, though I guess that one does not need to be a psychologist to know that.

On the Saturday morning, a small group of us including Vernon Hamilton, a noted expert on obsessionality, and David Warburton, set out by minibus for Pisa airport. The driver fitted exactly one's image of Latins, as he negotiated the bends in the road. At this stage, in their extreme discomfort on the back seat, Vernon Hamilton and his wife Betty tried some 'cognitive psychotherapy' on me, to the amusement of the other passengers.

'Are you afraid right now?'

'No. Or rather any fear I might feel is being attributed to the prospect of flying.'

'Good, because you should really be frightened of this journey. Flying will be safer and more comfortable than being in this mini-bus.'

'Yes. I understand all that, but it isn't really a question of statistics.'

'What are you scared of then?'

'Dying. It's all a question of mastery. I feel that I can influence this driver in some strange way.'

On arriving in one piece at Pisa airport, I proceeded to buy a ticket for London. David Warburton used his knowledge of psychopharmacology to devise a schedule of wine ingestion. The logic was simple: the alcohol level in the blood should rise at its sharpest as we boarded the aircraft. David confessed that even as an inveterate traveller he had his fears. 'Alcohol and mastery are the solution; organize your environment when you get on the plane,' he said. 'Ask for a newspaper and a bloody Mary. Have the stewardesses running around you. This will create the feeling that you are master of what goes on.' He then gave me still more the impression of mastery by describing the layout of Pisa airport, the wind direction, the hills that had to be cleared by the aircraft. We observed pilots doing checks of their wing flaps and watched take-offs and landings. It helped to see the faces of pilots. All this made it seem human.

I felt that I could perceive the alcohol soaking into my brain, as our flight was called. My emotion was now one of positive excitement rather than fear. I felt some anxiety as the plane accelerated down the runway but soon the alcohol soothed such lingering doubts. On hearing that I hadn't flown for 16 years, Captain Godfrey asked me into the cockpit and explained the controls. This was just fantastic; I loved it. On arriving at London, I realized I had totally conquered my fear – a testimony to simple exposure as therapy. Now there would be no stopping me; I had 16 lost years to make up.

I had always wanted to visit the Orient: Japan, China or Thailand, but fear of flying had made this impossible. Now, on earning my wings, I immediately consolidated the gain by booking a flight to Bangkok, to take a much-needed holiday in November. I borrowed the Linguaphone 'Teach yourself Thai' course from the library. By November, I had 'mastered' enough to feel confident with some very small 'small-talk'.

I was able to consume surreptitiously a can of wine before take-off at Heathrow. It was in a calm mood that I boarded the 747, and took into my hand the good-luck charm that a friend had given me for the journey. Take-off was fearless, even exhilarating, as was the rest of the 12-hour journey. Conversation with other passengers was aided by British Airways' regular supply of food and drink. Stepping out of the temperature-controlled plane at Bangkok airport really was like opening an oven door, and the 'Land of smiles' soon lived up to its name. I fought off successive waves of touts and took a bus for Bangkok city. Its traffic had been described to me, but the reality surpassed any description. The crazy driving, the heat, the noise, the choking pollution, a particularly obnoxious strain of mosquito – I wondered what the people have got to be so cheerful about, but perhaps such speculation is naive. The effect is infectious; even the European tourists start smiling at each other.

I travelled a bit around the country and visited a remote settlement of huts where the locals made me welcome. My few Thai expressions came in useful. When they were combined with some English, sign language and drawings, we understood each other reasonably well. I regretted that I had not learned to speak more Thai. After leaving the settlement by a dirt track, I started walking down a road, not knowing where I was heading. Two youths on a motor bike passed, looked at me and stopped. I was greeted with the standard question that Thais love to ask of anyone looking at all foreign:

'Where you go?'

'I go to the town.'

'It's a long way. If you buy me some petrol, I'll take you.'

'How about your companion?'

'He can wait here till I come back for him!'

As we set off dodging the holes in the road and swerving round bends, I suddenly remembered the promise I had faithfully made to my friend in England who gave me the good-luck charm – that I would at all times take care. We arrived safely at our destination and I gave the young man some money for petrol.

Obsessional thoughts were at a very low frequency and intensity. I speculated that the familiar environmental trigger-cues with which they had been associated over the years were mainly absent here; in Bangkok there was little to prime them. One day I experienced the thought sequence (1) Caucasian male approaching, (2) looks like Bertrand Russell, (3) Russell is dead and (4) the inevitability of death. This stood out as being a rare occurrence of an obsessional thought. Whatever the explanation, Thailand was heavenly and free of distractions, at least of the unwanted sort!

It was with a lump in my throat that I boarded the 747 for London. I took no alcohol but felt no fear. Could the emotion of sorrow at leaving new-found friends be inhibiting expression of fear? For whatever reason, I felt sure I had now completely cured my fear of flying. I watched the lights of Bangkok receding below as we headed west.

Looking at my behaviour in learning Thai also demonstrated clearly that I was, as always, obsessed with efficiency. Washing up or shaving did not represent an efficient use of time if the mental machinery were lying idle. Learning Thai by the cassettes *and* shaving was an efficient use of time. Time was treated as a commodity like money or petrol. I was trying to maximize my efficiency, as one might do with a racehorse.

I was, though, enjoying Thai very much, and I couldn't wait to get back onto the 747. This year, 1987, had been a good year. City University had awarded me a Doctor of Science for my contribution to psychology. I had no more night terrors, and thanks to Clomipramine, unwanted thoughts were under control. Next year, 1988, looked like being even better.

PART 2
What is obsessional disorder and what can be done about it?

10
The nature of the problem

Obsessional disorder presents a peculiar challenge and often formidable difficulty for not only the sufferer but also the doctor, psychiatrist and researcher. It is so hard for the non-sufferer to appreciate just how much distress is caused by obsessional disorder. For such activities as checking, the person is tempted to apply simple rationality – why don't they stop? Worse still, the behaviour can evoke the response – snap out of it or pull yourself together. Anyone working with obsessionals can tell you that, in the extreme, the problem can be every bit as debilitating as any known mental disorder.

Some notable investigators have occupied themselves with obsessional disorder, for example Sigmund Freud (1856–1939) and the distinguished French psychologist Pierre Janet (1859–1947). Janet is relatively unknown in the English-speaking world. His classic work on the subject of obsessionality, entitled *Les Obsessions et la Psychasthénie*, has never been translated into English. In my view, this has been a profound loss to psychology. Given the demise of French as a second language in the English-speaking world, researchers and therapists often have, at best, only a second-hand contact with Janet's work. Janet made a meticulous and extensive study of obsessionals in Paris. His work is beautifully written in a simple unaffected style, with a maximum of sympathy for his patients and their own insight, and with a minimum of unsupported speculation. His theoretical speculations were always modestly made, with extensive reference to the work of antecedent researchers.

Freud, a rather different personality-type to Janet, expressed a strong interest in obsessional neurosis, and two of his most celebrated cases, that of *Wolf-man* and *The Rat Man*, were apparently obsessional neurotics. There is some suggestion that Freud personally had experience of the obsessional phenomenon, and he certainly believed that it would be a very fruitful area to investigate in the future. Unfortunately, the efficacy of psychoanalytic techniques has not lived up to this promise, though some features of the disorder as experienced by the victim are often well described in the psychoanalytic literature.

Exactly what is obsessional disorder?

What are obsessional experiences and who suffers from them? There is some difficulty in describing exactly what is an obsessional disorder but perhaps the problems are less than for the diagnosis of other mental disorders. There is a fairly good consensus as to its definition and diagnosis, possibly better than for, say, schizophrenia.

Obsessional thoughts consist of a mental image or idea that has a feeling of compulsion. The compulsive quality of the thought overrides any resistance that the victim can offer. The thoughts are perceived as alien and often bizarre or morbid. (It is often possible to detect a change of heart rate associated with the obsessional subject experiencing the unwanted thought.) The sufferer tends to show brooding, doubting and speculation.

A major problem with pure obsessions, i.e. those unaccompanied by bizarre behaviour, is that, by definition, the disorder cannot be observed by others. Indeed, behaviour might look amazingly normal. On the other hand, where compulsive behaviour is concerned, this is often either washing or checking. It is easy to define and measure. Though bizarre, it is not morally unacceptable, and so one might expect fairly truthful accounts from the sufferer.

Commonly having meticulousness as a character trait and generally being articulate, means that obsessional patients can often provide their doctor with reliable data on their behaviour. My own doctor once told me that he would like to be able to test all of his new drugs on me. Interestingly though, Pierre Janet reported inordinate trouble in getting his patients to confess the truth about their thoughts. These days, as in Janet's time, sometimes patients are simply too embarrassed to come clean and speak the truth. They prefer to skate around the central problem, discussing only such things as 'general unease' or 'low spirits'. One cannot overstate the importance of the patient being as honest as possible, as soon as possible. Once under care, obsessionals are good patients in general, and having started on a course of treatment tend to see it through conscientiously. On the other hand, the caregiver runs the risk of being inundated with both spoken and written data obtained by the patient on their condition.

What is and *isn't* an obsessional disorder

The common use of the word 'obsession' is distinct from both an obsessional personality and an obsessional problem. Only the last two are discussed in this book. We commonly describe people as 'obsessional', without their so-called obsession being a problem to them. For instance, great inventors and scientists are often described as 'obsessed' with their intellectual challenge. They might ruminate for years on end, before finding a solution. The great composers, such as Schumann, have vividly described the endless toil that is necessary to achieve perfection. Our lives are richer as a result of such dogged persistence. These are totally different mental and behavioural phenomena to what we mean by the expressions 'obsessional thoughts' and 'obsessional behaviour'. In obsessional disorder, we are concerned with phenomena that seriously *trouble* the subject. By stark contrast, Schumann didn't resist his musical thoughts; on the contrary, they were part of his calling.

Some people might commonly be described as being obsessed with sex or the pursuit of money. However, I would not describe this as an obsessional problem. These individuals are not, we imagine, engaging in such behaviour as a way of neutralizing an unpleasant intrusive thought. The more usual erotic thoughts might well be distracting or frustrating, but would not normally be considered unpleasantly intrusive. In the present context, enjoyable thoughts or impulses are not termed 'obsessional'.

Neither is the spontaneous and unprovoked nature of a thought sufficient to classify it as a problem. Both Beethoven and Mozart have described how some of their creative ideas just came from 'nowhere'. Going from the sublime to the ridiculous, I am sure that I am no exception in frequently having just one line of a current pop song on my mind for ages and being 'compelled' to sing it. This certainly causes no pain to me; indeed, I greatly enjoy it, though I can't speak for those within earshot.

Consider the man who spends each day standing at Oxford Circus in London with a banner proclaiming 'Eat less protein. Protein stimulates sexual passion.' He might be said by some to be obsessed with his eccentric cause. In this context, the term has pejorative connotations, implying that his time might be better spent doing something more fruitful. However, in my terms, he is not exhibiting obsessional behaviour, since he does not resist his calling. The behaviour fits his life's goals. It would be inappropriate in a free society to suggest that he might consider changing his behaviour or need psychiatric intervention.

Although we clearly need caution in our use of the word 'obsession', the everyday usage does have a vivid meaning and presumably people will go on employing it in this sense. We simply need to take care not to include the dedicated scientist or police officer or the religious fanatic when discussing the subject at a medical level. To contrast the lay usage of 'obsession' with our true quarry, obsessional disorder, consider the intrusive thoughts described by John Bunyan, which acted against his life's purpose:

'... *if I have been hearing the Word, then uncleanliness, blasphemies, and despair, would hold me as Captive there; if I have been reading, then sometimes I had sudden thoughts to question all I read; sometimes again my mind would be so strangely snatched away, and possessed with other things, that I have neither known, nor regarded, nor remembered so much as the sentence that but now I have read.*

Sometimes again, when I have been preaching, I have been violently assaulted with thoughts of blasphemy, and strongly tempted to speak them with my mouth before the Congregation.'

These thoughts vividly illustrate our usage.

The dictionary definition of obsession is somewhat nearer the medical usage. The origin of the word is the Latin *obsidere*, which means to besiege. Definitions of the verb 'to obsess' generally involve 'to beset', 'to assail', 'to possess', 'to harass like a besieging force or an evil spirit'. The *Oxford English Dictionary* shows a significant change of emphasis between the early and late 17th century. Compare the following two definitions of 'obsession':

'The hostile action of the devil or an evil spirit besetting any one; actuation by the devil or an evil spirit from without; the fact of being thus beset or actuated',

and

'The action of any influence, notion or "fixed idea" which persistently assails or vexes, especially so as to discompose the mind'.

Coming to more recent times, *Chambers's Everyday Dictionary* captures an aspect of obsessional rumination in its definition of 'obsession' as 'morbid persistence of an idea in the mind: a fixed idea'.

My usage of 'obsession' conforms to the definition given by Graham Reed,[1] as applied to an individual who suffers constantly from '... intrusive and persistent mental events, which he usually recognizes as being foolish and unacceptable but which, despite all his efforts, he is unable to dispel.'

The meaning we are using here emphasizes the unwelcome nature of the intrusion, that these thoughts are in some sense imposed upon the conscious mind against its wishes. Care in our definition will help us to distinguish the condition from other distinct disorders that have some properties in common with it.[2] Repetitive mental events, even associated with repetitive movements, are found in a variety of disorders that one would not want to call obsessional, such as schizophrenia and some diseases of the nervous system. This is a vital consideration for a doctor providing a diagnosis. If the patient realizes that the actual thoughts causing the trouble are senseless or illogical this can serve as a valuable guide to the existence of an obsessional problem, but it should not be regarded as a necessary condition. Lewis[2] adds:

'Critical appraisal of the obsession, and recognition that it is absurd represents a defensive, intellectual effort, intended to destroy it: it is not always present, nor is the obsessional idea always absurd.'

More crucial and exclusive a criterion for Lewis is that the victim *resists* the intrusion. I would prefer to say that the subject *in principle* opposes the thought and has opposed it. In practice, in some cases, after a very long while, the subject has simply given up the struggle.

We are concerned then with thoughts that are frequent, unpleasant and, in general, resisted. Our criteria for obsessionality are not met by pleasant thoughts, which might still invade the stream of consciousness, but are not resisted. For practical purposes, our criteria would also rule out the experience of *occasional* unpleasant intrusive thoughts as being obsessional. A survey carried out on London students showed that most of them experienced thoughts, both positive and negative, that were perceived as intruding.[3] The thought content often did not differ very much from that of sufferers from obsessional disorder. What distinguished these so-called 'normal' thoughts from those creating a serious problem was that the abnormal obsessional thoughts last longer, are more intense and occur more frequently, are perceived as more alien and accompanied by stronger urges to neutralization, are more strongly resisted and are harder to dismiss. Similarly, many people have small rituals that they feel the need to observe. These are, of course, quite different to debilitating obsessive-compulsive disorder.

Interestingly, obsessional patients are more easily able to evoke their unwanted thought upon request than are normal subjects. The thought has a low threshold, as if it is permanently primed. Paradoxically, in this respect, obsessional patients could be said to have more control of their thought content than do non-obsessional control subjects.

To summarize, obsessional thoughts are treated as a special group deserving of therapy because of their quality, frequency and the resistance that they evoke.

How many people suffer from the disorder?

Some estimates had in the past put it as high as 1–2 per cent of the American population who in some way or other suffer from an obsessional problem. The latest and astonishing estimate is that up to five million Americans suffer from it.[4] The chances are that everyone knows well at least one person with the condition. As a percentage, Britons are probably not far from the American estimates, though this is speculation. However, the number of patients complaining primarily of obsessional disorders is a small percentage of those receiving psychiatric care (something like 3 per cent of those patients treated for neuroses), so it is possible that someone seeking medical help could find themselves to be their doctor's first patient with this condition. Hence, the doctor might be unsure about therapy or medication. Giving a precise figure for the incidence of the disorder based upon those seeking psychiatric help is however almost impossible due to the overlap of obsessional disorder with other conditions, such as anorexia nervosa, panic disorder, phobias and depression.

Obsessionals are more secretive than other sufferers from psychological problems and so it is the more serious disorders that tend to get seen by the medical profession. Without doubt, very many simply suffer in silence. Sometimes even the most severe cases only receive medical attention after heavy persuasion from relatives or close friends. The relatively small number of obsessionals as a percentage of psychiatric patients means that well-controlled studies are difficult to do, just because of the shortage of available subjects outside the main population concentrations.

Nature and nurture

Is the disorder inherited? Some authorities argue that it is. One problem here concerns the relatively small number of sufferers that are 'out in the open'. Ideally, one might like to compare identical and fraternal twins, brought up together or apart. However, the reader will doubtless appreciate the rarity of finding such subjects amongst available obsessionals. Although genetic transmission of obsessional-compulsive disorder as such is difficult to show, there is good evidence for an inherited tendency to general neuroticism ('emotional oversensitivity'), which for some subjects *might* reveal itself in obsessional problems.

Might the tendencies be passed on by children imitating their parents? Again it is difficult to do the necessary observations, but imitation of specific behaviours 'seems unlikely to happen often. Imitation of overall strategies for dealing with the world, such as timidity and caution, seems more likely. By genetics or by environmental observation, or more likely a subtle interaction of the two, the child might well come to acquire a tendency to timidity and overdependence. Some experts would regard this as fertile soil for the later growth of obsessional disorder. It appears that the illness is relatively common amongst the relatives of obsessionals. Their home environment tends to be excessively controlled. However, the number of sufferers coming from perfectly normal backgrounds makes any simple and unqualified appeal to 'faulty upbringing' suspicious. Parents should not blame themselves.

Age of onset

Obsessional disorder usually reveals itself between the ages of 20 and 30 years, though obsessional patients commonly report a variety of neurotic symptoms (or 'oversensitivity') exhibited in childhood. Phobias and mild compulsions are commonly part of the childhood experience of adult obsessional patients. Obsessional traits are also commonly shown prior to the full-blown emergence of the disorder, though this is by no means always so.

Obsessional disorder is uncommon in children, though it does sometimes occur. Indeed, it is even seen in its full 'adult' form in some children. This can occur even where there is neither indication of obsessional personality prior to the disorder nor evidence of obsessionality in the parents.

The average age at which professional help is sought is around 28 (I was 29), though there might have been considerable trouble for years before this. It is rare to find the onset beyond the age of 40. The majority of Janet's patients were between 20 and 40. Some investigators see the significance of the age factor as being that onset is rare outside what might be termed the active and striving period of life. The course of the trouble is sometimes up and down, commonly with two really bad periods in a lifetime. Stress or fatigue are likely to exacerbate the condition. For other sufferers the intensity of the problem is nearer constant, sometimes for life.

Is onset associated with a particular event?

According to a survey in Sweden, obsessionals can sometimes accurately date the time of onset of their symptoms.[5] For one patient, a pregnant woman, onset was while she was cleaning fish. Holding the dead fish appeared to be the cue to provoke thoughts of the transient nature of life. Another female patient was mincing meat and became obsessed with the thought that she could mince the flesh of her husband. The onset was not uncommonly associated with trauma that involved pronounced bodily anxiety symptoms, such as abnormal breathing or activity of the heart. This anxiety could be caused by, for example, the death of someone near to the subject. For some subjects, at the time of onset there might have been bodily disturbance with no obvious cause, such as the feeling that they will stop breathing. Temperature stress; a particular occasion involving excessive consumption of alcohol; pregnancy and abortion; sexual and marital problems were also represented amongst patients trying to date the time of onset. Some investigators report that the precipitating factor occasionally involves unexpressed anger. In other cases, it is not easy to determine the precise age of onset of the disorder, since this is gradual. In some 30–50 per cent of cases no precipitating event could be found. In some cases, during the course of depression, obsessional disorders arise and outlast the depression itself.

The nature of the thoughts

The essence of the problem is that the thoughts are perceived as alien to the person's lifestyle, his or her ambitions and desires in life. They can disrupt the subject's work and pleasure alike. The victim is unable to relax and accept the thought as irrelevant to his life. He usually feels compelled to offer some kind of resistance to it. The reaction and responses are likely to be much the same even after years of innumerable repetitions of the same theme.

The patient's subjective report that the thoughts are unwanted is crucial for classification of the disorder. Without this, even the content of the thoughts cannot be used unambiguously to identify an obsessional problem. For example, consider a patient whose problem consists of ruminating over why God created the world. Of course, some of the greatest intellects in history have occupied themselves with just that type of question, but one would not want to describe them as having psychiatric problems! What to them evoked pleasant awe, reverence, fascination and welcome challenge, would, by contrast, torment the obsessional patient.

Imagine two men both experiencing the identical set of thoughts, whose content is that they are worthless individuals. The one man might indeed feel that he is one of life's failures and do nothing to resist the thoughts. The second might resist the thoughts, recognizing that they are totally at odds with the true assessment of his worth. Only the second would be characterized as having an obsessional problem.[6]

Although obsessional thoughts occur spontaneously, without prompting from outside, they can also be provoked by certain external stimuli (e.g. passing a cemetery). Most obsessionals who present themselves for treatment are easily able to evoke the obsessional thought in response to instructions from the therapist. This is important where treatment requires the patient to entertain the obsessional thought. By contrast, once evoked, it is difficult to dismiss the thought, and the length of this time appears to give some measure of the severity of the discomfort that the intrusions cause. A radical change of environment can sometimes produce temporary relief from obsessions. New signals from a novel environment possibly inhibit the well-established obsessional signals in the brain.

The amount of resistance that subjects can muster in reply to an intrusion will normally vary over time. Their 'will-power' fluctuates. The following are typical reports from an obsessional:[7] 'I've been fighting it today, using all my will-power. Last week, I just didn't feel up to it.' 'I usually struggle with it. Today, I just feel too exhausted.' Another subject was ab'e to escape from his ruminations after receiving news of promotion. 'I just feel on top of the world. I could handle anything . . .' One patient was particularly vulnerable at the times of her menstruation and when she suffered bowel trouble. 'There's too much stacked against me . . . It's bad enough fighting it at the best of times, but right now I feel helpless – I haven't the will-power to go on.'

Content of obsessional thoughts

Pure obsessional thoughts (i.e. not involving compulsive behaviour) can, to a large extent, be divided into three categories: religious, sexual and violent. Religious ruminations seem somewhat less popular now than was the case in the past, as might be expected from the decline in influence of the church. At one time the condition we now term 'obsessional disorder' was described as *religious melancholy*, indicating its affinity to what we would now term 'depression'. A typical obsession of this class (in so far as any obsession can be described as 'typical') might be the fear of shouting 'Jesus is a bastard' in church on Sunday. The sufferer might feel a behavioural impulse, for example that they are about to shout obscenities in a public place, and feel themselves resisting this impulse. Pierre Janet encountered a relatively large number of patients suffering from this kind of obsession. Their thought content was a compound of sacred and profane aspects: examples included thoughts of a soul contaminated by excrement and a sexual perversion committed in church. For years, Claire, one of Janet's patients, had suffered some 200 times a day from the intrusive thought of the juxtaposition of a penis and the bread of holy communion. In some cases, months elapsed before the patients would confess to Janet the true nature of their thought content. In the meantime, Janet and the patient would go around in circles getting no nearer than discussing vague approximations to the central theme. Such patients often had a history of spending time in extensive philosophical speculation and rumination before developing a specific obsessional problem.

In the 17th-century autobiography of John Bunyan, *Grace Abounding to the Chief of Sinners*, we have a textbook case of intrusive thoughts of a religious nature:

'But it was neither my dislike of the thought, nor yet any desire and

endeavour to resist it, that in the least did shake or abate the continuation or force of strength thereof; for it did always in almost whatever I thought, intermix itself therewith, in such sort that I could neither eat my food, stoop for a pin, chop a stick, or cast mine eyes to look on this or that, but still the temptation would come, Sell Christ for this, or sell Christ for that; sell him, sell him.'

Sometimes he was assailed with fears concerning future damnation, and at other times hair-splitting existential dilemmas troubled him. The inner words 'Sell Christ' tormented him very much. The following quotation from his autobiography suggests that at other times the intrusive images were of a visual kind:

'Also when because I have had wandering thoughts in the time of this duty, I have laboured to compose my mind and fix it upon God; then, with great force, hath the Tempter laboured to distract me and confound me, and to turn away my mind, by presenting to my heart and fancy the form of a Bush, a Bull, a Besom, or the like, as if I should pray to those . . .'

Sexual themes for intrusions include seeing oneself, or those near to one, being in a perverse sexual role, such as committing rape. Violent themes, taken in the broadest sense of the word, include the thought of assaulting someone, being contaminated with cancerous material or simply watching a coffin containing mutilated bodies. Again, compounded sacred and profane thoughts of a kind can appear here. For example, Janet treated five Parisian mothers who were tormented by thoughts of damaging their babies with a sharp knife.

Sometimes the victim is tortured by unwelcome thoughts that lead to neither overt behaviour nor a covert neutralizing thought. Examples include the thought 'Christ was a bastard' or the image of mutilated corpses or decomposing foetuses. As a percentage of the total suffering from obsessional-compulsive disorders, the pure ruminator is probably in a minority, though the size of this percentage might well have been underestimated. For all practical purposes, I should be regarded as fitting the pure ruminator category, as my compulsive behaviour has always come in short phases and has never been serious enough on its own to ask for treatment.

Obsessional ruminations can be found at either extreme on a scale running from profound to trivial. Most normal, non-obsessional people almost by definition are able to avoid both extremes either for all or most of the time. Obsessionals worry unduly about, for example, why an apparently omniscient God allows evil, whether the world has existed for ever or how many strokes of a toothbrush are required to clean the third tooth on the left-hand side. They might be concerned about the possibility of life after death or whether a discarded milk bottle top has been left lying in Main Street. The content of most normal thoughts has more to do with realistic and purposive activities – have I enough money for the children's holiday? There is, at least in principle, if not in practice, a solution to such problems.

The obsessional thought can sometimes be one of *depersonalization* as reported by a number of investigators including Janet. The obsessional is troubled by the thought that he has lost his personality, that in some sense he is not 'himself'. The *Journal Intime* of the Swiss writer Henri-Frédéric Amiel reveals such a feeling:

> *'Life is merely the dream of a shadow; I felt this with new intensity this evening. I perceive myself only as a fugitive appearance, like the impalpable rainbow that for a moment floats over the spray, in the fearful cascade of being that falls incessantly into the abyss of the days. Thus everything seems to me a chimera, a mist, a phantom, nothingness, my own individuality included.*

Neutralizing thoughts

For some ruminators, an intruding thought is invariably countered by a neutralizing thought that seems to help to reduce its negative impact. For example, a thought such as 'the devil is good' might be countered by 'I remain a Christian'. The obsessional thought 'God is mad' might be countered by the thought 'I remain a Catholic'. Such a covert neutralizing action might serve to lower the anxiety level of some obsessional-compulsive patients.

Some obsessionals accompany the neutralizing thought with a simple voluntary muscular exertion that seems to drive home the resistance. A good example of this was given by John Bunyan in his autobiography:

> *'This temptation did put me to such scares lest I should at sometimes, I say, consent thereto, and to be overcome therewith, that by the very force of my mind in labouring to gainsay and resist this wickedness my very Body also would be put into action or motion, by way of pushing or thrusting with my hands or elbows; still answering, as fast as the destroyer said, Sell him; I will not, I will not, I will not, I will not . . .'*

Obsessions and compulsive behaviour

The relationship between obsessions, compulsions and urges, can be illustrated by considering a 20-year-old student.[8] The patient experienced the frequent intrusion of the painful thought and image that his parents were in imminent danger of sexual assault. The intrusion was usually associated with the urge to protect them from this threat. To do this, the student engaged in rituals of handwashing. Although he admitted to the irrationality of his behaviour, he showed little ability to resist it.

Another case concerned a 47-year-old married woman. She had suffered for 36 years from obsessional thoughts and the associated compulsive rituals of repetitive behaviour, such as walking up and down stairs. The obsessions were first of swear words but later developed a sexual theme. Her extreme anxiety was able to be allayed by performing the ritual.

The distinction between a pure obsession and an obsession accompanied by a behavioural urge can be illustrated by considering another patient, a young computer clerk. The problem, as she described it, was one of 'mental paralysis'. This was caused by repetitive and disturbing thoughts concerning something that happened when she was a child. An old woman whom she occasionally visited had died suddenly and the patient was tortured by the thought that in some mysterious way she had killed the old woman. These thoughts had no accompanying urges to do anything. However, this same patient also was troubled by urges to expose herself when confronting a group of men. Like most such cases, the urges were resisted. Interestingly, from the patient's report, the urges appeared to have no prior accompanying obsessional ideas.

Another patient had been very seriously disabled by a fear of cancer. In order to counter this threat, she went to inordinate lengths in washing herself. Her hands were cleaned and disinfected hundreds of times each day, during the course of which the skin of her hands would be damaged and her washing water would be bloody. Still the ritual persisted undeterred. This example can be used to illustrate the important point that compulsive behaviour is often directed towards attainment of a *goal* or *purpose* such as cleanliness. In a situation like this, the behaviour in itself does not usually constitute the purpose; it can therefore be described as 'goal-directed'. The goal might be perfectly normal, such as to get clean hands; it is just the effort expended to reach the goal that is abnormal. Similarly, the compulsive checker has the goal of, for example, establishing security in order to prevent harm in the house.

In other cases, the end point might seem bizarre or unattainable. There are situations where performance of the behaviour itself, the 'ritual', might seem to be the end point; the subject must go through an elaborate sequence of particular body movements. For instance, a person might need to turn around in the street exactly five times, or touch a post three times. In cases like this, though, anxiety might be reduced or, in the subject's consciousness, there might well be some future unwanted event that is warded off by their behaviour.

Some sufferers manage to lead amazingly normal lives in spite of what would appear to most people to be an utterly crippling burden. For example, a spell of four or more hours spent in the bathroom each morning can sometimes be integrated into the daily routine and the person might still manage to lead a successful professional life. Not surprisingly, obsessional-compulsive behaviour often disrupts the patient's sexual life, particularly where the obsession concerns contamination from others. However, in many cases, patients with very serious compulsive disorders still manage to engage in full and vigorous sexual behaviour.

The most common type of obsession appears to involve three stages, consisting of (1) obsessional thought, (2) compulsion and (3) ritual. For example, the person might be plagued with the thought that their body has been contaminated. This would be associated with the urge to wash or take a shower. Given the availability of washing facilities, an extensive washing ritual, sometimes lasting hours, would follow. The three stages, the 'triad', though abnormally and grossly exaggerated in terms of behaviour, nonetheless might be felt to have some intrinsic logic.

Other triads would seem, to the non-obsessional, to have no possible logic. For example, a person living in London might feel compelled to wash his hands in order to protect an uncle living in Edinburgh.

Finally, it is possible to find ritualistic behaviour without prior obsessional thoughts. A person might simply take hours to get dressed, and find themselves quite unable to speed up. The behaviour is ritualistic with a fixed order of doing things. However, there is relatively little, or no, fear of untoward consequences of not performing the action correctly.

Suppose I believe it makes good sense

Obsessional-compulsive problems are particularly difficult to treat in those cases where the victim feels that her fears are realistic, a situation which is given the technical description *overvalued ideation*. Dr Edna Foa[9] describes a particularly difficult and tragic case of this kind. Judy was a 37-year-old artist, with three children aged 8, 6 and 3 years. Her specific fear was of transmitting leukaemia germs to her husband and children. The following is an extract from the first interview with the patient:

Therapist: I understand that you need to wash excessively every time you are in contact, direct or indirect, with leukaemia.

Patient: Yes, like the other day I was sitting in the beauty parlour, and I heard the woman who sat next to me telling this other woman that she had just come back from the children's hospital where she had visited her grandson who had leukaemia. I immediately left, I registered in a hotel and washed for three days.

Therapist: What do you think would have happened if you did not wash?

Patient: My children and my husband would get leukaemia and die.

Therapist: Would *you* die too?

Patient: No, because I am immune, but they are particularly susceptible to these germs.

Therapist: Do you really think people get leukaemia through germs?

Patient: I have talked with several specialists about it. They all tried to assure me that there are no leukaemia germs, but medicine is not that advanced . . .

Linking the experience to gaining understanding

There have, broadly speaking, been two main approaches to the study of obsessional phenomena: considering either the *form* or the *content* of the experience. Psychoanalysts have been most concerned with interpreting the content of the experience, probing for a so-called deeper and symbolic significance. Graham Reed's approach,[10] by contrast, is to examine the form, noting that virtually anything, from one's own death to tiny morsels of dog excrement on the lawn, can constitute the content of the thought. In this respect Reed follows in the tradition of Pierre Janet. Arguing that the content is too variegated to form the basis for understanding and therapy, Reed instead asks such questions as – how does it feel to be subject to obsessional intrusions? How powerful do you perceive them to be? Under what circumstances do the thoughts become most insistent? By probing the form rather than the content of obsessions, Reed feels that we can develop models with explanatory power. My own approach has been very much influenced by the outlook of Janet and Reed. This theme will be developed later.

11
Overlap and confusion with other conditions

There are a number of behavioural phenomena and psychiatric disorders that have important features in common with obsessional-compulsive disorder, but with which it is useful to attempt to draw some distinctions. Some so-called normal rituals are similar in important ways to obsessional-compulsive disorders. The disorders that are similar to obsessional neurosis include depression, phobias and morbid preoccupations. However, we should be careful not to overstate the distinctions, since, over a period of time, a given subject might move around between these disorders or suffer from a combination of several at the same time. The science and treatment of behaviour rarely deliver neat, watertight boundaries. Nonetheless, trying to define some distinctions can be valuable in understanding exactly what obsessional-compulsive disorder is.

Rituals and premonitions

Humans try to effect changes in both this world and the next by the performance of rituals. Sir Aubrey Lewis[1] made the apposite comment:

> 'It has been said, somewhat metaphorically, that the obsessional lives in a peculiar world, peopled by demons – of dirt, decay, death, sexuality, cruelty, murder – whom he seeks to propitiate or drive off by ceremonies and rituals, as savages do. Superstitious observances have something in common with obsessional ones.'

Similarly, Arthur Guirdham[2] notes the obsessional's: '. . . atoning and self-punishing symptoms which so resemble those of the ritualistic religions'.

Premonitions are also of interest here. Guirdham observes:

> 'The differentiation between a premonition and an obsession can be an agonizing problem for a person suffering from an obsessional state. Strictly speaking, the two states of mind are essentially different. In a premonition the individual feels something dreadful is going to happen. In an obsession he feels it may happen, and especially if he does not

perform his usual placatory ritual. It is obvious that in actual practice it is difficult for any obsessional to be certain whether he is dealing with a premonition or an obsession.'

The subject of rituals forms the crux of one line of argument on obsessional disorder.[3] Rituals include throwing spilt salt over the shoulder as a means of preventing bad luck, rain-making dances in African tribes and complex sequences of public prayer and devotion. These are performed in order to cause a desired future consequence (e.g. rainfall or the admission of a soul to heaven) or to avoid a future negative consequence (e.g. bad luck or eternal damnation). What labels such purposive activities as 'rituals' is that the behaviour is not related to the associated future state by any rational justification. However, though I appreciate this argument, trying to decide what *is* or *is not* rational raises tortuously complex questions.

The rituals of primitive tribes appear to be connected with situations of personal danger and threat over which they otherwise have little or no control, such as drought, death, illness and childbirth. In general, rituals are more evident in children and primitive tribes, who have relatively few other means of gaining some prediction and exerting control over their environment. Non-believers are more likely to turn to religious rituals when they are placed in a situation of anxiety over which they can exert no control. They feel helpless. Examples include being in a storm at sea or on a battlefield. Objectively it might be argued that the ritual does not change the course of events, though the ritualizer might not see it that way. It might, however, alleviate the anxiety. In his own eyes and the eyes of any others present, it might help to confirm the ritualizer as a member of the community of concerned and deserving individuals.

Touching wood occasionally, going to church three times on Sunday, making the sign of the cross in the heat of battle or performing tribal rain-dances do not, of course, make one a candidate to visit a psychiatrist. So, in distinction, what do we mean by *'obsessional* rituals'? There are three important differences between obsessional and non-obsessional rituals.[4] First, the obsessional often repeats his activity many times, whereas the non-obsessional tends to run through a given sequence once. However, this distinction is not an absolute one. Secondly, the performance of obsessional rituals often fails to reduce the subject's level of anxiety. The anxiety level is sometimes even increased. By contrast, non-obsessional rituals appear to decrease anxiety. The third distinction is that normal rituals usually appear in situations of unambiguous threat, such as drought, epidemic or war. They also occur in situations of *anticipated* serious threat, such as displeasing God or condemnation to hell-fire. Often the obsessional is concerned with situations that appear highly improbable, such as whether cancer can be contracted through door handles, or trivial, such as whether a row of figures really add up. Sometimes the concern is with something that most people would consider both highly improbable and trivial. Again though, we should consider this third distinction to be a generalization and approximation, rather than being absolute.

Occasionally, for devout individuals, obsessional disorder attaches itself to their traditional religious rituals. These rituals become grossly exaggerated. This is well known in both the Roman Catholic and Jewish faiths. Within both faiths, procedures are available for assisting therapy.[5]

Morbid preoccupations

It is useful to distinguish between obsessional ruminations and *morbid preoccupations*.[6] A morbid preoccupation is where the thought has a rational basis and concerns 'realistic problems or experiences which give rise to unhappiness'. There is no inconsistency between the thought and the remainder of the personality and lifestyle of the sufferer. By contrast, obsessional ruminations concern thoughts that are at odds with the sufferer's personality and personal history. Morbid preoccupations do not evoke the resistance that is associated with obsessional ruminations. Mrs P's case illustrates the meaning of morbid preoccupations.[7]

Mrs P, a woman of 45 years of age, had been healthy psychologically. She married a man much older than herself, who then showed physical and mental deterioration. Looking after him imposed a terrible strain upon Mrs P, who carried on full-time employment. Such were the problems that Mr P had to be admitted to a geriatric ward. Mrs P then suffered severe depression which forced her to be admitted to hospital. Worrying thoughts never left her: these thoughts concerned whether she would ever be able to care for her husband again, and whether she was wrong to have agreed to his admission to a geriatric ward. These thoughts were such that she was unable to concentrate on other tasks. Clearly, they had a rational basis in terms of the context of her life, and we would term this a 'morbid preoccupation'.

Psychotic disorder – am I going mad?

Obsessional disorder needs to be distinguished from psychotic delusions, where the sufferer reports that he or she is being driven by mysterious forces from outside. Obsessional disorder does not lead to insanity, except in very rare cases. Obsessionals remain in touch with conventional reality in areas of their life apart from the obsession. Obsessionals attribute the source of the thoughts to their own minds; they have *insight* into their condition and usually recognize that their behaviour is, at least in part, irrational. The schizophrenic would not normally regard his thoughts as senseless nor would he try to resist them. However, in the past, there is evidence for considerable misdiagnosis of obsessional disorder as schizophrenia. This probably still occurs in a number of cases.

Only a very small percentage of obsessionals go on to develop schizophrenia, a percentage that is no higher than for other psychiatric patients. However, there is a grey area here and it concerns the factor of religion, an area that is a minefield of problems. It is interesting that some figures in history (e.g. John Bunyan), who would now be termed 'obsessional', did attribute their blasphemous ruminations to Satanic influences. Earlier dictionary definitions of obsessions spoke of being 'actuated by the devil'. Bunyan referred to being assaulted by the 'tempter' and, as a boy of nine, being afflicted in his sleep 'with the apprehensions of Devils, and wicked spirits'. Stanley Rachman and Ray Hodgson[8] note that:

'Bearing in mind the blasphemous content of many obsessions, it must be said at the outset that attributing the cause of obsessions to the intrusions of the Devil is more immediately understandable than ascribing them to the vagaries of infant bowel training'.

Noting that relatively few obsessionals become schizophrenic, Sir Aubrey Lewis[9] writes:

'The surprising thing here is not that some obsessionals become obviously schizophrenic, but that only a few do. It must be a very short step, one might suppose, from feeling that one must struggle against thoughts that are not one's own, to believing that these thoughts are forced upon one by an external agency ...'

Since obsessionals tend to be inveterate and well-practised daydreamers, when bizarre thoughts arise, the obsessional might be particularly well equipped to identify the intrinsic source of the thoughts.[10]

Phobias

Obsessional-compulsive problems are similar in some important respects to phobias and a large percentage of obsessional-neurotics show evidence of phobias as well. Although a distinction between the two conditions is usually worth drawing, there exists a grey area where the disorder can have features of both a phobia and an obsession. A phobia often relates to more or less distinct objects in the external world, such as snakes or open spaces. The sufferer might go to inordinate lengths to avoid contact with the object of the phobia but, once out of reach of the relevant object, can sometimes more or less switch off. The external object itself or approximations to it can form an obvious target for therapy. By contrast, the obsessional usually carries the problem around with her, however much objective disconfirmation of the need to worry is presented. The object of the obsessional's thought is usually intangible and invisible, e.g. hidden germs or a concept 'what would have happened, if . . .?' 'Was I really responsible for the death of the old lady?' Some of Pierre Janet's patients were tormented by philosophical doubts of the kind 'Suppose there is no God?' and 'Suppose there is a force of evil at work'. Obsessions have to do with *events* rather than objects, and these events usually have personal reference to the sufferer.[11]

The similarity and difference between clear-cut cases of phobias and obsessions is richly illustrated by the following account.[12]

> '*Obsessionals similarly say they fear situations, but in order to avoid them, they spend so much time scanning their environment and monitoring their own actions and thoughts that a particular problem is created by their extreme effort to avoid the feared stimuli. They "create" so to speak, in their internal representation of the world, the very environmental situations that they strive to avoid, even when these situations are factually absent'.*

A phobia can sometimes take on features almost identical to obsessional disorder. Jane, a patient of Dr Isaac Marks, was a 20-year-old university student. She suffered from a phobia about pigeons. In the street she needed to make detours to avoid seeing them and they formed the content of her nightmares. Jane needed to check doors and windows at night to make sure that a pigeon could not enter her house.

Of the more common obsessional-compulsive disorders, some washing rituals probably come closest to phobias. Indeed, aspects of the two conditions can appear to merge into one and attempting to draw a clear distinction could be highly misleading. A fear of germs might lead the sufferer to take active steps, such as washing, in which case we would term it 'obsessional-compulsive disorder'. At other times, the subject might simply withdraw from perceived sources of contamination, behaviour that we might term 'phobic'. A fear of contamination can, for example, prevent the sufferer from visiting towns associated with contamination and confine him or her to a room in the house.

Diagnosis of a condition as obsessional or phobic can often depend crucially upon the subjective report of the patient. For example, a patient of Dr Thomas Insel was afraid to leave his apartment. However, as Insel points out, it would have been misleading to define him as agoraphobic, since his fear was specifically of what could happen to the apartment if he relaxed his vigilance.

In some cases it might seem that a phobic condition arises from an underlying obsessional disorder. An example of this, a woman of age 32 years, was described by Dr Isaac Marks. She had been seen by 43 casualty departments of different hospitals over a three-year period. At times her fear concerned an imagined cancer of the stomach, at other times a brain tumour and thrombosis. Every part of her body had been X-rayed, but no abnormality was ever revealed. Each clean bill of health was greeting by, in her own words, the feeling of being 'rejuvenated – it's like having been condemned to death and given a reprieve'. Within a week, any such euphoria had subsided to the point where she was seeking a new hospital for another examination. The obsessional content clearly emerged in her discussion with Dr Marks:

'I am terrified of the idea of dying, it's the end, the complete end, and the thought of rotting in the ground obsesses me – I can see the worms and maggots'.

For many obsessional problems, such as rumination on a hypothetical past event or an existential dilemma about sin, the distinction from phobias is clear. The ruminator is obsessed with some event that might have happened or will happen in the future, such as a rape or death. Similarly the compulsive checker is usually not trying to avoid contact with a particular here-present external object. Rather, one might speculate that their motivation arises from the desire to avoid an unspecified and undesirable state of affairs that might prevail in the future, such as a gas explosion or a break-in.

However, concerning the area of overlap, Isaac Marks, in his book *Living with Fear*, uses the expression 'obsessive phobia' to refer to the syndrome that incorporates features of both phobia and obsession. He defines this as:

'An obsessive phobia is not a direct fear of a given object or situation, but rather of the results which are imagined to arise from it'.

Two of Dr Marks' patients illustrate clearly the distinction between an obsessive phobia and the more standard phobia. A man feared contamination by dogs, and spent time trying to avoid contact with dog hair and any possible traces left by dogs. He resigned from his job on finding out that a dog might have been present once on another floor of the office block. He would engage in compulsive washing rituals following any such 'suggestion' of contamination. Interestingly, the patient would prefer to touch a dog with his hands rather than let it come into contact with his clothes, since he reckoned hands to be more easily cleaned than clothes. On close examination, it would be inaccurate to term this patient a 'dog phobic'. Another patient's obsession was that injury could result from small glass splinters that *might* be on her carpet, but which could not be seen. She was less afraid of those splinters that she actually could find and remove by her own hand. The description 'broken-glass phobia', without further qualification, could prove highly misleading in, for example, psychotherapy. It was not broken glass as such that she feared but the consequences of hidden bits of glass.

Gilles de la Tourette syndrome

Obsessional-compulsive disorder is different from Gilles de la Tourette syndrome, though there are similarities and a significant percentage of patients suffer both.[13] Some researchers speak of a genetically acquired proneness towards both. Gilles de la Tourette syndrome is characterized by tics, repetitive motor acts usually described as involuntary, such as facial grimaces or jutting out a leg. Unlike the actions in obsessional-compulsive disorder, these involve a local, circumscribed part of the body and, in the mind of the sufferer, can lack an end point or purpose. Although the repetitive checking or handwashing of obsessional-compulsive disorder might at one level be described as stereotyped, they need not consist of the repetition of simple acts. Rather washing might be performed by using a variety of different movements. What is repetitive and stereotyped need not be the actions, but the elusive goal or end point, to establish cleanliness. The patient's own perceptions are different in the two conditions, obsessional disorder having a 'whole person' frame of reference.[14] The Tourette patient is likely to report 'My *arm* twitches', whereas the obsessional is likely to report '*I* have to move my arm'. The Tourette patient might be concerned because he utters obscenities in public, whereas the comparable obsessional would worry because he *might* utter them (but doesn't). However, the two conditions sometimes coalesce (as with Samuel Johnson, described later), and a patient in Rome[15] illustrates this.

Rita was 18 years old and single. She was brought to psychotherapy as a result of multiple tics and habit spasms. She had earlier been diagnosed as suffering from Tourette syndrome. However, psychiatrists examining Rita at the clinic described the spasms as *voluntary*. On the basis of carefully questioning Rita, it was found that the spasms served to divert her attention from intrusive images of death and death-related themes; they were a mechanism for cancelling death-related images. Rita feared that if she were not able to cancel the images, and they were able to persist in her consciousness, then tragedy would befall her family. Her compulsion was experienced as one of actively shaking the unacceptable thoughts out of her head; the muscular activity was felt to be correcting the weakness associated with the intrusive image.

Not uncommonly for obsessionals, Rita's thinking processes reveal an assumption of some omnipotence, of 'mind over matter'. An omnipotence, a kind of capacity for magical thinking, characterizes quite a few obsessionals.[16]

Not altogether surprisingly, Rita's boyfriend and parents did not understand the logic behind her behaviour, and tried to make her stop shaking her body. Rita was unable to explain her behaviour, for the simple reason that to do so would involve uttering such unutterable words as 'death'. The attempts to make her stop served only to exacerbate the condition, creating a vicious circle. Rita's case is a good example of where interpersonal pressures can affect a disorder. Further, Rita epitomizes a way in which so many obsessionals construe the world, and which might prove relevant to therapy.[15]

> *'Rita cannot afford to be negligent toward her intrusive images even for an instant; she must always watch out and never leave the slightest room for those images. Therefore, however bizarre the intrusive images may be, the problem-solving mechanisms in these patients shows rules based on the belief that perfection and certainty are possible in the relationship between human beings and reality.'*

Rita benefited from behaviour therapy. The treatment started with such words as 'death' being gently whispered in her presence, and progressively moved to where Rita was able to read aloud passages from books containing death-related themes. She was even able to walk in a graveyard accompanied by a therapist.

Anorexia nervosa

Anorexia nervosa might be classed as an obsessional-compulsive disorder. It overlaps considerably with disorders normally classed as obsessional, in terms of its population of sufferers. It is sometimes felt that anorexia nervosa is a disease of modern times. Although it might be more frequent now, there is well-documented evidence that it has been around for a long time. Pierre Janet subsumed the phenomenon under the heading of obsessional disorder and treated a substantial number of anorexics. The feminist writer Susie Orbach in an interesting review[17] sees this disorder and conventional obsessional-compulsive behaviour as, in some ways, alternative strategies for coping with psychological pressures. They are ways of gaining some kind of mastery.

The anorexic could be described as *obsessed* with attaining slimness or having a *phobic* avoidance of fatness. In anorexia nervosa, we see the same perverse logic in terms of the difference between the patient's perception of an aspect of reality and the consensus view, and the same resistance to rational persuasion. In both sufferers, we often see a considerable amount of guilt. There is also a pathological exaggeration of reasonable goal-seeking, in this case to attain slimness. There is the dilemma of whether to eat or not, analogous to the obsessional's decision of whether to wash the hands or not. However, a distinction with more conventional obsessional disorders is worth drawing, if only because of the type of victim of anorexia nervosa, predominantly young women, and the specialized therapy techniques for this condition.

Sometimes a conventional compulsive behaviour gets woven into the lifestyle of the sufferer from anorexia nervosa. For example, Padmal de Silva recalls treating two cases of this kind. In one, the young woman insisted on leaving a particular segment of food on her plate uneaten. This of course served to reduce the amount she needed to eat. In another, eating was invariably followed by a complex exercise ritual, which served to burn off some calories. The patients that Janet treated showed self-induced vomiting, the same concern with exercise and the same paradoxical fascination with food that modern clinicians report.

In this context, it is interesting that Janet also treated a number of patients whose obsession concerned shame about the appearance of various parts of their body. For example, the patient might be tormented by the idea that his nose is too large, even though there was no objective support for this notion. These days, the occasional female patient seeking treatment for the size of her breasts, might more usefully be treated as suffering from an obsessional thought.[18] Also in his study of obsessionals, Janet included discussion of self-mutilation and hair-pulling.[19]

Depression

Obsessions were once regarded as merely an aspect of depression, but now the condition is recognized in its own right. The 'pure' obsessional patient does not exhibit the more obvious signs associated with depression, such as loss of appetite and early-morning waking. However, there are important features in common between obsessional disorder and depression. Also a given patient will commonly suffer from both conditions, either simultaneously or in succession. Whereas the 'pure' obsessional will usually complain of being bombarded with thoughts that have at most only a tenuous link to her earlier experiences in life, the depressed victim is likely to focus upon something more obviously central to her life, such as the loss of a partner or a feeling of worthlessness. The feeling of depressives is sometimes one of suicide – that they are both helpless and hopeless. By contrast, suicide amongst obsessionals is rare: even the most seriously tormented do not usually try to escape their torture this way. However, if the obsessional problem gives way to depression, the danger of suicide increases.

There is an important, but usually unrecognized, common feature in the two conditions: a perception of helplessness. This is likely to be a helplessness with life in general for the depressive, but a helplessness perceived specifically in the face of the intrusion for the obsessional. In spite of the feeling of helplessness, pure obsessionals often still manage to muster resistance. Many endogenous depressives exhibit:[20]

> '... the self-crucifying characteristics of the obsessional temperament. Forty years ago, before the terms endogenous and reactive came into use, the melancholic was described as having a characteristic pre-existing temperament. He was exceptionally scrupulous and honest, highly conscientious, a hard worker, self-critical and with a marked attention to detail.'

This description is virtually identical to that of the obsessional personality.

I would prefer to see pure depression and pure obsessional disorder located at two ends of a continuum, with an area of overlap between. At one end there are pure obsessions with no sign of depression. At the other end there is depression but not obsession, for example the thoughts are ones that relate directly and logically to the person's lot in life. The area of the spectrum between the extremes has features of both. At a point in time a given subject might be located at a particular point on this spectrum, but might move around from nearer to one end or to the other over the course of their disorder. At any point on the continuum there will be a thought content, the negative aspect of which can be accentuated by a factor such as stress.

Appetitive urges

Obsessional-compulsive behaviour is distinct from what I would term *appetitive urges* or, as some might term them, *appetitive compulsions*. By this term, I mean such things as apparently compulsive gambling, drug addiction and some forms of sexual activity. On close examination, the distinction turns out to be more elusive than appears initially.

In each case, we see an element of profound conflict. Like the hand-washer, the heroin addict might admit that her habit is self-destructive but report that she is unable to give it up. If only she could break free from the cycle of injection and unpleasant withdrawal. The compulsive gambler is locked into a similar cycle that has an overall destructive effect on his life. In each case, as with obsessional-compulsive disorder, there is a vicious circle and an observer viewing it from a dispassionate vantage point often cannot see why the subjects don't stop.

So much for the similarities, now for the differences. Appetitive urges involve what I would term 'incentives'. Another expression often used is 'positive reinforcer'. The unnatural agents, heroin and cocaine, act on the central nervous system like very powerful biological reinforcers. In a sense, they cheat the natural pleasure system by infiltrating and overwhelming it. An engagement with positive reinforcers, sex, food, drugs and money is therefore rather different to the obsessional-compulsive who is essentially trying to *escape* from or *avoid* a negative event, such as contamination or illness or any one of thousands of tragic events.

The gambler derives pleasure in the casino. These reactions stand in contrast to the obsessional-compulsive who would be most unlikely to report deriving pleasure from hand-washing or the anticipation of it. At best the behaviour serves very temporarily to lower anxiety level, though even attaining this beneficial outcome is by no means assured.

In the subject's view of the world, the compulsive hand-washing might serve an obvious goal like turning contaminated hands into clean ones or it could be in the service of a more abstract goal such as preventing a tragedy befalling a distant relative. This places obsessional-compulsive disorder in distinction to an activity such as 'compulsive' sexuality which is not performed with an *ulterior motive*. The intrinsic pleasure of sexuality is itself the goal.[21]

In trying to clarify true obsessional-compulsive disorder and place it in distinction to the condition I term 'appetitive urge', a remark[22] is very relevant here:

'. . . compulsive behaviour seems never to be anti-social; the suggestion that child-molesting or fire-raising are traceable to irresistible compulsive urges comes better from the mouths of defence lawyers than from those of diagnosticians.'

Another useful means of conceptualizing the distinction is to consider the type of therapy that is appropriate in each case: for obsessional-compulsive disorder this is often exposure to the feared stimulus. The inappropriateness of this to appetitive urges such as heroin or gambling is obvious.

12
Who are the victims of the disorder?

What kind of people develop obsessional-compulsive disorder? Is there a typical sufferer? I shall try to outline some of the features that characterize the obsessional-compulsive patient. However, as with all stereotypes, this process is fraught with difficulty; there are always important exceptions to any such generalization.

Sufferers from obsessional disorders often can be shown to have had what is known as an obsessional personality (described below) before the start of their troubles, but this is not so in every case. Also, an obsessional personality will not inevitably lead to obsessional-compulsive disorder. We need to be very careful on this point. Sufferers from obsessional neurosis usually show high levels of general anxiety and often low mood (bordering on, if not involving, depression).

Are the sufferers male or female?

Of the large sample of obsessional patients seen by Pierre Janet in late 19th-century France, women outnumbered men by over 2 to 1. However, these days, the sexes are about equally represented amongst obsessionals overall. Among compulsive checkers, males and females are roughly equally represented; compulsive cleaners tend to be more often female than male.

Comparing different societies

Obsessional-compulsive disorder is not a recent phenomenon; it has been well documented over a long period. In early times, obsessional-compulsives were said to be possessed by demons. In European monasteries during the 16th century, techniques of thought stopping were employed. Shakespeare described the hand-washing compulsion of Lady Macbeth. We have already described Bunyan's intrusive thoughts. Though the general themes remain rather consistent, the specific content of obsessions changes somewhat over time, reflecting contemporary fears. For example, syphilis is less common as an intrusive thought content now, and

AIDS is clearly emerging as a dominant theme.

There is a remarkable similarity in the general themes that appear as the content of obsessions in Africa, Asia, Europe and America. For example, amongst a population in Chandigarh, India,[1] the dominant themes that emerged were dirt and contamination, aggression against the self, including death, orderliness, sex and religion. There were doubts of the kind 'Did I lock the door?' A 41-year-old lawyer was obsessed by the notion of drinking from his inkwell. A 23-year-old student was bothered because she couldn't remove a current pop song from her consciousness. Interesting cultural variations on the general themes were also evident. For example, some people expressed doubts and fears concerning physical contact with beggars and people of lower caste. A study of Hong Kong Chinese found fear of penile shrinkage amongst a couple of patients, which was attributed to the prevalence of such sexual themes in Chinese folk beliefs.[2]

Padmal de Silva, who is Sri Lankan by origin, has documented the similarity between the descriptions and treatments for intrusive thoughts appearing in early Buddhist writings and those of modern behavioural psychology.[3] Intrusive thoughts are clearly no modern middle-class Western phenomenon. They were around to trouble the unfortunate in the 5th century BC, for example, interrupting the meditations of Buddhist monks. Indeed, one Buddhist discourse is devoted entirely to techniques for controlling them.

What is obsessional personality? – a problem

There exists an 'obsessional personality' (also known as 'compulsive' and 'anankastic') and its associated traits are listed below.[4] Amongst other means, this personality type can be formally described in terms of the way a subject answers a particular questionnaire designed to identify the obsessional personality.[5] It is the widely-recognized collection of a number of traits in an individual that identifies the obsessional personality. However, only a fraction of people with this personality type go on to exhibit obsessional illness. Considering the reciprocal relationship, a significant percentage of obsessional patients showed no sign of obsessional personality prior to the illness.

The relationship between obsessional personality and obsessional disorder is a hotly debated one. Should obsessional disorder be seen as an extreme case of obsessional personality? Can we usefully see them lying on a continuum? Insight into the processes underlying obsessional personality might also illuminate obsessional disorder. We need to ask how the obsessional personality copes with the world, in the hope that we can see where things can go seriously wrong.

Some people think that the obsessional personality is fertile ground on which obsessional illness is easily able to grow. Others express it as the obsessional personality type being analogous to the property of brittleness of, say, glass. Knowing about this property tells us that in response to the impact of a stone the glass is more likely to break than would non-brittle material.

What traits, attributes and abilities does the obsessional personality typically possess? Usually, obsessionals are found to have a higher than average intelligence. They tend to be more unstable/neurotic and more introverted[6] than the general population.

It is vital not to assume that obsessional personality is synonymous with having an obsessional disorder. The package of personality traits (e.g. orderliness and cautiousness) that characterizes the obsessional can add up to a viable person whose life is in harmony. Such an individual might well exploit their obsessional traits to good use. By contast, the obsessional *problem* acts against the goals, standards and self-image set by the victim. Use of the expressions 'obsessional personality' and especially 'compulsive personality', for subjects not having the disorder, can be something of a misnomer: these people do not resist their behaviour. However, this usage is standard in the literature. I shall refer to the 'obsessional' as meaning someone who both suffers from obsessional disorder and exhibited obsessional personality prior to the onset of illness.

What characteristics comprise the obsessional personality?

Obsessionals have particular difficulty handling uncertainty; they need to feel sure of things and have control. To *be in control* of themselves and their social and emotional commerce with the world is a deeply felt need amongst obsessionals:[7]

> *'Manipulating, categorizing, measuring and otherwise ordering representative bits of the universe at large – data, matter, numerical ratios, energies, ideas, etc. – are reassuring to him, providing symbolic confirmation of his illusion that ultimately – through alertness, discovery, reason and effort – he can predict or otherwise control the behaviour of his universe.'*

Obsessionals have a strong need to make decisions. However, perhaps paradoxically, rather than removing uncertainty by making a somewhat arbitrary choice, given the opportunity, they will postpone final decisions in the hope of gaining more information.

For example, if given a choice of time for the next appointment, obsessionals often have difficulty deciding which to accept, weighing up the pros and cons of each.[8] Obsessionals are characterized by the desire for certainty, somewhat cruelly associated with the inability to attain it; the world of statistical chance is essentially an alien one. They have a tendency to ruminate 'What if . . .?'[9] The obsessional is indecisive – not having enough information available to make an unambiguously correct decision, trying to take too many factors into account to be able to arrive at a decision.

Investigators commonly observe a tendency to perfectionism in obsessionals. They believe that an absolutely correct solution to human problems is possible and this can give rise to awful dilemmas. The obsessional's indecisiveness represents an unwillingness to accept a provisional or 'working' solution and the need to scan for imperfections in any such solution. The virtues of alternative solutions are constantly weighed up in the interests of the perfect solution. The obsessional tends to compare his actual performance with ideal standards, and to be strongly goaded by any disparity. Disparity is associated with tension and self-criticism. For example, in the past, when religious influence was stronger, obsessionals tended to compare their behaviour and thoughts with what was proper according to religious mores and dogma. Even in these somewhat secular times, a religious flavour is evident in the way that many obsessionals view the world.

The obsessional tends to persist, not giving up until he is 'there', and there usually means a score of 100 per cent. The craving for perfection is usually, of course, frustrated. Completion evades its pursuer. Two terms seem appropriate here: 'inconclusiveness', which characterizes the failure to attain the goal, and 'assimilation', which is desired but not attained. The dilemma felt by many obsessionals arises because it is impossible to please everyone.

The obsessional is typically always busy but never finished. In case the reader by now feels unduly sorry for the obsessional, an optimistic streak should also be recorded: against all contradictory evidence, obsessionals commonly feel that tomorrow will be better than today, that the world will eventually yield to control.

Obsessionals often report a feeling of 'generalized tension': that something not done should be done. Some investigators see this as a tendency to be hyperalert and watchful, ready for any problem that might be confronted in an often-hostile world. We might expect this to be associated with a frequent and inappropriate triggering of stress hormones. Obsessionals tend to experience what is termed *subjective discomfort*. This is not easy to define, but is not as strong a negative emotion as depression, and is by no means confined to obsessionals. It is a distress with no obvious source.

Hans Eysenck[10] refers to something very similar, if not identical, as *free-floating anxiety*.

Obsessionals tend to suppress anger and outward display of emotion, and are prone to episodes of depression. Obsessionals are often controlled, avoiding undue emotional expression. Orderliness also emerges as a clear character trait, though there are exceptions to this, as a moment's glance at my bedroom would prove. Indeed, the tendency seems to be for the obsessional's tidiness to be somewhat superficial. I could name one obsessional who perfectly fits Graham Reed's description[11] 'The top of the anankast's dressing table may be exceedingly clean and neat, objects upon it being arranged with fussy precision, but the interiors of the drawers may tell a different story, underwear and socks being crammed in quite haphazardly.'

The obsessional is generally cautious, reliable, thorough, precise, punctual (particularly in the demands made upon others), conscientious, trustworthy, fair and well organized. Things are done methodically and systematically. She will try to impose a *pattern* upon objects and events. For example, to the obsessional, it is probably more important than to others that pictures should hang straight. The obsessional is disturbed by imbalance and asymmetry. For instance, some obsessionals insist that their feet should touch the floor at exactly the same point in time on rising in the morning. The obsessional loves to impose order on things; routines are valued, events are programmed in advance. Precision in the use of words also emerges as a trait. Some have observed the need for accuracy in the behaviour of their obsessional patients. Filling in a form is carried out with meticulous attention to detail. Recall of personal details is often performed with inordinate precision, and emphasis is placed upon exact dates. Professor Reed characterizes this as a need to 'dot every i and cross every t', slightly pejoratively expressed as a tendency to pedantry. Every factor needs to be taken into consideration, even those which by popular consensus would be seen as trivial, peripheral or irrelevant. The obsessional can suffer from 'not seeing the wood for the trees'. Such a person is an expert hair-splitter.

Researchers into obsession have observed an intolerance of ambiguity, which might be seen as an aspect of the need for precision. Plans need to cater for every possible contingency – leaving nothing exposed to the vagaries of chance. The obsessional does not like loopholes, but loves clean-cut boundaries.

The obsessional is able to show a single-minded pursuit of goals, exhibiting high levels of concentration. However, daydreaming is also well represented amongst obsessionals. There is an element of paradox here; obsessions, which are by definition intrusions into the overall goal- and aspiration-setting of the individual, can coexist with otherwise excellent pursuit of goals. The obsessional will overcome obstacles to reach a goal, and the intrusions are just one more obstacle to be overcome. This personality type shows a preference for doing things one at a time, and doing them well. This ruthless single-mindedness can be a source of both awe and immense frustration to those living with obsessionals.

The obsessional doesn't like putting things off to the last minute, and hates being caught without a plan and in need of making an impulsive decision. Planning ahead is important to the obsessional. Improvisation is not a talent well represented amongst this group. They are often timid, sacrificing their own interests in preference to a fight.

The picture of the obsessional painted by Arthur Guirdham[12] is that of a misunderstood, self-sacrificing and tortured martyr standing firm on moral principles in an often hostile environment. The obsessional's heroic story as relayed to Guirdham was commonly – 'I come to you with my troubles, doctor, but the people who come to me with theirs don't seem to realize that I have any'. Possibly Guirdham's own obsessional traits might have coloured his favourable perspective, and a somewhat less flattering portrait of the obsessional personality was painted by Alfred Adler[13] in 1912:

'He is a person who feels that he is set apart from other individuals; who thinks only of himself; who is imbued with self-love, and has no interest in the general welfare'.

With the exception of Adler's opinion, it might be felt that the traits listed so far are by no means entirely undesirable ones in general, but there is also a somewhat more unattractive side to the obsessional character. Other traits include inflexibility, rigidity, obstinacy, irritability, moroseness and over-submissiveness.

Obsessionals are said to tend towards parsimony and hypochondria, and some have noticed a willingness to accept superstition. My impression is that religious beliefs are rather commonly held by obsessionals. Some report that their compulsive activities are attempts at repentance for their sins.

Concerning superstition and the subject's perception of what causes what in the world, one of Dorothy Rowe's observations[14] could be relevant to understanding the bases of obsessional disorder:

'The obsessional introvert cannot appreciate the privacy and limited power of thought. He has been taught that he can sin by thought alone. Thinking murder is as evil as doing murder.'

Some investigators identify two subgroups of obsessional personality, the one subgroup being people characterized by uncertainty, doubting, vacillation, whereas the others show the traits of inflexibility, irritability and stubbornness.

A fondness for collecting things is often shown. Time is precious to the 'typical' obsessional and is not something to be wasted on activities that lack a purpose. In the context of a preoccupation with the importance of chronological time, obsessionals often tend to be forceful and successful people who belong to the 'time is money' mode of thinking.[15] Obsessionals are often masters of wit, by which means emotions are often tersely expressed.[16] Samuel Johnson is a good example of this.

Amongst obsessionals, there is evidence of dichotomous thinking: the need to categorize into distinct groups, and to apply all-or-none logic. They tend to overestimate the probability of harm. The obsessional can appear to be unresponsive to rational debate. However, apart from obsessional personality traits, which, it must be repeated, are usually, but not always, present, sufferers from obsessional disorder tend to be very normal, and with 'intact personalities'. The typical one has been described as being 'correct, upright and moral', and aspiring to 'high standards of personal conduct'.[17]

The obsessional likes to abide by regulations, to show loyalty to the institution with which he is associated. Chains of command tend to be acceptable. They tend to be conscientious and to conform to the moral rules and standards of their society and to display a great sense (some might say 'inflated' sense) of responsibility. Indeed, Pierre Janet used the term *les scrupuleux* (the 'scrupulous ones') to describe obsessionals. Principles tend to be put before self-interest. Obsessionals often come across as self-righteous and demanding of others.

One is struck by the general consensus of agreement as to what are the defining character traits of the obsessional. However, we must never be complacent. In case the reader is being lulled into feeling that the obsessional personality is well defined and consistent, another observation will shatter the calm. Some note that, in direct contradiction to conventional morality, there are cases of what would be described as sexual perversion amongst obsessionals.[18]

Some clinicians come to apparently opposite assessments of character traits of obsessionals. For example, they have variously been described as both immature and mature, self-deprecating and arrogant, as well as both timid and aggressive. There are several possible explanations for this. First, there could be ambivalence, 'bipolarity' or 'counter-personality' within a given individual. Obsessionals might swing from one extreme on a scale to another, depending upon the context in which they find themselves. Also, as Graham Reed points out, on some character traits when comparing between individuals there could be just as much variation as in non-obsessionals. Finally, different clinicians might be applying different assessment criteria. For example, Reed has heard the promiscuous lifestyle of a female patient described as evidence of both 'shallow affect and loose morals' and as 'an anankastic searching for perfection'.

Obsessional disorder, crime and the law

It is very rare that an obsessional who ruminates about, for example, committing an unacceptable sexual act or performing violence actually puts into practice the content of the obsession. Often obsessionals can derive some comfort from knowing this. Pierre Janet, after studying numerous obsessionals haunted by thoughts of damaging their loved ones or committing suicide, could not find a single example of where an obsessional actually performed the act. Similarly, Graham Reed, [19] after extensive study of obsessionals in Canada, cannot recall a single case in which the antisocial behavioural content of an obsession has ever been put into practice.

Where the behaviour associated with the obsession causes 'incidental' harm, the behaviour will usually be executed. A good example of this is severe skin damage caused by extreme handwashing. Where the behaviour suggested by the obsessional thought would involve direct harm to the subject (e.g. suicide) or to another (e.g. stabbing a child), it will almost never be put into practice. In the overwhelming majority of cases, obsessionals do not come into conflict with the law. A very rare exception to this came to the attention of Barnsley magistrates in England in 1987. Prosecuting counsel, Mr Martin Lord described the antisocial behaviour of a Mrs Janet Dyson.

'She creeps up neighbours' driveways, or climbs over their fences, to peer through their windows, rummage through their dustbins, and peek through their letter boxes'.

Mrs Dyson's obsession began 18 years earlier when she was 34 years old. At one time her snooping took 90 per cent of her waking hours, but had been reduced to 25 per cent. Neighbours had been driven to moving house and to exhaustion and the prospect of nervous breakdowns, the court was told. Defence counsel, Mr John Dearden argued:

'This is one of the most bizarre cases ever to come before the court. She checks everything in the house before going out, but cannot control an urge to check the property of others.

There is nothing the court can do to stop her urge. The only answer is for neighbours to ignore her.

She has suffered from an obsessive compulsive neurosis for 18 years. The symptoms are that she goes round checking everything in the house – gas taps, water taps, windows and doors before going out.'

Mrs Dyson was bound over for two years in the sum of 100 pounds after admitting that she caused a breach of the peace.

Occasionally, an obsessional will come into conflict with the law as an indirect rather than direct consequence of the disorder.[20] For example, a woman patient washed her hands as much as a hundred times each day, occupying hours of time and causing bleeding from her skin. The size of her salary was not sufficient to pay for the quantities of soap and disinfectants that were necessitated by her behaviour. She was arrested for shoplifting, and the bizarre twist to the story was that, because of the wear on her fingers, it proved impossible for the police to take any fingerprints. Interestingly, the subject's perfectionism did not extend above the elbows; the rest of her body was left unwashed.

A perfectly innocent obsessional might sometimes come under suspicion as a result of his actions. For example, a motorist repeatedly checking a certain street for the victim of a car accident could well alert residents and police. In a case such as this it might be useful for the obsessional (or his doctor) to contact the local police and explain the situation (take this book along!).

Marriage and the family context

Problems within the family caused by obsessional disorder can be quite horrendous. In some cases, the situation is possibly even worse for other family members than for the obsessional. Some obsessionals are able to dominate their families completely with their rituals, to the extent that literally every action in the household rotates around their cleaning. The bathroom might be put out of bounds to other family members for hours on end each day. Consider the case of a 28-year-old female teacher, who spent three hours each evening checking doors, gas taps and windows before retiring to bed. Another case concerned a 19-year-old male clerk who needed four hours each evening to do the same task, only getting to bed at 3-4am.

Occasionally the obsessional is brought for treatment under pressure from other family members and against their own wishes. Consider a patient of this kind, Mrs X.[21] At the initial interview, Mrs X was accompanied by a somewhat desperate and angry Mr X. Over a twenty-year period, Mrs X had insisted that the family repeatedly move house in order to get away from their home's contamination. Each new house, it was supposed, would represent a clean break, but of course it didn't, and the unfortunate family again found themselves confined to the dining room in order not to contaminate the remainder of the house. At the interview it was very clear that the husband rather than the patient was seeking help, though it must be added that such cases are exceptional.

Obsessionals are commonly either single, divorced or separated. To what extent this might be due to 'free choice', or to the difficulty for both the subject and their partner of living with the demands of the obsessional personality and disorder is almost impossible to say, if it is even a meaningful question. The so-called 'full-time obsessionals' are particularly prone to marital problems, as one might expect. The more covert or 'part-time obsessionals' are less prone to marital problems.

For some patients, obsessions appear to be directly related to marital problems. In some cases, clear improvement followed divorce. Marital therapy appeared useful to others. In marriage, obsessionals have a relatively high probability of being infertile.

The obsessional personality and other associated disorders

The obsessional personality is, relative to the non-obsessional, likely to develop obsessional disorder. However, there are other disorders that also seem to find the obsessional personality to be fertile ground. These include peptic ulcer, colitis, hypochondria, anorexia nervosa and phobias. Some writers on the subject of the so-called psychosomatic disorders particularly associate *mucous colitis* (the 'irritable colon syndrome') with the obsessional personality.[22] It might be expected that the condition would be able to set up a vicious circle with the obsessional thoughts. Sweating, faintness and palpitations are also sometimes experienced.

Obsessionals and the Puritan personality

It would be interesting to know whether Puritans are particularly prone to obsessional disorder. By the expression 'Puritan', I refer particularly to the faith that reached its fruition in 17th-century England and later in America. Typically, the Puritan is someone of uncompromising morality. As Monica Furlong[23] remarks, concerning such a personality:

'It is not so much that he does not see, and rue, the cost of standing out against established opinion or mass opinion, as that he feels he has no choice.'

Adjectives used to describe the 17th-century Puritan include honest, brave, conscientious, suspicious, efficient, self-analytical, melancholic, God-fearing, hardworking and dutiful. Well-represented qualities include thrift, punctuality, pedantry, tidiness, rationality and perseverance. To the Puritan, above all else, life is a journey towards a future goal. Joy and relaxation, if to be attained at all in this life or the next, are for the future. For the present, there is work that needs to be done. In the words of Monica Furlong:

'Work, being both practical and often far from enjoyable, was a natural sphere of Puritan activity. It supplies the continual spur, the kind of perpetual discomfort, with which the Puritan was most comfortable.' The journey forward is a hard one, fraught with danger. The Puritan is like an athlete under gruelling training, always trying still harder. Even one slip on the hazardous journey could turn into a fall towards eternal damnation; perfectionist standards, total self-control and permanent vigilance against the devil, are therefore demanded. Time is not something to be wasted on pleasurable but pointless activities, such as dancing. In meeting the demanding standards, extensive self-analysis combined with absolute truthfulness are needed.

The 17th-century Puritan and the 20th-century obsessional share a faith in perfectionism as a *goal* of behaviour. The Puritan tended to believe that perfectionism as a desirable goal was attainable, if at all, then only after a long struggle, and possibly only in the next life. The obsessional is inclined to feel that it is within earthly reach. Indeed, occasionally an obsessional believes he has already achieved perfection.

I see distinct Puritan traits in my own make-up. I still find it very hard to relax if someone around me is working. For example, on visiting Helen's parents, I would find it quite impossible to sit and read in the presence of their cleaning lady. I felt most uncomfortable attending our Christmas party at Lancashire Polytechnic, since it was held in a room exposed to the road where people were going about their business. Time is of great importance to me, and needs to be put to productive use.

The obsessional personality, creativity and the famous

When obsessionals can use their traits of orderliness and meticulousness, combined with persistence, to good use, then the results can be extremely beneficial.[24] Samuel Johnson and Charles Darwin are good examples. The works of both reflect their personality; both made a virtue of collecting, organizing, ordering and refining details. Jerome Singer argues:[25]

'At its most creative, the obsessional style has been manifested in the philosophical construct of Immanuel Kant, with its incredibly detailed logical structure and its call for the highest level of morality.'

Singer's observation leads to a particularly challenging aspect of obsessionality: its possible association with creativity. Creativity is normally considered to require an ability to explore new and incongruous ways of looking at the world, to develop novel syntheses. It would seem to call for flexibility and non-comformity.[26] This would seem to demand mental skills quite the opposite of the rigidity and concern with minute detail that characterizes the obsessional. Looked at in these terms, one might suppose that the possession of obsessional traits would be a major handicap, as much a burden to creativity as carrying a heavy lead weight around the neck to an athlete's performance at the high jump. The puzzle is that an array of famous names shows that obsessionals are very well-represented amongst the creative.[27] Of those showing obsessional symptoms and traits, there are the composers Rossini and Stravinsky, the diarist Amiel, the playright Ibsen and the novelists Dickens and Proust. There are also poets, writers and essayists, Bunyan, Swift and Johnson. Obsessional traits were shown by Beethoven,[28] and the philosophers Rousseau and Pascal.[29] Later I shall discuss obsessionality in the writers Hans Christian Andersen and George Borrow, the philosopher and theologian Søren Kierkegaard and the film-maker Woody Allen. One might also offer the theologian Martin Luther and I would tentatively suggest inclusion of the biographer James Boswell and the writer Thomas de Quincey. Clear signs of obsessionality are to be seen in the composer Eric Satie.[30]

It is indeed surprising to find obsessionals so well represented amongst creative people. However, in the light of the obsessional's preference for fixed order and pre-set rules, it is even more surprising to note that creative obsessionals include a significant number whose work formed a radical departure from the status quo, for example, Allen, Ibsen, Darwin and Stravinsky. In matters of worship and theology, Luther, Bunyan and Kierkegaard each posed a serious challenge to the established church. Samuel Johnson's creative writing served as a vehicle for advancing profound social change and justice, such as opposition to slavery and colonialism.

What could it be that creative obsessionals possess that overrides the qualities that do not lend themselves to creativity? I would suggest one such attribute is dogged perseverance, but I suspect that this is not enough. A suggestion as to what else might contribute will be made later, after discussing the obsessional's mode of handling information.

Certain obsessional ways of doing things, such as neatness, orderliness and routines might be seen simply as setting the scene within which perfectionist creative talent can most efficiently flourish. Anthony Storr[31] describes the work environment of Rossini, Stravinsky and Ibsen in such terms. Occasionally the detailed content of obsessions might directly lend itself to literary or philosophical themes. Storr argues that reading *Gulliver's Travels* reveals something of the content of Swift's own obsessions. For example:

'... *during the first Year I could not endure my Wife or Children in my Presence, the very smell of them was intolerable; much less could I suffer them to eat in the same Room. To this Hour they dare not presume to touch my Bread, or drink out of the same Cup; neither was I ever able to let one of them take me by the hand.*'

Coping with an obsessional personality as a partner

It is worth adding a few words about the social interactions between obsessionals and non-obsessionals, quite apart from coping with the experience of obsessional *disorder*. Information on the obsessional personality can help to avoid misunderstandings. Obsessionals tend to be goal-orientated, purposive and planning in their actions. Gratuitous remarks do not come easily to them, and are often not understood as such when spoken by others. Anything that you say to an obsessional is likely to be seen in terms of a plan, a meaning for life. The obsessional might well ruminate over any 'throw-away' remarks to extract a serious design behind them. Obsessionals tend to intellectualize a great deal. I would imagine that if the verbal and non-verbal signals are in conflict, the obsessional would tend to put more weight on the verbal signal than would a non-obsessional.

The obsessional sometimes has difficulty accepting that others are not obsessional, often judging their behaviour by his own standards. This can occasionally be seriously misleading. The obsessional often has an urge to reform his partner to match an ideal standard. Not surprisingly, the partner commonly resists the conversion process.

A tendency for obsessionals to tell their partners everything has been noted.[32] Of course, whether this proves to be good or bad will depend to some extent upon the partner and what they are told!

A brief look back

To reiterate the main message, there exists an obsessional personality that is prone to exhibit obsessional disorder. The disorder can sometimes make better sense seen in the light of how the personality functions. Sometimes it is convenient to refer simply to 'the obsessional', meaning someone with both the personality-type and some signs of disorder. Very many of those suffering from obsessional disorder have an obsessional personality. However, two things complicate the picture. The disorder sometimes appears in a personality not characterized as obsessional. Certainly not every person with an obsessional personality exhibits obsessional disorder. In discussing how to treat this condition, it is the disorder and not the personality that is being targeted. The personality-type is not one that is a viable candidate for reform. Indeed, most people of this kind probably feel that it is the rest of the world that needs changing. The disorder is quite another matter and the sufferer desperately craves a cure.

13
Professional help

Broadly speaking, there are four main types of treatment available for obsessional disorder, some of which I have briefly described earlier. First, there is treatment that tries to oppose directly the intrusion, such as thought stopping. Secondly, there is the exposure technique, e.g. exposure to the repeated presentation of the spoken content of the obsession. Paradoxical intention falls into this category. Thirdly, there are techniques that try to reshape the thinking process, for example, cognitive psychotherapy. Fourthly, there is physical intervention with drugs, electric currents or even, in the most extreme cases, brain surgery. In Britain, one would normally be referred by one's own doctor to a clinical psychologist for behavioural treatments. Drugs could be prescribed by the doctor.

Behaviour therapy

The type of treatment given depends to some extent upon the theoretical orientation of the therapist. A physical analogy can illuminate this.[1] Suppose a skier breaks a leg. One might argue that the first priority is to repair the broken leg. As secondary considerations, we might ask whether the ski-slope could be restructured or the patient taught to ski better. By analogy, the primary problem with an obsessional-compulsive disorder or phobia is considered to be the abnormal *behaviour* itself. This is the behaviourist approach, sometimes called behaviour therapy. It is often said in criticism of this approach that it fails to address the problem underlying the behaviour. The behaviourist would answer that we have no evidence that there is anything of significance underlying it. Even if one concedes that there might be, then behaviour therapy is still seen as the appropriate tool.

The treatment of phobias and obsessions by behaviour therapy is one of the success stories of clinical psychology. Where overt behaviour is involved, then such therapy has brought relief to a very large number of patients. One such technique is *response prevention*: for example, the therapist might sit with the patient encouraging him not to make the response, such as hand-washing. Where a fear of some future consequence is involved, the technique of *behavioural modelling* has proved useful. Suppose a person is afraid of going into a shop in case he gets contaminated. Entry into a shop might be followed by extensive washing rituals. In such a case, the patient might be encouraged to visit a shop with the therapist. The therapist would thereby demonstrate that no harm comes to people who visit shops.

Some patients can be used to illustrate details of the techniques.[2] Let's return to the case of Jane, whose pigeon phobia was described on page 91. Treatment for Jane consisted of gradually bringing her into contact with the dreaded object, in spite of the obvious fear that this evoked. First, the therapist asked Jane to hang pictures of birds in her room. She was then instructed to purchase dummy birds and to get used to handling them. In her first session of therapy, she managed to handle a pigeon that was being held by the therapist. At the next session, she was able to accompany the therapist to a park where pigeons were feeding, even though she screamed when a bird came particularly near. The story had a happy ending; at the follow-up interview one year later, Jane reported no fear of pigeons.

The logic underlying treatment of an illness phobia is the same as that described for the pigeon phobia, but the form of the treatment is necessarily different. For example, someone with a cancer phobia needs to be exposed *in his mind* to the stimulus of his own cancer. To do this, the therapist might ask the patient to imagine that he has cancer, and has only six months to live. He needs to settle important family business. The patient is asked to imagine that he has been shown an X-ray that reveals cancer, and told that although this might at first seem unreal, then the truth will later hit him. In pursuing therapy of this kind, the patient's family would be instructed not to give reassurance to his questions of the kind 'Am I really ill?' Such reassurance would normally bring temporary relief, but at the price of strengthening the disorder in the long term.

Treatment of obsessional-compulsive disorder is similar to that for phobias, but can be more lengthy and tortuous. The nature of obsessions is sometimes such that one cannot get a purchase on them as easily as on phobias. There is often not a feared *object* or *stimulus* out there that can form the target for exposure, unlike a phobia over a pigeon or an open space. Thus, Hans Eysenck once asked me 'How would you like to be shut up in a mortuary for a few hours surrounded by corpses?' To avoid conveying the wrong impression, I must add that Hans knew I was feeling relatively OK at the time and that I had a sense of humour. However, I suspect this drastic intervention might not work, since it would not tackle the personal frame of reference.

Obsessions so often take the form of a puzzle of the kind 'did I . . .? 'What if . . .? 'Suppose if . . .' However, in spite of these complications, a modification of the technique used with phobias has proved very helpful.

Consider Ann, a bank employee, 23 years of age.[2] Ann suffered from a variety of obsessional thoughts and associated compulsive behaviour, concerning the general theme of harm coming to herself, and, as a consequence, to her family. She worried about having become pregnant, in spite of being a virgin. Ann was afraid to visit the toilet after her boyfriend, in case she should 'catch' pregnancy. A wart on her finger was perceived to be cancerous and a source of infection to other members of her family. Objects were avoided because they might contaminate her with, as she perceived it, 'cancer germs'. Electrical switches were checked very frequently. Ann washed her hands 125 times each day, getting through three bars of soap a day.

The treatment consisted of Ann first being given certain targets to achieve, such as being able to cook a meal for her parents, without carrying out protective rituals. Ann was instructed to reduce slowly the number of times she washed her hands each day. Ann watched the nurse-therapist 'contaminate' herself by performing a behaviour that Ann would have feared to do. The logic was to expose Ann gradually to the feared situations in the hope that they would thereby slowly lose their fear-evoking potency. The family and Ann's boyfriend were involved with the programme. As an index of its success, after the 47th session Ann had reduced her consumption of soap to one bar every two weeks.

The significance of the success of behaviour therapy in the treatment of phobias and obsessional-compulsive disorders is both practical and theoretical. Help is available without the lengthy and expensive therapy procedures hitherto employed. In these terms, the problem is seen to be the phobia or the obsession *itself*, rather than something lying behind it. Isaac Marks[3] argues:

'There is no need to look for hidden origins to phobias and obsessions. They do not point to dark, unconscious secrets which have to be uncovered for treatment to succeed. The anxieties can be cleared by working on the assumption that the sufferer needs to get used to the situation which troubles him, without any need to reconstruct his personality.'

Paradoxical intention

A variety of exposure that has been used with some success in treating obsessions is that of *paradoxical intention*. Its essence is to expose the patient not just to the feared object or thought, but to a grossly exaggerated version of it. A patient who is obsessed with the thought that he might commit sexual assault in public is taken by the therapist to a public place and told to try to assault as many people as possible. He is typically quite unable to begin to do so, and often finds the notion ludicrous. Similarly, a stutterer is told to try hard to stutter as much as possible.

The therapy is attractive in part because of the intrinsically *paradoxical* nature of the obsessional phenomenon.[4] The patient is tempted to do something quite against her better judgement or feels compelled to think a thought quite at odds with the rest of her lifestyle. As therapy, the patient is instructed to dwell upon the thought, to expand upon it and convince herself of its validity.

Consider the case of the treatment of a 22-year-old male patient by this technique.[5] On visiting a movie, the patient was obsessed with the idea that he might have started a fire in the toilet, and would need to get up repeatedly to inspect the toilet. He did this up to twenty times in the course of a film. The instructions to the patient were as follows. When the urge to check next intruded, he should imagine that indeed a fire had broken out. The entire men's room is ablaze. Soon the cinema is an inferno. The fire rages out of control throughout the entire city, while the unfortunate obsessional who is the cause of it all is still seated in the cinema. On the next visit to the movies, the patient tried imagining this sequence. At first, he experienced acute panic, but this gave way to a calm feeling and a realization of 'how ridiculous it was to keep checking.'

An advocate of paradoxical intention who has reported success in its use observed:[6]

'Since most obsessional-compulsive patients are known to be perfectionists, the basic underlying theme must be – "Heck, who wants to be perfect! I don't give a damn!"'.

One patient suffered from obsessive doubts about whether he really loved his wife, and was asked to adopt the attitude 'Who wants to love his wife?'

Along similar lines was the treatment of a patient who was obsessed by the thought that the objects of the world might not be real.[7] Just before the Second World War, the man, a 41-year-old Munich lawyer, had read the work *Critique of Pure Reason* by the philosopher Immanuel Kant, and a sentence concerning the possibility of unreality '. . . was the truly decisive blow for me, all else had been only a prelude.' From then on, the patient was concerned to do everything 'one hundred per cent' correct. The symptoms improved somewhat during his period of war service. However, the symptoms later got much worse and he was unable to work. The obsessive thought of unreality was attacked with paradoxical intention; he was asked to practise the phrase 'Okay so I live in an unreal world. The table here is not real, the doctors are not really here either . . .' This appeared to be successful.

Paradoxical intention is a good example of where ideas deriving from different schools in psychology can sometimes be brought together. The irony is that paradoxical intention, rather than owing its genesis to rat-based analogies in the behaviourist movement, is usually attributed to the existentialist psychologist Viktor Frankl.[8] The unquestioned success of behaviour therapy even when using only *images* of the dreaded object, rather than real confrontation with it, depends upon the patient's peculiarly human ability to create fantasy upon verbal instruction. Frankl suggests that the patient should so exaggerate the situation, make it so absurd that she is able to laugh at it. Therein lies the paradoxical intention. The prescription is paradoxical, but so is the disorder. Interestingly, in the Morita school of psychotherapy in Japan one finds ideas similar to paradoxical intention. In describing their methods, Takehisa Kora[9] observes:

'. . . even a small dysfunction of mind or body results in an oversensitive reaction. In other words, they become hypochondriacal. People with a morbid fear of wandering thoughts, while studying, are more concerned with preventing the wandering thoughts than with studying, and they become trapped by their symptoms.'

Obsessions, unaccompanied by compulsive rituals, are less common than obsessional-compulsive disorders. Unfortunately, it is now clear that the outcome of therapy of any kind is not good for pure obsessional ruminations, certainly not as good as where compulsive behaviour is also involved. Paradoxical intention and drugs perhaps offer the best hope.

Cognitive therapy

Cognitive therapy works by the therapist questioning critically the assumptions on which the client appears to be operating. It was pioneered[10] primarily by working with depressives. A similar strand of the development of this technique is termed *rational-emotive therapy*.[11] Cognitive therapy might be helpful to some sufferers from obsessional disorder, where faulty all-or-none, 'black and white' logic tends to be endemic.[12] One way in which the logic of obsessionals is sometimes faulty is their tendency to overestimate the probability of negative outcomes: if harm can happen, it will. The psychologist establishes a rapport with the client and then asks questions to try to ascertain the major premises under which the client operates. Logic from which the disturbed mental state could derive support is unearthed and then challenged. Clearly, each client is likely to have slightly different patterns of thought and therefore slightly different counter-thoughts are suggested. One's ideological and religious beliefs might play a role in what is the best counter-thought. This kind of information will emerge in discussion with the therapist.

To try to modify the obsessional's feeling of harm coming is one possible approach to therapy, though this would depend upon the nature of the intruding thought. An intelligent obsessional troubled by a fear of death is likely to show resistance to anything suggesting the logic that it might not happen after all. Ruminators are sometimes secretive and suspicious, so the therapist might need to tread carefully and gently. Obsessionals often have multiple obsessions and to obtain access to all of them can require a lot of careful coaxing and confidence building by the therapist. There is sometimes a *network* of related obsessions. Unfortunately, it is still too soon to know whether the results of cognitive psychotherapy offer general hope.

Behaviour therapy and cognitive therapy compared

For pure obsessions, I suggest that it would be worth trying at first the technique of confronting *each* intrusion with the thought that the worst situation suggested by the intrusion does indeed, or will, prevail. This is the technique described earlier for someone who was obsessed by thoughts of cancer. She was asked to entertain repeatedly the *worst* features and logical conclusions that followed from her obsession. This can be very tough, but it could prove helpful. If no progress is made after a week or two, I suggest you give it up.

If this method of confrontation fails or if the subject feels more at home with reasoning, she can try the technique of cognitive therapy. She can see whether any subtle counter-thoughts help to ease the pain, by undermining any 'logic' that is strengthening the obsession. To do this she might need to make notes of what she is doing. If a basic philosophical dilemma underlies the obsession, then in the context of cognitive restructuring, it *might* help to read works of philosophy, literature or theology that address the issue. See how others have faced it. Feel part of a bigger community (Viktor Frankl[13] discusses some of the philosophical and theological issues surrounding obsessional thinking). Interestingly, Pierre Janet was occasionally able to help his patients by pointing to faulty theological reasoning underlying the problem. In this respect Janet was a kind of 19th-century cognitive psychotherapist.

On the other hand, an attempt at cognitive restructuring might make matters worse, for at least two reasons. First, it might suggest, or reinforce the notion, that a solution exists to what in fact will prove to be an insoluble problem. Second, the quest might uncover additional information that reinforces the problem. John Bunyan experienced this, though in the end he seemed to find an acceptable solution. Bunyan[14] prayed that the Lord would spare his wife from painful pangs, and when the pain lifted he took this to mean his prayer had been heard. However, rather than permanently comforting him, some 18 months later it served to strengthen his torment. The response to the prayer implied that God knew all that was happening in Bunyan's sinful mind. Henceforth the intrusion *Let Christ go if he will* triggered the painful thought *Now you may see that God doth know the most secret thoughts of the heart*.

Perhaps the most useful advice to the sufferer who tries cognitive restructuring is the general one to abandon strategies that don't appear to be working.

You can also try to experiment with arguing against the thoughts. Get a friend to play devil's advocate, by taking your position and you then argue against it. In this, as in other situations, play it by ear and note the reactions.

Let us consider a hypothetical obsessional, Jim. Jim had a religious upbringing. At age 25, Jim is assailed by the thought 'God is not good'. Jim might find that by reading works of popular theology and talking to a priest, he can undermine the logic. He becomes convinced that his fears are groundless, and the pain of the intrusions eases. He finds a matrix of social support. Suppose though that he can't find any useful and convincing answers and the problem seems just as bad or even worse. He might try confrontation with the worse possible consequence of his fear. This might be that God is evil, or indifferent to suffering, or that there is no God at all. Every time he ruminates he could try thinking that the very worse situation of all does indeed prevail.

Cognitive therapy, i.e. logical restructuring of thought is constructive thinking, but, in general, I am not yet optimistic about the outcome for obsessionals. The obsessional is an expert thinker, even without the help of deliberate restructuring or a cognitive psychotherapist, Trying to make sense of what is going on, to undermine its logic, to subvert it, is not something that I could strongly recommend in any but a few cases. For the obsessional doubt of the kind 'Did I cause a road accident?' I would rate the chances of cognitive restructuring working as being low. In my view, simply confronting in the imagination the worse possible situation is likely to prove more effective.

As far as any rational restructuring is concerned, Graham Reed[15] sums up very convincingly the nature of one problem:

> 'The vast majority of psychotherapeutic approaches rely upon the detailed examination of the contents of consciousness and attempt to "interpret" these. On the present theory, such activity can be of little

help and may well be actively harmful. It encourages the patient to engage in the hair-splitting, self-questioning, and circular arguments which are at the heart of his disturbance. He is being asked to practice the very cognitive activities which are causing him distress.'

Graham Reed argues that techniques which attempt to persuade sufferers of the irrationality of their obsessional thought content are almost doomed to failure, since, almost by definition, the obsessional acknowledges their irrationality.

Some other ways of treating pure obsessions

Satiation training consists in asking the patient to generate the obsessional thought and to hold it for about 15 minutes. A somewhat different technique, in which the therapist plays a more active role, is as follows.[16] The patient is first relaxed and asked to close her eyes. Then the therapist describes the content of the obsession and the patient is instructed not to avoid imagining any of the scenes. A patient whose obsessional thoughts consisted of hitting out in the direction of a child was treated in this way. The therapist suggested scenes that covered the content of the obsession, no more or less. Thus, the patient is prompted to think about hitting out at the child, but the therapist does not provide details about the consequence of the assault, such as it being fatal or superficial. To do so would mean going beyond the content of the obsession. The pauses are very brief, designed to be only of sufficient length to allow the patient to record his subjective level of anxiety. Usually, over the course of a 1-hour therapist-guided session, there is a decrease in the anxiety level. This method seems to help some patients, but by no means all. Sometimes the content of the thought can be undermined by such a technique even though the thought occurs just as frequently after treatment. For example, a lengthy and very realistic thought was reduced to a more vague and transient thought. In one patient, the thought of a knife being used repeatedly to slash at someone slowly converted itself into a neutral object gliding through the air.

For large numbers of obsessionals, the unwanted thoughts have been found to concern harm, done either to themselves or to others.[17] Such patients, reporting for example a fear of killing someone or killing themselves, have been found to be relatively unassertive. This has suggested the possibility that the obsessions concerning harm were connected with unexpressed feelings of aggression. The suggestion has led some to consider the possible therapeutic value of assertiveness training in helping the patients to handle their aggression better. Whether such training might help obsessionals who do not display an obvious lack of assertiveness remains to be seen.

Drugs

Obsessional-compulsive disorder is usually classified as a type of anxiety. However, anxiolytics (anti-anxiety drugs, such as Valium) are not effective in reducing its intensity. There is also an associated risk of addiction. Some argue[18] that anxiety is *caused by* the condition, rather than being its *cause*. Concerning drugs, the link with depression seems much closer than that with anxiety. There are several reports of success using the antidepressant Clomipramine ('Anafranil'), both for pure obsessionals as well as for those with associated rituals.[19] It is particularly effective where there is associated depression. As medication, only Clomipramine helped me. Occasionally, Imipramine ('Tofranil') helps.[20] Fluoxetine and Fluvoxamine are showing some hopes.[21]

There is a beneficial effect of clomipramine with both depressive and non-depressive obsessionals. Stopping the clomipramine treatment can result in a relapse. Patients often describe the effect of clomipramine as 'I still have the thoughts but they don't bother me as much. I've got so many other things on my mind now.'[22] Often activities that had been interrupted by the illness are able to be resumed, such as work and sports activities. This leads to a natural diminution of the problem. The aspect that the thoughts persist but are not so frightening was very much the way that I experienced the effect of clomipramine. It is also how some patients receiving brain surgery for chronic pain describe their experience. 'I can still feel it but it doesn't worry me so much.'

Clomipramine is often very effective in combination with behaviour therapy.[23] There is a delay of days or weeks between taking clomipramine and any therapeutic effect. The full effect might take 5–10 weeks to appear. Possible side-effects of this drug (weight gain, dry mouth, tiredness, excessive sweating, unsteady hands, drowsiness, problems with focusing the eyes, dizziness, constipation and difficulty in attaining orgasm) can sometimes be a problem (this seems a daunting list but there is no reason to suppose that all or even most of them will appear). It might be possible to find a low daily dose of clomipramine (e.g. 25mg) that has a marked effect on attentuating obsessional thoughts, but only minimal side-effects.

Of all the techniques available for the treatment of mental illness none evoke more fear and controversy in the general community than that of electroconvulsive therapy (ECT) and psychosurgery. ECT has not proved useful in the case of obsessional disorder, except where the disorder is accompanied by very severe depression. In such a case, it is most useful to see the ECT as affecting the depression rather than the obsessional disorder itself.

Psychosurgery

It is possible to envisage a rationale for psychosurgery. Repetition of a thought suggests repetition of activity in circuits of nerve cells and a well-placed cut might just break the circuit. These days, psychosurgery would be used in only the most extreme cases that have proved themselves resistant to less drastic interventions. Some authorities still consider it a viable procedure in such extreme cases. However, drugs and behaviour therapy offer a safer and more viable choice. A tragic case of psychosurgery concerned a woman who felt herself to be contaminated by things associated with death, such as cemeteries and coffins.[24] So serious was this fear that the patient was living a hermit's existence, confined to her bed and being fed by her husband. She was offered a form of behaviour therapy involving confrontation with the feared objects. However, so great was her fear that she opted to undergo psychosurgery which was viewed as a lesser evil. The psycho-surgery failed to relieve the situation and she then accepted behaviour therapy.

A fascinating anecdote is worth recording.[25] Tom, a 19-year-old, had suffered from obsessions regarding contamination since he was 10. By age 15, checking and hand-washing had become insufferable problems. Two suicide attempts were made, Tom believing that the sacrifice of his life would appease God and restore family harmony. Things got worse, with Tom also acquiring a chanting ritual. One day he complained to his mother about how awful life had become, to which she replied 'Go and shoot yourself.' In utter desperation, he took a .22 calibre rifle, and pointed it into his mouth. Tom felt that to fire such a shot would somehow answer his problem, which, apparently, is exactly what it did do, though not for any reason he could have anticipated.

Tom was found alive, but with blood on his face. The bullet was lodged in his brain, having penetrated the left frontal lobe for which Tom was given neurosurgery. From then on, and at a 2-year post-operation check-up, Tom's obsessional problems were minimal. Was it pure coincidence that Tom's self-inflicted psychosurgery was associated with a dramatic recovery from obsessional disorder? We cannot say. Possibly, the stay in hospital at a safe distance from the insufferable stresses of family life could be responsible. Possibly, '. . . the drama of the suicide attempt, with its attendant notion of "hitting bottom". . .'[25] could have played a role. Possibly, the change in the mother in the direction of taking a more sympathetic view of Tom was responsible. All of these factors could have played a role, in addition to any possible effect of damage to the brain tissue.

Final word

In summary, one can say that, of all the techniques available, that of behaviour therapy offers the most hope. Such techniques are very effective where compulsive behaviour is involved, and for pure obsessions some techniques work for some people in some situations. Paradoxical intention offers some hope. These techniques are quick, cheap and not too painful. In my view, clomipramine used in conjunction with such techniques could prove to be more effective than any other combination. Nothing is certain in the treatment of mental and behavioural disorder. There is no magic cure, but in this chapter I have done my best to give a fair assessment of the possibilities. The obsessional can derive some help simply from learning that assistance is available. Very many refuse to acknowledge that others have the condition, firmly believing themselves to be the only sufferer in the world. Contrary to what the sufferer might feel, he will not be thought to be 'crazy' on revealing all to a doctor or psychiatrist.

14
Self help – what to do and what not to do

On their own initiative, the patient and her family can achieve much, or conversely make some fundamental errors. Some useful advice can now be offered.

Even if the victim's attempts to block the ruminations themselves are not successful, she might have some success with stopping the process of 'ruminating about ruminations'. Any ruminations about ruminations need to be constructive ones, involving the planning of new experiences and modes of social interaction. (In the last few pages of his book, Graham Reed[1] gives examples of some mental exercises that might prove useful in changing the general way that the obsessional processes information.)

The patient can try to make a note of those situations in which she feels particularly bad, and attempt to avoid them in the future. Note any in which the ruminations appear to be less frequent or less intense and try to maximize such situations. Try to identify any 'dismissal tactics', those courses of action that are good at getting away from the thoughts. The patient might find music, sport or debate, or amateur dramatics, to be his or her own best dismissal tactic.

In general, one can probably do no better than listen to the profound wisdom advanced by Samuel Johnson:

'The safe and general antidote against sorrow is employment.'

Or, perhaps more specifically, when the problem is one of obsessional thoughts:

'Imagination never takes such firm possession of the mind as when it is found empty and unoccupied.'

One can see the rationale for this in terms of the brain's limited processing capacity. The brain is less likely to switch into fantasy when it is heavily engaged, particularly where there is a strong element of external pacing involved, as in social interaction. (B. F. Skinner[2] offers the same advice.)

When Boswell consulted Johnson about his own unwanted thoughts, he was told:

'For the black fumes which arise in your mind, I can prescribe nothing but that you disperse them by honest business or innocent pleasure, and by reading, sometimes easy and sometimes serious.

Change of place is useful . . .'

Johnson was emphatic (as was usually the case!) in his advice to Boswell on what *not* to do, and the reader who is in distress might experiment here also:

'. . . make it an invariable and obligatory law to yourself, never to mention your own mental diseases; if you are never to speak of them, you will think on them but little, and if you think little of them, they will molest you rarely.'

Alas, one needs to note that, in spite of his wisdom, Johnson appeared to be molested almost all of the time by unpleasant intrusions. In my view, whether it is beneficial for the obsessional to mention his 'own mental diseases' depends upon the purpose of mentioning them. Insight and help can often be gained from others. For some it might prove useful to know that they are not alone in their problem. However, the obsessional should avoid seeking pity.

I would suggest that trying to keep busy is a good idea. It would be good to establish practical and realistic goals. Being under a *little* pressure could be good news. A forced pacing of your day might help, with clear target times etc. A delicate balance needs to be found between, on the one hand, the desirable situation of being under sufficient pressure to occupy one's attention and generate and realize worthy goals and, on the other, the negative situation of being under stress. Each person needs to find a balance.

Checking

My experiences might be of some use to a person caught up in the ritual of checking. It occurs to me that it might (and no more than 'might') be of help to try in some way to *tag* your check unambiguously, so that later it can be made to stand out from the memories of previous checking experiences. Otherwise you are in a vicious circle, where each check increases the total number of checks, and makes it all the more difficult for the latest check to stand out.

Suppose that you telephone for a taxi and are locking the front door. You check the door and it is locked, but you check it again. Then the taxi arrives and you notice that, instead of the usual taxi driver, this time the driver is a Sikh in a turban. You go to give it one last check. While you are doing this, I would suggest that you say to yourself 'I'll call this check a *Sikh taxi-driver check*.' Then, on trying to recall the check in question when you are in the taxi, with luck it might stand out unambiguously from all other checks. For another example, try buying an evening paper and focus upon a piece of the day's news while you perform your checking. Then, on reading, say, that today is Thatcher's birthday, you might tag today's check as a 'Thatcher birthday check'. Another possible solution is to take an associate into your confidence, explain the problem to her, and ask her to observe your check. However, the confederate must be firm and not get sucked into the ritual. What is not enough to help the obsessional in this state is simply to try reassuring them in some general way like, 'I am sure you did lock the door. You always do, so don't worry about it.' In giving help, people can be more sympathetic than perhaps the checker realizes. However, the helper needs to exercise great care, and it is very important to fit in with any therapy that might be in employment at the same time.

Exercise, getting out and keeping busy

I suggest that the sufferer from obsessions and/or depression tries putting the following advice from Johnson to the test:

'. . . how much happiness is gained, and how much misery escaped, by frequent and violent agitation of the body.'

In this context, Johnson would doubtless have given his approval to today's jogging and aerobics, the 18th-century equivalent for him being a brisk walk from Lichfield to Birmingham and back. George Borrow found a similar solution to the problem of melancholic and intrusive thoughts, as described in *Lavengro*:

'I have come from some distance . . . indeed I am walking for exercise, which I find as necessary to the mind as the body. I believe that by exercise people would escape much mental misery.'

In an interview in *The Sunday Times*, Woody Allen relates his own somewhat similar experiences that offer the therapeutic combination of a certain amount of physical exertion and rich sensory stimulation:

'In every crisis in my life, the way I have responded is by immediately putting on my coat and walking the streets endlessly.'

It would appear that the streets of Manhattan have a beneficial effect on Allen that is similar to the one Samuel Johnson described for London: '. . . if there is not much happiness, there is, at least, such a diversity of good and evil, that slight vexations do not fix upon the heart.' At times of particularly acute mental agony, Johnson was known to spend all night walking the streets of London, his massive physique affording protection against the capital's numerous villains.

Some seem to find creative 'obsessions' themselves a good distraction from obsessional problems. For example, Woody Allen is quoted as saying '. . . if one can arrange one's life so that one can obsess about small things, it keeps you from obsessing about the really big things.' In this case, the really big things are death, ageing and the passage of time. The small things are presumably film making and acting.

In this context, rest and sedation might well be counter-productive.[3] They could present the obsessional with a golden opportunity to ruminate.

If the obsessional is leading a hermit's life, he should get out and about, and note what happens. Try taking a package-tour holiday. Try energetic sport, such as badminton or aerobics. Social sports might be most useful, and better than solitary pursuits such as jogging on one's own.

The company of others

Samuel Johnson recommended early rising (something he was not good at) as a means of reclaiming imagination, but perhaps most important of all to him was the company of others. He wrote: 'Happiness is not found in self-contemplation; it is perceived only when it is reflected from another.' Nothing could be worse than being alone, or going back to an empty house. To Johnson what was needed was conversation, '. . . where there is no competition, no vanity, but a calm quiet interchange of sentiments.' Sir Joshua Reynolds told James Boswell 'He has often begged me to go home with him to prevent his being alone in the coach. Any company was better than none; by which he connected himself with many mean persons whose presence he could command.' Boswell felt that playing draughts would have had a beneficial effect upon Johnson's mental state.

Buddhism and self help

Buddhist teachings offer help for eliminating unwanted thoughts. A hierarchy of therapeutic methods has been described; if the first fails to eliminate the intrusion, the thinker is to move down the hierarchy until a suitable one is found.[4] The first trick is to try to move to an incompatible thought; an intrusion of hate would need to prompt a thought of kindness. If that should fail, then the patient should try considering the harmful consequences of the intrusion. Next, distraction must be employed, for example, recall of something or engagement in a task. Fourthly, the long-suffering victim could try asking what is the cause of the thought, and finally, if all else fails, the command is to try to dominate the mind by, amongst other things, clenching the teeth and pressing the tongue hard against the palate. The latter is by analogy with a strong person restraining a weaker one.

Another piece of advice found in Buddhist teaching, having clear parallels with contemporary therapy, is to concentrate upon the unwanted thought – confront it, entertain it, dwell on it . . . It should then lose its evil attraction; it might even disappear.

Effects of alcohol and drugs

I would most strongly advise the obsessional to be very careful with alcohol consumption. Alcohol will most probably make the intrusions less frequent and less intense, for a while. As its effect wears off, it could well make them much worse for a long time. The danger is that the sufferer might associate the alcohol more closely with the good rather than the bad effects. It is *highly unlikely* that alcohol would have any net beneficial effect on this condition. Samuel Johnson was particularly careful in his advice on the use of alcohol (though, at times, having quite a reputation as a drinker). Unfortunately souls '. . . sometimes fly for relief to wine instead of exercise, and purchase temporary ease, by the hazard of the most dreadful consequences.' Johnson experimented with opium as a means of obtaining bodily and mental peace, though this did not have the same negative connotations in the 18th as in the 20th century, and therefore I would be reluctant to advise it today!

There is disagreement in the literature as to whether obsessionals are more prone than normals to drug abuse. Undoubtedly, a number turn to illegal drugs as an attempt at finding self-medication for the disorder.[5]

Alternative medicine and techniques

The sufferer can try yoga and/or transcendental meditation, but needs to see how they suit. In the literature on alternative medicine, there is considerable discussion of unwanted thoughts. The amount of space devoted to it supports the idea that such thoughts are much more common than is usually supposed. Perhaps alternative medicine forms a more natural resort for the obsessional – 'I am not ill, it's only my thinking that is odd.' I have no evidence on the effectiveness of alternative medicine, but neither can I dismiss it. In Bach flower therapy, White Chestnut (*Aesculus hippocastanum*) is recommended for unwanted thoughts.[6] There is even the occasional report of faith-healing working, though not surprisingly we lack controlled studies.

Prevention and some warning signs

Can one do anything to prevent obsessional disorder? I can give some cautious advice to parents, care-givers and careers advisors etc. Be open with your child. Tell them truthfully about life and its problems, good and bad. Encourage a richness of experience. Answer their questions truthfully. Of course protect your child, but don't be overprotective. Don't 'wrap the child in cotton wool'. Try not to make the child feel superior or inferior to others.

Both in Britain and Hong Kong it has been observed that the parents of obsessional neurotics tended, more than average, to have strict perfectionist standards that were expected of their children. So the advice to parents would be to avoid the setting of rigid and perfectionist standards. Goals should be accessible. Such advice is probably equally useful for the avoidance of depression.

Roger Pitman[7] offers advice to parents of children who appear to have a predisposition towards obsessional disorder:

'One should mistrust wisdom, overprudence and reflection in children. These children should be encouraged to confront reality and even be allowed to have dangerous experiences, which are exhilarating and increase self-confidence. They should be encouraged not to avoid fights with peers; concern about their futures is worth the risk of a few punches. The physical should be emphasized over the intellectual. They should not be given the chance to daydream, but pushed towards quickness, accuracy and practical activity. Unfortunately, the parents of these patients often do the opposite. Nothing makes a child timid like the presence of his parents, because in their presence he does not feel the need to make an effort.'

In my view, it is unreasonable to try to eliminate daydreaming. Rather, a reasonable balance between daydreaming and activity is desirable. Active sport (e.g. running) could prove to have a beneficial effect.

Jobs and career guidance

I would steer the ruminator away from jobs that encourage independent free-thinking, such as being an artist, writer, philosopher, poet or psychologist. This is unfortunate since ruminators probably make good philosophers. I would like to think that sometimes they make reasonable psychologists too! I suggest that they are steered towards jobs in which some kind of external pacing is involved and where there is limited time for free-floating thought. Possibly politics, social work, nursing or the probation service could make good careers. In 1938, Sir Aubrey Lewis[8] offered the advice:

'. . . it is usually better for an obsessional to have his day mapped out as far as possible, without frequent need of choosing between various courses of action; sub-editing a newspaper, for example, or speculating on the stock exchange are the reverse of ideal occupations for him.'

What can a partner or friend do to help?

Obsessions often involve not just the victim but also complex interactions with other members of the family. The whole family might sometimes be usefully brought into the therapeutic process. In some cases other family members are being used or exploited to serve the compulsive behaviour. It is not unknown for obsessionals to use their condition in order to manipulate others. Sometimes family members could be described as acting in collusion with the obsessional. In extreme but rare cases, the obsessional-compulsive will tyrannize other family members into submission, under threat of temper tantrums or physical abuse.

For the close companion of an obsessional neurotic, I can suggest some advice. However, if the patient is undergoing treatment, it is *vital* that the therapist be contacted. What could seem to be help might in fact be going counter to the treatment. For example, to comply with a patient's wishes for reassurance, or for leaving the bathroom unoccupied all evening, could directly hinder therapy. Fundamental reorganization of the household and its interpersonal relations might help to find a solution to the problem. If the other family members are complying under duress or threat, then clearly they are in a real dilemma. Isaac Marks[9] asks:

> *'Should they settle for a quiet life and just comply with the patient's weird requests to avoid upsetting him or her, or should they refuse and risk a flood of abuse pouring over them, not to mention the handicap to their own lives that will ensue? Gentle but firm refusal to comply is in fact kinder in the long run, despite the initial upset that this may cause.'*

Occasionally, an obsessional has been put off seeking professional help by being laughed at by family members when making the first step of 'going public'. The necessity to avoid this is, of course, obvious. Try to be as sympathetic as possible to the obsessional, but be careful to give practical help rather than pity. Pity might help to confirm the ruminator's fears that he or she is a most unfortunate soul to be suffering in this exceptional way, and could make them feel on the slippery slope to insanity. Undramatic, genuine sympathy and practical help are needed. If it seems appropriate, you might point out that relatively few obsessionals end up in mental hospitals and that all but the most severe cases are able to carry on working. (However, if the primary content of the obsession itself is a fear of insanity, avoid responding to pleas for reassurance.) Viktor Frankl[10] distinguishes between the fear that the *content* of the obsession arouses and fear of the obsession itself. It would seem that the situation is exacerbated by the patient's fear of the obsession itself; that it might lead to insanity or suicide. Frankl believes that overcoming fear of the obsession can set the scene for tackling the content. It is at this level, of breaking the vicious circle, that paradoxical intention enters the picture. There is not a high risk of homicide or suicide amongst obsessionals.

It might also help to point out that almost all people experience intrusive thoughts of an unacceptable nature at some time in their lives. Obsessional disorder is an exaggeration of this. The victim is not an evil person or one being possessed by a spirit, but simply one whose way of processing information has gone wrong. The victim is not being punished for his sins.

The partner as well as the obsessional might need to face the fact that stresses and tensions within the family could either have triggered the disorder or are serving to exacerbate it. There might be practical steps that can be taken to reduce conflict and stress levels within the family, and it is very strongly urged that these be followed. Marriage guidance counsellors and family therapy could well be useful. The family can often work as a team to correct what has gone wrong. They can try to agree to target goals (e.g. a gradual percentage reduction in time spent washing) and a system of rewards (positive reinforcement) agreed for attaining each successive goal. Praise can serve as an effective reward. Consent and trust are very important. In their desperation, other family members are sometimes tempted to try radical 'exposure therapy', such as surreptitiously switching off the water at the main supply while the obsessional washes. This is very likely to exacerbate the condition and is a temptation to be resisted. An unpleasant 'scene' is a likely outcome. A system that has been used very effectively in the United States consists of what is termed a *multifamily psychoeducational support group*. In this programme several families meet together with a professional.

For the obsessional phenomena themselves, I would advise the avoidance of homespun psychoanalysis and 'trying to get to the root of the problem'. Any restructuring of the obsessional's mental world that you might be tempted to try has probably been tried countless times already by the obsessional. Avoid at all costs advice of the kind 'you really must sort yourself out, otherwise you will ruin the rest of your life.' The obsessional needs no confirmation of that. Also avoid giving advice of the kind 'You must simply try harder to get rid of the thoughts. Make a really determined effort this weekend, for my sake' or 'Just stop washing for your sake and mine.' A conscious effort to get rid of the thoughts, in the absence of any 'tricks of the trade' such as a strategy of confrontation with the worst consequences of the fear, is almost certainly doomed to failure. In fact, it is likely to exacerbate the condition.[11] (The ruminator might even try to make no effort at all to oppose the intrusion and, perhaps with the help of a spouse, set aside a period of time each day in order to ruminate *actively*, a kind of homework. Intrusions at other times could be answered by the counter-thought – 'We will think about this some more this evening in the homework period.')

Listen particularly carefully to the subject's reports of what is good and bad for him. Obsessionals are usually articulate people who can describe their situation rather well. You could be of great help in, for example, planning ahead so as to avoid negative contexts. You might be invaluable in helping the sufferer to get into favourable contexts, for example travel or just getting out and about.

If compulsive checking is the problem, you might be in a position to offer significant help, but make sure that you really are lowering the obsessional's fear level on a long-term basis. You might be buying temporary peace at the price of exacerbating the condition in the longer term. For example, if the partner is tempted to accompany the checker on his rounds, this could strengthen the habit. On the other hand, to monitor progress as the obsessional tries to reduce his checking could be very useful. To make sure that you are not undoing the effects of any professional intervention, discuss all such issues with the clinical psychologist.

Believe the ruminator. Even if there are few outward signs of suffering, the person might be in considerable distress. Even when times were bad, I met people who found it very difficult to accept that I had any problem, simply because I seemed to be functioning normally. Obsessionals usually manage to carry on working normally, except in the most severe cases.

Walter Bate[12] in his biography of Samuel Johnson, discusses the subject of the relation of those suffering mental disorder to their companions:

> '*Only those who themselves have come close to mental breakdown – and not merely for a short while but for a period of some years – know how easy it is to disguise their situation from others unless living with them constantly (and even then it can be concealed to a surprising extent). Few people otherwise ever believe this is possible. It is too far from their own experience. But the truth is that most people, as Johnson often said, are far too preoccupied with their own problems, whether large or small, to pay close attention to those of others unless they are almost thrust into their faces.*'

Finally, if therapy for compulsive behaviour is successful, a vacuum might be left in the life of the patient. The six hours each day previously spent washing now need to be filled with something else. The more rewarding this something is, the less the chances of relapse. A partner could prove to be of invaluable assistance here. I wish you well.

15
Trying to solve the puzzle

Obsessions and compulsions are a profound challenge to psychology. Like other challenges, there is more than one logical starting point for an attempt to make some sense out of them. For a start, we could ask whether it is useful to regard obsessions as an illness. Alternatively, are they to be seen as just a gross exaggeration of normal thinking and behaviour? We cannot rule out the possibility that they serve some useful function, though I imagine we would need to stretch lateral thinking to breaking point to find one.

Is obsessional-compulsive disorder an illness?

There are several related answers to this. Let's first take an unambiguous illness, AIDS, in order to draw a comparison. Here we see a clearly identified target in the cells of the body, and specifying the target gives unambiguous pointers to the kind of treatment that is necessary. The disease was acquired at a particular time and in a particular way, and to some extent one can predict the onset of symptoms. Obsessional-compulsive disorder is clearly rather different.

It could be helpful to draw an analogy between obsessional illness and alcoholism. The disease label has not proved very fruitful in understanding the causes of alcoholism.[1] Rather, it is more useful to look at alcoholism as an exaggeration of behaviour that most of us can handle without too much problem. However, there is more than one valid way to consider a given phenomenon and the disease model was at least an advance over its predecessors. Hitherto, alcoholism had been seen as the outcome of weak will; essentially the sufferers needed to pull themselves together. The disease model suggests sympathy and help.

Advocacy of the disease model probably also has a subtle but profound influence on the patient. What is the patient's own self-image like? Does the sufferer play the role of a sick person? To label a problem as an illness might be perceived as placing the responsibility for getting better firmly in the hands of the caregivers. The sufferer and those around him might adopt a stance of passivity rather than active resistance. For obsessional-compulsive behaviour, the expression 'emotional and behavioural problem'[2] is preferable to that of disease. This relates to the continuity of development and experience that in some cases will lead to this problem. There is often not a clear moment of onset. In other words, the expression underlines the multiple factors involved. This prompts the question as to which factors promote and which discourage the emergence of the disorder.

Analogies might help to understand what is going on. Suppose the ruminator is like a computer that has been wrongly programmed and has got locked into a loop from which it cannot escape. Another approach is to ask – can we make sense of obsessional-compulsive behaviour from the viewpoint of the theory of evolution? Such deviant processes might represent the inevitable price some of us have to pay for the human species having the most sophisticated brain.

Such questions and any answers to them should not be thought to be mutually exclusive; it is in the best scientific traditions to attempt to tackle a problem in several different ways. The tentative answers will appear rather different according to the way that we approach the phenomenon. They will also depend upon *why* we are asking the question and what is in it for us in giving a particular answer. For example, there might be certain advantages in regarding obsessions as an illness. In the interests of getting resources allocated for treatment, we might wish to emphasize the disease model, the suffering, the loss of working hours and the hope of bringing relief. On the other hand, the disease model might prove to be fruitless in speculation as to the causes of the problem.

Animals under stress – a suitable model?

One approach that psychologists have taken in trying to understand human behaviour has been to look at animal behaviour. Then, if one can see similarities between the behaviour of animals and humans, by studying the animal's behaviour (the 'model') we might be able to cast some light on the more complex human situation. In several cases, animal studies have proved useful in enlightening abnormal human behaviour, for example in learning, obesity and anxiety.

However, one might suppose that obsessions present a peculiarly human challenge, since so much of the evidence for their existence depends upon spoken language. For the researcher into ruminations there might be no other source of evidence than the word of the subject. Although I think it is true to say that the rat model has so far not provided us with much insight into processes that underlie pure obsessions, nonetheless clinical psychologists who treat obsessional-compulsive disorder by behaviour therapy owe much to research on rats and dogs. For example, the response-prevention technique of trying to combat overt compulsions (described earlier) was inspired from studies with rats.

In the cases where obsessions are accompanied by bizarre compulsions of a ritualistic nature, it might be profitable to look at analogous behaviour in domestic animals, though caution is needed. There are cases of where animal behaviour seems to have the qualities of the bizarre, exaggerated and being out of context.

One situation in which such abnormal behaviour comes into sharp relief is that of intensive farming. Some of these abnormalities might have more in common with the human phenomenon of tics, but they might also have relevance for compulsive behaviour. Veal calves are raised in such a way as to preclude turning around and social contact is minimal. Such calves display odd movements. One of the best known of these is 'tongue playing', in which the tongue is rolled in and out or swayed from side to side.

As a means of saving space, pregnant sows are kept tethered. In this condition, the sows show a number of stereotyped behaviours such as sham chewing and biting of a bar. Socially housed pigs develop tail biting, by which means serious injury can follow and something like 100,000 pigs are lost each year in the Netherlands.[3] These behaviours are termed 'abnormal' since they do not occur if the animals are raised under more natural conditions. With all due respect to Samuel Johnson, I cannot help but think of behavioural abnormality in caged animals when I read James Boswell's account of Johnson's behaviour:

'In the intervals of articulating he made various sounds with his mouth, sometimes as if ruminating, or what is called chewing the cud, sometimes giving a half whistle, sometimes making his tongue play backwards from the roof of his mouth, as if clucking like a hen, and sometimes protruding it against his upper gums in front ...'

It is possible that further examination of abnormalities in domestic animals and the exercise of lateral thinking will be able to enlighten obsessional-compulsive disorder.

Does obsessional disorder serve a purpose?

If we consider compulsive behaviour in terms of Charles Darwin's theory of evolution, we might be led to look for some advantage that the behaviour confers. In these terms, obsessions might appear to be clearly maladaptive. They break up the flow of purposive activity in which the sufferer is engaged, activity that is directed to practical goals. In the extreme, social bonds and families are torn apart.

Some writers of a psychoanalytic persuasion[4] still suggest that, by emerging into consciousness, insistent and repetitive thoughts serve to distract the subject from more unpleasant material that is also being processed in the brain. However, Salzman admits that:

'The distracting or controlling function of such a thought is comparatively more difficult to recognize when the thought itself is extremely upsetting and disturbing',

while still believing in *displacement*:

'. . . the same basic process is operative when, regardless of how extreme or revolting an obsessive thought might be, it is still much less distressing than the idea it is covering up.'

As a personal view, I must add that nothing I have read convinces me that there is necessarily a hidden disturbing thought of this kind underlying obsessional thoughts.

Conditioning

Suppose we look at ruminations from the viewpoint of conditioning and learning. Hans Eysenck[5] argues that neurotic behaviour is an example of faulty learning, an aberration of a perfectly useful process of learning, as described by the Russian physiologist Ivan Pavlov. The essence of Pavlovian conditioning is that a relationship is established between two otherwise unrelated events. In Pavlov's famous experiment, an association was formed between a bell and food, so that the sound of the bell was able to stimulate salivation. The relevance of this model to obsessions is suggested in posing the question: 'how does a normally ignored or innocuous situation (e.g. a milk-bottle top lying in the street, counting numbers), one that evoked little fear or dread, now come to evoke disquiet, anxiety, dread or even terror?' Perhaps the best way of thinking about this is that there might be an element of accidental or chance association between one of a wide variety of thoughts and a mood.[6] There are a number of cases reported where the onset of obsessional disorder can apparently be traced to an association with a traumatic event.

In 1757, a case of this kind was reported by John Woodard. Following a series of awful family traumas, a woman bearing her sixth child observed a porpoise in the river Thames. She was delighted with seeing this creature. Alas, some 2 weeks later, she went on to suffer serious abdominal pain. At this point she recalled the porpoise and from then on was haunted by the obsessional fear that the animal would harm her baby.

Consider the following case, which could fit the conditioning model.[7]

'A person has an attack of dizziness on his way home from work.

After arrival home he opens the paper and sees the announcements of death, and he faints. Some days later he feels tired and becomes dizzy. These feelings link themselves to the previous experiences, situations of insecurity and to the possibility of death, with the development of a phobic obsessive syndrome as a result.'

The nervous system is programmed to scan for causes of significant events and often gets the cause wrong. Hit your finger with a hammer, and the chances are you will blame your boss, or wife or children, even though they might have had nothing to do with it. Similarly, if you become ill after eating Thai food, you might well go off Thai food even though it had nothing to do with causing your illness. So, maybe, obsessional rumination is the outcome of a hypersensitive nervous system possessed by some human beings – a species known for its richness of association formation.

The model of conditioning certainly seems relevant to obsessions, but just how relevant it is, only time will tell. It is interesting to note that a wide range of different situations can and do become candidates for obsessions. However, there are a number of more common themes, such as physical damage and contamination. The nervous system might be said to be 'prepared'[8] to form certain associations and not others. For example, in the case of phobias, it could be argued that we are strongly prepared to develop spider and snake phobias and not prepared to learn, say, gramophone-record phobias.

Let's now consider the situation when the obsession is well-established. There might be an *incubation* of fear.[9] Once acquired, fears can grow stronger with the passage of time. Each experience of the fear serves to strengthen it. Once the association gets triggered by some chance event it is self-reinforcing. A similar logic might be applicable to the origin of phobias.

For the sake of completeness in the discussion of learning, I must add that animal behaviour can also be changed, 'shaped', by techniques of reinforcement, described by B. F. Skinner.[10] Reward the appropriate behaviour, and one can train a rat to press a lever to obtain food or teach a pigeon to steer a missile. Conversely, if negative consequences follow behaviour, then the tendency is for the behaviour to stop, though this is more complex. Viewed in such terms, the origins of obsessional thoughts and much of compulsive behaviour make little sense. There is no obvious reward to the sufferer. Indeed, the sufferer might report extreme discomfort as a result of them and go to great lengths to get rid of them. However, in terms of inter-family dynamics, we need to consider that some forms of compulsive behaviour can involve subtle reinforcement. The behaviour can serve to manipulate family members. In some cases, family members can unwittingly help to maintain the behaviour by, for example, complying with the wilder excesses of the obsessional-compulsive's demands or giving repeated reassurance.

Mood state and stress

Obsessional ruminations about unambiguously negative themes, such as death and injury, can fit a model in which a negative mood accentuates certain negative thoughts. Thus we might want to see the phenomenon of rumination in terms of an exaggeration of a normal brain process that links moods to thoughts. There might be a kind of mutual support between the thought, or *cognition*, and mood. Stress, for example, of a general kind, not necessarily caused by events related to the specific content of the obsession, might serve to accentuate the specific thought, and so the vicious circle would continue.

Some studies have shown that obsessional patients are more likely to be affected negatively by depression and hostility, rather than anxiety.[11] Occasionally a female patient will only report compulsive symptoms at the time of menstruation. (Stress is also known to exert a bias towards depression.) With repeated cycling within the vicious circle, a broader range of stimuli in the environment might become associated with the circle, so as to be able to trigger it. It might be relevant in this context to note the observation that obsessionals commonly find that a change of environment can bring temporary relief.[12]

Viewing obsessions in this way suggests that probing the initial cause of the vicious circle is unlikely to be fruitful, if even a meaningful exercise. Rather, it is possible that all that can meaningfully be looked at is how the circle can be broken.

Is my brain malfunctioning or damaged?

Consider the computer analogy and the situation where something goes wrong in the way that a computer works. A vital caution to note about analogies is that they are no more than analogies. They are examples that are in some way analogous in their working to the system under investigation; they are not *identical*, so sooner or later we will doubtless find their explanatory value limited. For example, some would argue that the computer analogy doesn't begin to do justice to the richness of the human brain and experience. Nonetheless, such a 'simple' analogy might help us initially to pose relevant questions and clarify our thinking.

Broadly, we could identify two classes of reason as to why a computer might malfunction. There could be something wrong with the computer itself; some of its circuits might have been put together wrongly or someone with a pair of wire-cutters might have tampered with it. A sharp-eyed computer engineer might be able to spot the defect simply by examining the computer itself, without even plugging it in and switching on the power. The defect means that the computer gives a bizarre output even though appropriate information is fed into it, and it might be necessary to return the machine to the manufacturer. Alternatively, it might be a perfectly intact computer; there is nothing defective to be seen by examining it. Rather, something could be wrong with the program that is being run on the machine; in computer jargon, 'there is a bug in the program'. For either reason, the computer could present us with bizarre information. My own hunch is that obsessional disorder has features comparable to both of these classes of abnormality. Therefore, useful as the computer might be initially in clarifying our thinking, I would not want to overstate the distinction in the two types of malfunction.

We should at least consider the notion that there might be some physical abnormality, such as brain damage, a hormone excess or deficiency, underlying obsessional disorder. There are a few reports in the literature of the onset of obsessional disorder immediately after traumatic injury to the head and also accompanying the onset of epilepsy. Some even believe that traumatic birth contributes to the condition.[13] A survey on some patients in Chichester, England did indeed find an increased incidence of reported traumatic birth in the obsessional group, as compared to a control group.[14] However, even if this relationship were firmly established, we would not be able to conclude unambiguously that obsessionals suffered brain damage. An alternative explanation might be that, in traumatic cases, mother and baby were separated immediately after birth. For a more zany explanation, some [15] appeal to memory: the obsessional remembers the 'agony of being born'.

There is some evidence of brain abnormality in obsessionals, specifically in the temporal and parietal regions of the brain.[16] There appear to be some abnormalities in the patterns of electrical activity of the brain, the electroencephalogram (EEG). Map reading and spatial skills are said to be deficient (they certainly are in my case!). Some samples have found obsessionals more likely to be left-handed than control subjects. Tantalizingly, there is also some evidence for temporal lobe disorder in night terror sufferers.[17] Whether or not it confirms brain damage, the relationship between sleep disorder and obsessional illness might prove revealing. The sleep of obsessional-compulsive patients is certainly abnormal.[18]

Another possible type of abnormality that we need to consider concerns the chemical state of the brain, the activities of its transmitter substances that convey signals from one nerve cell to another. There are some suggestions based on the therapeutic success of the drug clomipramine with obsessionals that there might be an abnormality in the brain's chemical messenger, serotonin.[19] Clomipramine appears to restore the normal level of serotonin at certain key sites. Other drugs, effective against depression but which do not affect serotonin, do not help to combat obsessional-compulsive disorder.

Stress

An experiment was performed in which groups of normal subjects were exposed to films judged to be stress-inducing.[20] The background to this experiment was the observation that, following a traumatic experience, many people report intrusive thoughts and nightmares. In the experiment, intrusive, distracting thoughts increased after exposure to a gory stress-evoking film, as compared to a neutral film. A film with a depressing theme also aroused unwanted intrusions. At times of sadness, intrusive thoughts are more frequent. A situation of uncontrived stress has also been studied.[21] Mothers whose children were admitted into hospital for surgery were observed. Unpleasant and intrusive thoughts were more frequent in this group, as compared to a control group. In World War II, airmen reported an increased frequency after exposure to the stress of combat.

The phenomena of nightmares and night terrors might also provide a useful lead here. Stress increases the severity and frequency of nightmares.[22] In my own experience, I am convinced that night terrors were more frequent at times of stress, such as when I was in a situation of ambivalence about important decisions I had to make. Though the stress was not caused by any death-related events, it seemed to be accentuating the death-related night terrors.

A feedback explanation of obsessional disorder?

In 1985, a new explanation of obsessional disorder appeared, based upon negative feedback, long familiar to engineers.[23]

The everyday examples of negative feedback control are legion. Take the thermostat that helps regulate the temperature of a room. The occupant returns from holiday, and the room temperature is, say, 15°C. He sets the thermostat at, say, 20°C, and switches the heating on. The setting of 20°C constitutes the *set-point* or *goal* of the system. The temperature of 15°C is the *actual* value of room temperature. In effect, the thermostat performs the operation of comparison between the goal and the actual value and the system is constructed in such a way that action is taken to bring actual value to the goal value. In this case, heating effort is exerted. When the room temperature reaches 20°C, actual temperature and the goal temperature are equal and heating switches off. If room temperature falls, heating is automatically switched on to bring it back to 20°C. The system is called 'feedback' because the actual state is fed back and compared with the desired state. It is called *negative* feedback because any difference, or deviation, between goal and actual state tends to be *self-eliminating*. Deviation drives the system so as to eliminate deviation.

Let us take the situation of hand-washing. There is a goal, a criterion of cleanliness that is being strived for. The actual state of cleanliness, as perceived by the subject, is compared with this desired state. For most of us, we rapidly reach our goal. The difference between desired state and perceived actual state is soon eliminated, and we turn the tap off and then grab a towel. According to the feedback model, it is useful to see the compulsive hand-washer as someone who is unsuccessfully striving to reach the goal of cleanliness. The feedback pathway and comparison process are abnormal. Desired state is compared with the *perception* of actual state, but for the compulsive hand-washer the hands are perceived as still contaminated in so far as the behavioural decision-making process is concerned. In these terms, the fundamental problem in obsessional-compulsive disorder is the existence of a mismatch between what is desired and what is achieved.

In the context of such a property of negative feedback systems, a comment on the anorexia sufferer's 'relentless pursuit of thinness' might well also prove relevant:

'But the satisfaction of achieving the goal is denied the anorectic, for she is never able to recognize that she is, in fact, thin.'[24]

This model of obsessional-compulsive disorder immediately offers possible insight. For example, rather than simply asking what makes people compulsively wash their hands, sometimes it might be appropriate also to ask what prevents them from stopping, and switching to the next logical activity. Indeed, in general there is nothing so abnormal about hand-washing; it is the length of time the obsessional devotes to it that is abnormal. Furthermore, from discussions with compulsive hand-washers, it would seem that they experience distress not so much when they start washing, but specifically at not being able to stop.[25] They often report, not so much that they are under the control of some omnipotent force, but that they experience frustration at their lack of will in not being able to quit. One might see here some rationale for why the therapist can sometimes help the patient by specifying a criterion of when to quit. For example, 'Rather than wash for 4 hours, wash for only 3 hours at first'. The therapist is providing the needed feedback, the criterion of completion.

The condition termed 'primary obsessional slowness' might also be understood in these terms. As an example to illustrate this condition, a patient might simply take an inordinately long time to get dressed but would not be trying to avoid some harmful or catastrophic outcome. In such terms the subject would find it very difficult to reach the criterion 'I am now correctly dressed'.

Occasionally it has been maintained that there is a link between obsessional disorder and the conditions of stuttering and stammering. Anecdotally, a tendency for stutterers to be obsessional has been noted but I know of no reliable evidence on this point. It is very tempting to speculate here, given that the essence of stuttering is a failure in a negative feedback system; the subject has inadequate feedback from the spoken sound to continue normal speech production and 'gets stuck'.

A negative feedback model would appear to be more insightful than some other possible models. It emphasizes that compulsive behaviour is not something that is generated purely internally by a buildup of energy or simply by a defective bit of the brain's machinery. Rather, the experience of compulsion and the associated behaviour arise in the subject's interaction with his environment. The system is not like a pressure cooker that has to let off steam once in a while to maintain internal pressure within safe limits. Stopping the compulsive behaviour would not be expected to lead to a buildup of pressure that will cause trouble elsewhere. By analogy, it would not be like jamming up the outlet of a pressure cooker, which would be expected to cause a rupture in the wall of the appliance.

Under the directions of a therapist, the obsessional is able to refrain from engaging in compulsive behaviour with no harmful effects. On a longer time-scale, curing a compulsive disorder would not be expected to lead to problems elsewhere, i.e. to the condition termed *symptom substitution*. It is not as if some kind of psychic energy must be discharged somewhere and the compulsive behaviour is the vehicle for this, as suggested by Freud. The fact that symptom substitution does not occur following the behavioural treatment of compulsive disorder is an argument against the Freudian model of neurosis.[26]

The negative feedback model provides insight into the indecisiveness of the obsessional.[27] This is characterized as two control systems being in conflict. Bearing this analogy in mind, consider a 21-year-old male patient, Hank. Hank needed to spend 15 minutes adjusting water temperature before taking a shower.

Fine adjustments were made to get things 'just right'. On one occasion, a friend asked Hank to go to a baseball game. Hank in fact wanted to visit a racetrack, but agreed to go with the friend to the baseball game. Hank drove his friend towards the baseball game, but as they got nearer, Hank's urge to be at the racetrack grew. Much to the friend's disappointment, Hank turned the car around and targeted it upon the racetrack. However, as the racetrack got nearer, so Hank's guilt intensified. He again turned the car around and pursued the original course. A series of such oscillations was ended by Hank parking the car midway between the two goals, at which point the friend took over the driving.

Hank also reported great difficulty in ordering from a menu when there was more than one desirable dish. The waiter would end up oscillating between Hank and the kitchen in response to Hank's vacillations of desire. Each time a choice was made, attention was soon shifted from the chosen item to the unchosen one, which then competed for dominance.

There is another general feature of the negative feedback model that is interesting. Consider a man at a fête trying his skill in not letting the two bits of wire touch each other. Watch his exact movements as he has two or three goes at it. The goal is always the same, to steer the loop along a middle course. However, on close examination, it will be seen that the actual movements are different from game to game. The behaviour is not stereotyped. He will try slightly different strategies as he gets better at it. This is like the obsessional; typically, he will use different hand movements, different ways of rubbing the soap, but always striving for a match with the same goal of perfect cleanliness. Similarly, the compulsive counter will try different mental tricks to reach perfection.

The obsessional-compulsive is often engaging in action that is logical in terms of an attempt to gain control. Hand-washing is a logical action suggested by the perception of contaminated hands. In normal subjects, and indeed for the obsessional prior to the onset of the disorder, the action of washing would generate negative feedback to alter the perception of dirtiness or contamination to one of cleanliness. However, under obsessional conditions the perception does not change with effort exerted; normal feedback does not occur and the system is said to have gone *open-loop*. Worse still, the system can generate a vicious circle, known also as exhibiting *positive feedback*. That is to say, the longer the subject washes her hands, the more she perceives them to be contaminated, and so the more she washes them, and . . . Anxiety might even increase in parallel. How does she ever manage to stop? One imagines that, after hours of washing, another goal will be able to take control, such as the growing attraction of sleep as a result of exhaustion or the fear of future exhaustion.

Pure obsessions

I believe that for my own obsessional thoughts, the two bits of information, desired and actual, are compared in an attempt to eliminate a disparity. The evidence is based largely upon my own subjective experience. As documented earlier, the intrusions often came in response to situations that in some sense highlighted disparity. Stimuli confirming the transitory nature of existence were commonly triggers, but so were the diametrically opposite class of situations underlining the present and future goodness of life. Information relevant to future attainment was a strong trigger to death themes, such as: *cue* – 'you speak good German' → *mental response* – successful assimilation into Germany during my future study leave. By contrast, pieces of information relevant to the past, e.g. 'what a great summer school in 1978', were not trigger cues, unless they served to trigger an intermediate thought sequence '1978' → 'seems like yesterday' → 'time flies' → 'can't stop it' with an accompanying negative emotion.

My feeling is that where two bits of information are incongruous, triggering the one can serve to excite the other. The system then searches for the possibilities for correcting the disparity. When my lifestyle and prospects were not so good, as on returning from Denmark, the intrusions were very much less intense.

Though my observations arise from my own subjective states, I am not alone in thinking along these lines. Pierre Janet used the expression *l'association par contraste* to describe a very similar phenomenon, and noted that, for example, loving parents would often be obsessed with the thought of selling their loved ones to the devil or mutilating them with a knife.[28] The latter was particularly common amongst his patients. Janet also discusses the blasphemous thoughts of John Bunyan, which were experienced in a religious context, as an example of obsessions acting in opposition to the current intention. My own self-observations in this area also coincide with those reported by the 19th century writer Thomas de Quincey. In his classic, *Confessions of an English Opium-Eater*, de Quincey recorded:

> '. . . the exuberant and riotous prodigality of life naturally forces the mind more powerfully upon the antagonist thought of death, and the wintry sterility of the grave. For it may be observed generally that, wherever two thoughts stand related to each other by a law of antagonism, and exist, as it were, by mutual repulsion, they are apt to suggest each other. On these accounts it is that I find it impossible to banish the thought of death when I am walking alone in the endless days of summer; and any particular death, if not actually more affecting, at least haunts my mind more obstinately and besiegingly, in that season.'

Obsessional thoughts and compulsive behaviour

How does compulsive behaviour become associated with obsessional thoughts? I suggest that there are several ways. First, the behaviour might be acquired somewhat arbitrarily as a trick for terminating, or at least reducing, the intensity of the thought. As an example of this, consider the following patient, a highly intelligent 47-year-old teacher, Linda.[29] She had suffered for 36 years from compulsive thoughts and rituals. At the age of 10 she was preoccupied with a passage from the Bible 'to blaspheme against the Holy Ghost is unforgivable'. Later she was to be troubled by the intrusion of such words as 'damn' and 'bloody' into her consciousness. Linda discovered that the anxiety that these thoughts evoked could be reduced to some extent by the repetition of an apparently arbitrary activity a set number of times. When she was 13 years old, the intrusive words were of a sexual nature and she was obsessed by the thought of sexual relations with the Holy Ghost. Again though, repetitive acts, such as walking up and down the stairs, served to allay the anxiety. I suggest that such arbitrary rituals are analogous to mental rituals in that they are acquired by trial and error and retained because they serve to allay the discomfort.

In other cases, rather than arbitrary activity, the behaviour might be one that has traditionally been performed in solving problems similar to that presented by the obsessional thought. For example, in our culture, washing of some sort is traditionally a response to the perception of dirt or impurity, both physical and, in some cases, moral. For example there is 'cleanse yourself of sin' and 'wash your mouth out for saying that'. Checking by means of inspection, seeking personal reassurance or making a telephone call are perfectly normal responses to uncertainty. These actions only become abnormal because of the intensity and frequency with which they are performed. I suggest that such extensive behaviour is analogous to obsessional rumination. It is not arbitrary and, albeit grossly exaggerated and ultimately fruitless, it represents a natural and logical means of attempting to find a solution.

In some cases, the compulsive behaviour is perceived by the subject to provide information relevant to the obsessional rumination, presumably via some supernatural route. Pierre Janet saw a number of patients of this kind. For example, Vy was tormented by doubts as to whether he really believed in God. In walking the streets, he felt that relevant information could be generated by observing whether he was able to avoid treading on the shadows of trees. If he succeeded, this was a sign that he believed in God. If he failed, this indicated non-belief.

Creativity

How is it that obsessionals are often able to show creativity? The obsessional trait of dogged persistence is sometimes seen as a blind obedience to a fixed course of action, the antithesis of what is needed for creativity. A rather different consideration might be that obsessionals set high, indeed perfectionist, goals which they attempt to reach by a variety of strategies. Suppose such writers as Swift ruminated endlessly trying to match an actual phrase to an idealized state. Investigation of creative talent and working style shown by obsessionals could be useful. In this regard we have rather a good account of John Bunyan's thought processes, in his work *Grace Abounding to the Chief of Sinners*. We know that Bunyan was a formidable hair-splitter. Convinced that he had committed the ultimate sin, that against the Holy Ghost, he tried countless times to match his sin against those recorded in the Bible. Each time he failed, finding ever more original reasons for why his own sin was worse. In other words, his neutralizing thoughts were always inadequate. Each novel approach led to the same conclusion:

> *'This one consideration would always kill my Heart,* My sin was point-blank against my Saviour, *and that too, at that height, that I had in my heart said of him,* Let him go if he will. *Oh! me thoughts, this sin was bigger than the sins of a Countrey, of a Kingdom, or of the whole World, no one pardonable, nor all of them together, was able to equal mine, mine out-went them every one.'*

In this quotation we see good examples of the tendency to categorize in extremes rather than shades of grey and the perfectionism of some obsessionals. However, I imagine that a process of challenge of ideas against a perfectionist standard would, if anything, be compatible with creativity.

Anthony Storr reaches a similar conclusion:[30]

'Some forms of creativity are clearly related to the obsessional's wish for order. The fact which does not fit into the current scientific hypothesis may give rise to the same irritation as the crooked picture, the dirt in the corner, or the clothes dropped on the floor. It is something outside the ordered scheme, and therefore out of control.'

Storr argues that the pursuit of science has intrinsically something of an obsessional activity about it. Advance in science depends upon producing theories that are able to account for otherwise aberrant findings. He notes the case of a scientist who would make the angry comment 'I'll beat the bastard' in the face of technical problems.

The tendency to what is termed *overinclusion* has been noted in creativity. This refers to a tendency to attend to information that might seem to be irrelevant to the task in hand. The similarity of this to obsessional thinking hardly needs pointing out. The production of major creative work involves the use of imagery and metaphor, and in these capacities the obsessional is well represented. In the case of highly creative female musicians, a tendency towards solitary hobbies and individualistic creative activity has been detected.

In summary, obsessional ruminations remain in some respects an enigma, and it would be foolish to try to dress it up to be otherwise. However, there are a few leads and I believe the feedback model (see page 139) to be the most promising.

16
Some famous thoughts

'O God, grant me repentence, grant me reformation. Grant that I may be no longer disturbed with doubts and harrassed with vain terrours'
Samuel Johnson, Prayers and Meditations, *March 29th 1766*

In this chapter, I look at some famous people whose lives can illuminate the understanding of obsessions. It might also be that the sufferer from obsessions can gain some help from looking at the lives of others with similar experiences or whose writings are relevant.

Samuel Johnson

Researchers into Johnson are fortunate in having what is perhaps the most famous biography of all time, James Boswell's *The Life of Samuel Johnson*, where they can find in detail what Johnson liked, disliked, ate, drank, thought and feared. Boswell's work, a brilliant insight into the mind and behaviour of one man, is itself a classic of English literature. We might well know more about Johnson than about any other person who ever lived.

The interaction between the two is especially revealing: the prudish and 'very English' Johnson and the much younger and usually more liberal-minded upper-class Scotsman Boswell, who had earlier tasted the temptations of London and caught venereal disease. Boswell gives a vivid account of their regular meetings, dining at the Mitre Tavern, where he soaked up the wisdom of Johnson, such as 'Endeavour to be as perfect as you can in every respect.'

Although Johnson at times comes across as 'holier-than-thou' and dogmatic, he managed to blend the qualities of kindness, genius and clowning. He gave insight to every situation, profound and trivial. So often one feels 'If only then I had thought to say that.' For example, on being asked by a woman to account for a mistake in the dictionary he had written, Johnson offered the incomparable 'Ignorance, Madam, pure ignorance.' I can think of occasions, while teaching at summer schools, when I would have been well served to have had that particular expression available.

Samuel Johnson ('Dr Johnson') writer, poet, critic, sage, philosopher, biographer, moralist, wit, formidable debater and conversationalist *extraordinaire*, was born into a humble household in Lichfield in 1709. The birth was a very difficult one. His father was a not-very-successful bookseller and suffered from melancholy. Mrs Johnson could be characterized as showing more than average anxiety. Samuel felt that he inherited his own tendency to melancholy, a 'vile temperament', from his father.

At an early age, the boy was instructed by his somewhat austere and over-scrupulous mother on the two possible fates that await the soul: heaven or torment. It is not difficult to see the family as a fertile breeding ground for Samuel's later agonies of guilt. At school, the young Samuel showed himself to have a desire to excel, an incredibly good memory (which he showed later in life as well) and to be competitive, but curiously to have also a streak of indolence.

He didn't join in activities with other pupils, though his incomparable intellect was held in awe by fellow-pupils. One day, while sitting alone at home reading *Hamlet*, he was so overcome by fear of the ghost that he moved nearer to the door that opened to the street. Samuel would spend hours wandering the fields and lanes around Lichfield, preferably in the company of a companion, Hector. However, Samuel's lengthy speeches were not addressed to Hector as part of a normal interaction, but represented thinking aloud. Samuel showed some signs of rebellion about going to the same church as his parents, and later Boswell noted:

'At the age of ten his mind was disturbed by scruples of infidelity, which preyed upon his spirits, and made him very uneasy' and '. . . he began to think himself highly culpable for neglecting such a means of information, and took himself severely to task for this sin, adding many acts of voluntary, and to others unknown, penance.'

Johnson gained a place at Oxford University, but tragically because of economic circumstances he was unable to remain a student. To his immense disappointment, he was forced to return to Lichfield. Without any logical reason, Johnson blamed himself. He came near to suicide and feared for his sanity. Intense anxiety was accompanied by feelings of hopelessness and helplessness.[1] From reading accounts of Johnson's later cycles of behaviour, between the lows of inactivity and the highs of extreme exertion, I suspect that he might be described as manic-depressive. Periods of idleness, characterized by daydreaming, would be interrupted by fanatical concentration and incredible energy.[2] Boswell noted that 'A horrour at life in general is more consonant with Johnson's habitual gloomy cast of thought.' In case the reader should gain the impression that psychiatric problems are associated with only the tender and the meek, Johnson would disconfirm this. In physique, he was by all accounts about as feeble and weak as a full-grown grizzly bear.

Johnson exhibited tics and various other compulsive manner-isms; on occasion he was the object of some ridicule in public. Years later, on the subject of these movements, Boswell quotes a letter from Sir Joshua Reynolds:

> '*These motions or tricks of Dr Johnson are improperly called convulsions. He could sit motionless, when he was told to do so, as well as any other man; my opinion is that it proceeded from a habit which he had indulged himself in, of accompanying his thoughts with certain untoward actions, and those actions always appeared to me as if they were meant to reprobate some part of his past conduct. Whenever he was not engaged in conversation, such thoughts were sure to rush into his mind; and for this reason, any company, any employment, whatever, he preferred to being alone . . .*'

In 1737, Johnson and a friend, David Garrick (later to achieve fame in the theatre), left Lichfield to make the 120-mile journey to London, into the unknown. Life in the capital was not easy for Johnson, at first leading a precarious existence as a hack-writer. However, the city's ceaseless stimulation afforded him some escape from ruminations about guilt. Estranged from his wife towards whom he felt great responsibility and guilt, Johnson led something of a waif's life for a while.

His behaviour was exemplary, showing great financial generosity not only to his wife, but also to almost anyone in need. Johnson collected a circle of misfits and eccentrics, with whom he would spend long hours. His close friend Mrs Thrale described how Johnson 'nursed whole nests of people in his house, where the lame, the blind, the sick, and the sorrowful found a sure retreat from all the evils whence his little income could secure them.'

The obsessional trait of accuracy and meticulousness, an ability to 'split hairs', was put to good use by Johnson in producing his dictionary. He insisted upon exact use of rules and words. For instance, he criticized Boswell for saying to *make* money, insisting that this implied to *coin* money. In Boswell's words, the students of Johnson were urged to show 'perpetual vigilance against the slightest degrees of falsehood.'

Boswell describes a scene concerning Johnson in his thirties, at a stage in his life when he had already written speeches for foremost politicians. Johnson had been asked to dine at the home of Edward Cave, and another distinguished guest, Walter Harte, had been invited. On arriving, Johnson felt ashamed of his shabby clothes, so before the other guest arrived, hid himself behind a screen, where later his meal was surreptitiously served. During the meal, Harte praised a recent book that Johnson had written. Cave was later to explain to Harte how happy his comments had made the invisible

Johnson dining behind the screen.

Johnson found a poor woman lying exhausted in the street and unable to walk. He promptly lifted the unfortunate soul onto his back and carried her to his house, whereupon he discovered that she was a prostitute. Johnson cared for her until she was well and then tried to point her towards a virtuous occupation. He was known to enjoy the company of such women, though feeling great pity for their lot in life. This observation, and the fact that he kept some very disreputable male company, has raised the question as to whether he ever gave in to temptation. My guess is not, but of course we cannot be sure. We know that he had to stop visiting David Garrick at Drury Lane theatre, the reason being simple. Given Johnson's uncompromising moral principles, he couldn't bear the sexual passion aroused by Garrick's actress companions.

Johnson's reputation as a skilled raconteur is beautifully illustrated in Boswell's biography:

> '. . . *he had accumulated a great fund of miscellaneous knowledge, which, by a peculiar promptitude of mind, was ever ready at his call, and which he constantly accustomed himself to clothe in the most apt and energetick expression. Sir Joshua Reynolds once asked him by what means he had attained his extraordinary accuracy and flow of language. He told him, that he had early laid it down as a fixed rule to do his best on every occasion, and in every company; to impart whatever he knew in the most forcible language he could put it in; and that by constant practice, and never suffering any careless expressions to escape him, or attempting to deliver his thoughts without arranging them in the clearest manner, it became habitual to him.*'

Sir Aubrey Lewis noted:[3]

'I have been impressed also by the frequency with which obsessional patients who are depersonalized complain of this necessity for inner verbal repetition of all they hear and precise verbal formulation of their own thoughts.'

As an account of intrusive thoughts, it would be difficult to improve upon Johnson's;

> '. . . *an irresistible obtrusion of a disagreeable image, which you always wished away, but could not dismiss, an incessant persecution of a troublesome thought, neither to be pacified nor ejected. Such has of late been the state of my own mind. I had formerly great command of my attention, and what I did not like could forbear to think on . . .*'

In addition to Boswell's biography, we have Johnson's *Prayers and Meditations*. These are very revealing of the obsessional personality, showing a mind gripped with guilt, doubts about worthiness, and fear of insanity and death. The same theme occurs again and again:

the request for forgiveness from sin, strength to overcome indolence and, finally, a smooth transition to the after-life. So keen was Johnson to obtain eternal life that he even asked a man condemned to die at the gallows, a Dr Dodd, to make a last plea on his behalf.

Johnson managed beautifully to weave personally held fears and aspirations into his stories, a classic being *Rasselas*, the tale of an Abyssinian prince who abandons the comforts of his palace to discover the secret of happiness. Rasselas searches far and wide, consulting a wide variety of people and seeing the wondrous sights of the world. He attends the lectures of distinguished philosophers at university, but alas finds that, in spite of eloquent academic arguments on the nature of happiness, in private their lives are as prone to grief as those of lesser mortals. Despairing of ever finding an answer, Rasselas turns to the advice of a friendly and hospitable hermit living in a cave, only to discover that, lacking the opportunity for distraction, the unfortunate hermit is bombarded mercilessly with intrusive thoughts. The reader is expected to arrive at the conclusion that the elusive state of happiness is not to be found in this world, but, God willing, in the next.

A striking contradiction in Johnson is the disparity between what he achieved and his own perception of his worth, about which so many of his obsessional thoughts concerning indolence turned. It is true that Johnson had phases of relative inactivity, but to all but a mind torn by the guilt of perfectionism, these would fit very easily into context. His productivity defies belief; in just a few years, he produced a comprehensive dictionary, involving consideration of around 250,000 quotations. Yet Johnson still ruminated richly about his indolence.

Johnson displayed sheer honesty, an intolerance for cant and affectation. For example, when a devout man, James Beattie, told Johnson that he had been '. . . at times troubled with impious thoughts', he got the reply 'If I was to divide my life into three parts, two of them have been filled with such thoughts.' Herein lies a paradox: the obsessional, a person characterized by extreme persistence and dogged determination, should be so easily able to be distracted from his goal. Johnson describes another aspect:

'If all the employments of life were crowded into the time which it really occupied, perhaps a few weeks, days, or hours would be sufficient for its accomplishment, so far as the mind was engaged in the performance.'

Johnson exhibited the obsessional trait of anticipation that things might get better. This emerges in his conversation with Boswell:

'He asserted that *the present* was never a happy state to any human being; but that, as every part of life, of which we are conscious, was at some point of time a period yet to come, in which felicity was expected, there was some happiness produced by hope.'

Johnson, who described himself as unsettled, as a 'kind of ship with a wide sail, and without an anchor', went on to argue that *present* happiness is possible only under the influence of alcohol. With the help of wine, he was able (in his own words) 'To get rid of myself, to send myself away.'

Johnson prepared himself for future disasters so effectively that this caused difficulty in enjoying the present; he was determined not to be caught unawares by the future. Walter Bate[4] writes: 'Over and over in the moral essays he had tried to control this habit of "anticipating evils", to realize its insidious effect when it was carried too far, and to replace it with the "habit of being pleased". But this habit had long since become too closely interwoven with his own sense of identity and self-preservation.'

Walter Bate describes Johnson's need to:

'. . ."divide up" the welter of subjective feeling and reduce to manageable units, which we also see in his constant resort to arithmetic and counting. An example would be his blowing out his breath loudly like a whale when he finished a lengthy remark or a dispute, as if to punctuate it and give it finality . . .' Johnson found that the exercise of mathematics provided great pleasure and some escape from painful ruminations on guilt, the prospect of insanity and death.

Boswell describes a compulsive behaviour that was shown by Johnson:

> '*He had another peculiarity, of which none of his friends ever ventured to ask an explanation. It appeared to me some superstitious habit, which he contracted early, and from which he had never called upon his reason to disentangle him. This was his anxious care to go out or in at a door or passage by a certain number of steps from a certain point, or at least so as that either his right or his left foot, (I am not certain which,) should constantly make the first actual movement when he came close to the door or passage. Thus I conjecture: for I have, upon innumerable occasions, observed him suddenly stop, and then seem to count his steps with a deep earnestness; and when he had neglected or gone wrong in this sort of magical movement, I have seen him go back again, put himself in a proper posture to begin the ceremony, and, having gone through it, break from his abstraction, walk briskly on, and join his companion.*'

With the help of an opera-glass, looking from a room in Bedford Street, a certain Mr S. Whyte was able to observe Johnson's locomotion in Henrietta Street:[5]

> '*I perceived him at a good distance walking along with a peculiar solemnity of deportment, and an awkward sort of measured step. Upon*

every post as he passed along, he deliberately laid his hand; but missing one of them, when he had got at some distance, he seemed suddenly to recollect himself, and immediately returning carefully performed the accustomed ceremony, and resumed his former course, not omitting one till he gained the crossing.'

Johnson left a vivid record of his fear of the passage of time. For example: 'I have now begun the sixtieth year of my life. How the last year has past I am unwilling to terrify myself with thinking. This day has been passed in great perturbation. I was distracted at Church in an uncommon degree, and my distress has had very little intermission.'

On this same day Johnson recorded in his *Prayers and Meditations*:

'This day it came into my mind to write the history of my melancholy. On this I purpose to deliberate; I know not whether it may not too much disturb me.'

In spite of the suffering experienced by Johnson, Boswell observed that he rarely, if ever, complained. In Boswell's own inimitable style 'What philosophick heroism was it in him to appear with such manly fortitude in the world, while he was inwardly so distressed!' He was much engaged by attempting the resolution of problems, whether personal or national, rather than whining about them.

We might see a dread of mortality in Johnson's comment to Sir Joshua Reynolds:[6]

'It has often grieved me, Sir, to see so much mind as the science of painting requires, laid out upon such perishable materials: why do you not oftener make use of copper? I could wish your superiority in the art you profess to be preserved in stuff more durable than canvas.'

Time was particularly precious to Johnson in the context of getting older, something about which he was much disturbed to be reminded. During the course of a confinement to bed, he counted the days, which came to a total of 129. '. . . more than the third part of a year, and no inconsiderable part of human life.'

Johnson was disturbed when Boswell reminded a family with whom they were staying that it was September 18th, Johnson's birthday. The day '. . . fills me with thoughts which it seems to be the general care of humanity to escape.' The night before his 66th birthday, this time spent in France, was a sleepless one as Johnson wrestled with the implications of advancing years. Johnson's thoughts turned even more strongly to the meaning of life, the existence of evil and its relevance to the possibility of an after-life:

'It is scarcely to be imagined that Infinite Benevolence would create a being capable of enjoying so much more than is here to be enjoyed, and qualified by nature to prolong pain by remembrance and anticipate it by terror, if he was not designed for something nobler and better than a state, in which many of his faculties can serve only for his torment . . .'

Johnson showed exceptional courage in the face of danger, until seized by the prospect of death. Even when sailing in a tempest off Scotland, Johnson was observed to be lying in his bunk, quite calm and with a greyhound cushioned against his back to help him keep warm. The idea of death aroused his fear, in a more abstract sense. He appeared to fear annihilation even more than the torments of hell. Although Johnson was a believer in the after-life, it was the *uncertainty* regarding his salvation that seemed to cause him most torment.

A friend from Lichfield, Anna Seward, tried to reason with him that annihilation was not something to fear: 'the dread of annihilation, which is only a pleasing dream.' He was, of course, unconvinced: 'It is neither pleasing, nor sleep; it is nothing. Now mere existence is so much better than nothing, that one would rather exist even in pain, than not exist.' Johnson's fear of annihilation led him to a great interest in supernatural phenomena, such as London's numerous ghost 'sightings', as possible evidence of life after death. One is reminded of Woody Allen's appeals in his films that God should just give one little sign of his presence.

In 1776, Boswell persuaded Johnson to discuss thought control, or, as they termed it, 'management of the mind'. His answers are interesting from the viewpoint of modern psychotherapy: one must '. . . divert distressing thoughts, and not combat with them.' Boswell asked Johnson whether it was possible to 'think them down', and was told 'To attempt to think them down is madness'. I must agree with Johnson.

In 1779, Johnson was deeply moved by the death of David Garrick. He was occupied by memories of the day, 42 years earlier, when they had travelled to London and was observed 'bathed in tears' at the funeral. Johnson had earlier denied that Garrick was ill; the mere possibility that a friend might die was unthinkable. He hated to part from any situation, since this had broader connotations, so when some good friends moved from Streatham to Brighton this seemed like a permanent 'goodbye'.

Just before his death, Johnson asked Sir John Hawkins where he would be buried. 'Doubtless in Westminster Abbey' was the reply. Johnson clearly had a feeling that this would be so. He had shown a reluctance to enter the Abbey over the preceding years but even in such a situation his wit did not desert him. On being asked by Lady Knight to join her for a visit to the Abbey, Johnson replied 'No, not while I can keep out.'

In the last 100 years or so, there have been several analyses of

Johnson's condition. One[7] contains an interesting speculation that Johnson's behavioural problems arose from the effects of lack of oxygen at birth.[8]

Søren Kierkegaard

Søren Kierkegaard, philosopher and theologian, was born in Copenhagen in 1813. Kierkegaard was eventually to be termed the father of existential philosophy. Psychologically speaking, he might be described as a full-time depressive with a *morbid preoccupation* and a part-time obsessional. However, he appears to have stretched philosophical rumination to its limits. I can think of few better prescriptions for obtaining a feeling of depression and existential fear than to read either Kierkegaard himself (which is hard going) or the excellent biography by Josiah Thompson[9] (much lighter). For example, one of Kierkegaard's better-known works, *Fear and Trembling*, is an analysis of the agony experienced by Abraham as he prepared to sacrifice Isaac.

As a child, Søren had been termed 'the strange one' by other children. He would wear the same formal costume to school each day, unlike the informality of his classmates. Essentially a loner, introverted and melancholic, he lived a cocooned existence, brought up under the strict control of a devout father, himself a chronic depressive. Obedience to father was the rule. Young Søren would spend hours with his spinning-top – lost in thought. The father had demanding standards concerning such things as exactly how to polish shoes and at what time it was no longer safe for Søren to go out. They would sometimes spend long periods walking up and down their room hand-in-hand, while the father described to the young Søren imaginary street scenes in Copenhagen that they were passing.

Later, Søren's university tutor was to have been exasperated by his: '. . . irresistible urge to sophistry, to hair-splitting that come out on all occasions.'

Kierkegaard's aim in life might be described as one of completion or accommodation – of finding a master key, or to use his own words: '. . . to clarify and solve the riddle of life has been my constant wish.' To this end, he showed an insatiable appetite for writing, performed while alone, but sometimes in evening dress as if to be entertaining company. In the toil of writing, he was able to escape from some of his torments. Kierkegaard gives us vivid insight:

'So I fared forth into life – initiated into all possible enjoyment yet never really enjoying, but rather (this was my single pleasure with respect to the pain of melancholy) working to produce the appearance that I enjoyed. I was acquainted with all sorts of people, yet it never aroused my mind that in any of them I had a confidant. . .'

Jolly, witty, argumentative in company, 'enjoying' good food and wine, and yet through it all so clearly the ruminative, the melancholic, stares out:

'I have just now come from a party where I was its life and soul; witticisms streamed from my lips, everyone laughed and admired me, but I went away – yes, the dash should be as long as the radius of the earth's orbit – and wanted to shoot myself.'

'The whole of existence makes me anxious, from the smallest fly to the mystery of the Incarnation: everything is unintelligible to me, most of all myself . . .' 'I suffer as a human being can suffer in indescribable melancholy, which always has to do with my thinking about my own existence.'

'The terrible thing about the total spiritual incapacity from which I suffer is precisely that it is coupled with a consuming longing, a spiritual passion.'

He appears to have been tormented by guilt associated with the feeling that he had let his father down. In addition to endless philosophical ruminations, there is evidence of conventional obsessionality. Things in his room were maintained in meticulous order. He insisted that his servant, Anders, should always maintain the room temperature at exactly 13¾°C. He kept 50 cups and saucers in his cabinet, one pair in each of 50 patterns. His guests were asked which pair they wanted their coffee served in, and then required to justify their choice. On walking the streets of Copenhagen, he always kept to the shadows and would never step over a sunlit patch.

Kierkegaard's biographer notes:[9]

> '. . . the ritual elements but also the studied regularity of the meals – bouillon on 29 out of 31 days – points to a life that has withdrawn into an aesthetic cocoon. Protected from distractions and interruptions by his faithful Anders, his rooms kept a constant 13¾°C with just a trace of Eau de Cologne in the air, Kierkegaard has succeeded in keeping that 'infected' world he hated at a distance.'

There were moments of light relief in Kierkegaard's life. In fact, he was capable of displaying an impish sense of humour and wasn't past a cruel practical joke. The melancholic philosopher was surprisingly good with children; an accomplished story-teller, he was easily able to switch into a world of fantasy. In these, and some other regards, there are close similarities with his even more famous fellow-countryman, Hans Christian Andersen, whom he would sometimes encounter in the street during his strolls around Copenhagen. Both appeared to have lived a large part of their lives in what is best described as daydreams.

Hans Christian Andersen

Hans Christian Andersen was born to poor parents in Odense, Denmark, in 1805. Fortunately, because of Andersen's enthusiasm for writing everything down, not least that which concerned himself, a mountain of material was left for posterity. Hans Christian was born into a family in which folklore, magic, superstition and rituals played an ever-present role. Death omens, ghosts and fortune-telling were much in evidence. The morbid, dramatic and romantic were to hold a life-long fascination for him. Somewhat predictably, he was scared of the dark and frightened to walk past a churchyard. Sometimes the young boy was sent on an errand that involved passing a demolished convent. This place was considered haunted; it seemed to emit a strange light, but believing that spirits cannot cross water, he felt safe upon reaching the far side of the river. Hans Christian's father suffered from occasional depression, was prone to spells of silent rumination and was devoted to his son.

In 1811, when Hans Christian was six, the great comet appeared in the sky. His own life-story records that he believed the superstition regarding the destruction of the earth that would be caused by the comet.[10] 'I expected every moment that the comet would rush down, and the day of judgement would come.' A belief in divine providence over his own life was something that accompanied Andersen for all of his days.

Odense jail and lunatic asylum, both of which he visited, held an irresistible mixture of terror and fascination for the young Hans Christian. His mother and grandmother spoilt him, protected him and inculcated the belief that he was somewhat different from other children – a natural genius. Hans Christian didn't play with other children, and was regarded as very odd and prudish. He preferred the company of his toys and puppets, his dolls and books. Some time was devoted to praying. He would spend hours in the garden inside a tent improvised from his mother's apron, engaged in making dresses for the dolls, or just ruminating. 'I was a singularly dreamy child, and so constantly went about with my eyes shut, as at last to give the impression of having weak sight, although the sense of sight was especially cultivated by me.'

Andersen opens his autobiography with 'There is a loving God, who directs all things for the best.' Nonetheless, in Andersen's belief system, it was worth keeping God informed of one's wishes. His autobiography shows his wish to test the control of destiny, a factor of much interest to students of the obsessional personality. After being told about the omniscient and omnipotent nature of God, he recorded:[11]

'That idea occupied my whole mind, and towards evening, as I went

*alone from the court, where there was a deep pond, and stood upon
some stones which were just within the water, the thought passed
through my head, whether God actually knew every thing which was to
happen there. Yes, he has now determined that I should live and be so
many years old, thought I; but, if I now were to jump into the water
here and drown myself, then it would not be as he wished; and all at
once I was firmly and resolutely determined to drown myself. I ran to
where the water was deepest, and then a new thought passed through
my soul. "It is the devil who wishes to have power over me!" I uttered
a loud cry, and, running away from the place as if I were pursued, fell
weeping into my mother's arms.'*

(Similar childhood testings of God were recorded in John Bunyan's
Autobiography of a Soul and J.-J. Rousseau's *Confessions*.)

Hans Christian was drawn to the theatre, and tried writing and
performing plays, using his parents as an audience. The child loved
the limelight that these plays and his fine singing voice provided.
Acting became such an 'obsession' that his parents were led to
wonder whether their much-loved son was mad. The plays often
had morbid and macabre themes, one being an adaptation of
Hamlet. Being told that royalty probably addressed each other in
foreign tongues, he devised a hybrid language for the royal parts. In
one, a princess greets her father, the King, with the original, if
somewhat inelegant 'Guten Morgen, mon père! Har De godt
sleeping?'[12]

Hans Christian's mother had designs on him becoming a tailor
or bookbinder, but his ambition was to be an actor. Overwhelming
egocentricity and self-confidence would not permit a humble job;
he craved public recognition. The boy protested to his mother that
he had read stories of many men from humble origins who went on
to better things.

When he was 14, Hans Christian's mother waved him off on the
mail-coach for Copenhagen, where he was determined to seek his
fortune.[13] When the boat arrived at Zealand, his reaction was to fall
down on his knees and pray for God's help. After some tears and
further prayers on the way, he finally arrived at the big city.

Life was to be far from easy. Naive and trusting, but driven by an
overwhelming ambition, he encountered numerous frustrations
and hardships. He found a tiny room but for which he could not
raise enough money for the deposit. Hans Christian's reaction on
finding himself alone in the room of this potential landlady shows
an affinity for superstition. '. . . I seated myself on the sofa, and
contemplated the portrait of her deceased husband. I was so wholly
a child, that as the tears rolled down my cheeks I wetted the eyes of
the portrait with my tears, in order that the dead man might feel
how troubled I was, and influence the heart of his wife. She must

have seen that nothing more was to be drained out of me, for when she returned to the room she said she would receive me into her house for the sixteen rix dollars. I thanked God and the dead man.'

Still, life was tough. Andersen was excessively clumsy in his movements, somewhat weird in looks and often treated as a joke by Copenhageners. However, he could not face the humiliation of returning to Odense. Suicide, though seriously contemplated, was not an option, since it was a sin.

Throughout his life, literally from the moment of birth onwards, Andersen spent an inordinate amount of time in tears: tears of sorrow, of joy, of sentiment, of excitement, of awe for the singing of Jenny Lind, and occasionally of unambiguous manipulation. Regularly he prayed that things might get better, and, when they did, God was thanked. In the end, Hans Christian was admitted briefly to the ballet, his first appearance being as one of a group of trolls. The memoirs record:

'. . . our names stood printed in the bill. That was a moment in my life, when my name was printed! I fancied I could see in it a nimbus of immortality. I was continually looking at the printed paper. I carried the programme of the ballet with me at night to bed, lay and read my name by candle-light – in short, I was happy.'

Andersen's talents were to move from the ballet to that of writing stories and poems, for which he was soon to be famous throughout Denmark, and ultimately the world.

He had a genius for inventing situations of fear and seemed to have been as afraid of hypothetical and highly improbable events as of immediate real danger. He had an obsession about dying from drowning or fire, or as the victim of murder. His fear of seduction, robbery, dogs and losing his passport seemed to be carried with him wherever he went. He also suffered from agoraphobia, being unable to cross a large crowded square without an escort.[14]

Considering such a daunting list of dangers, one might have supposed that Andersen would have spent his life in the relative safety of a house, but nothing could be further from the truth. Not only did he never have a home of his own, preferring to stay with friends or in hotels, but his autobiography describes the life of a fanatical traveller, constantly on the move and meeting people in Sweden, France, England, Italy and Holland. Even in unambiguously dangerous situations, after much ruminating, curiosity was sometimes able to dominate over caution.[15] Some obsessionals are nothing if not stubborn and determined!

An impression of the thoughts that troubled Andersen for so much of his life can be gained from the following entry in his diary, concerning the Franco-Prussian war in 1870:

'The war in France overwhelms me, I am suffering from *idées fixes* which make me mad; the terrors of France are constantly showing themselves before me as if I had to live through them myself: I see myself pierced by bayonets, the city is burning, friends are dying, or I dream of being thrown into prison.'

Andersen was a man of high moral standards, prudish and a bachelor. He probably never had any sexual experience, though he recorded fascination with prostitutes he saw in Naples, as if torn between approach and avoidance. Wolfgang Lederer[16] describes him as '. . . Forever an "applicant", forever insistently ingratiating, but never frankly asserting himself.' He was essentially a loner, despite being known by a vast circle of contacts throughout most of Europe, Kings and Queens, composers and writers, from whom he endlessly solicited praise and appreciation of his own fame.

His life was a textbook case of obsessional rumination: something he had just eaten would poison him, he would miss an important connection unless he arrived very early, he would be returned to poverty; some trivial event would be blown up out of all proportion and be seen as leading to his death.

A process of competition between thoughts is recorded by a friend, William Bloch[17] describing a visit to Vienna:

'Andersen was choking and had to leave the table, accompanied by our host and hostess, and everything was very quiet while Andersen was heard coughing and spitting in the other room. Against the protest of the hostess he maintained that there had been a pin in the meat; he had swallowed it and could clearly feel it sitting inside him. That evening and the following day he was very worried about the consequences. His anxiety was so pronounced that it had completely removed his fear that a little spot above one of his eyebrows might grow into a large excrescence which would cover the eye, which again had made him forget that he might rupture himself because I had touched his stomach slightly with my walking stick, which again made him abandon the thought of having hydrarthrosis of the knee, something he was much concerned about when he arrived in Vienna.'

Andersen was able to ruin an evening out by imagining that he had forgotten to lock the front door. In the course of a night he needed repeatedly to rise in order to check that he really had extinguished the candle by his bed, though he never failed to do this very carefully on retiring. On sending letters, he would worry that he had mixed up envelopes. On one occasion, having written to King George of Greece, he became obsessed that he had written 'Otto' instead of 'George'. Another obsession was that he had paid the wrong amount of money in a shop.

The dark side of Andersen's personality emerges very clearly in his autobiography, and these writings are of importance in the study of the obsessional personality.

'At the end of October, 1845, I left Copenhagen. Formerly I had

*thought when I set out on a journey, God! what wilt thou permit to
happen to me on this journey! This time my thoughts were, God, what
will happen to my friends at home during this long time! And I felt a
real anxiety. In one year the hearse may drive up to the door many
times, and whose name may shine upon the coffin! The proverb says,
when one suddenly feels a cold shudder "now death passes over my
grave". The shudder is still colder when the thoughts pass over the
graves of our best friends.'*

The theme of avoiding harm appears in so many of Andersen's
obsessions, even though the logic that might lead to harm would
seem to be somewhat convoluted. For example, he was once given a
banknote in his change in a restaurant in Frankfurt, and later
discovered that the note was no longer legal tender. He described
this later in a letter to a friend in Frankfurt, and posted the letter,
only to find himself occupied with the thought that it could lead to
the waiter being fired. So he returned to the post office and
retrieved the letter.

To use Andersen's own expression, he was able to 'plague
himself to the most exquisite degree'. He wrote this in his diary on
the day in which he paid a visit to the tailor's to collect a coat. On
finding his coat was not ready, the tailor loaned him another. This
troubled Andersen much, since he was afraid that the coat might
belong to someone else. The person might come up and say
'You're wearing my coat!'

He noted that the essence of his creative work consisted of
allowing his imagination to flow, but that this same imagination was
the source of so much inconvenience:

'I possessed a peculiar talent, that of lingering on the gloomy side
of life, of extracting the bitter from it, and tasting it; and understood
well, when the whole was exhausted, how to torment myself.'

'I betrayed more and more in my writings an unhealthy turn
of mind. I felt an inclination to seek for the melancholy in life,
and to linger on the dark side of things; I became sensitive,
and thought rather of the blame than the praise which was
lavished on me.'

However, the melancholy needs to be put into context; Andersen
also vividly recorded moments of immense joy in his life.

Andersen took action to preempt the danger contained within his
fears.[18] For instance, he carried a rope in his trunk, just in case
there should be a fire and then he would be able to descend from
the window. Somewhat more bizarre was his fear of being buried
whilst still alive, and to prevent this he would leave a note by his bed
with 'Jeg er skindød' written on it (meaning 'I only appear to be
dead', or 'I am in suspended animation'). He repeatedly requested
friends to promise to cut an artery before sealing his coffin.
Andersen's ability to allow the anticipation of disaster to detract

from the pleasures of good things to come is illustrated on the occasion of being given the freedom of Odense, the realization of the fortune-teller's prediction. He predicted that someone would spoil the big event, possibly by trying to murder him.

Literary fame would also appear to have set the scene for ruminations and self-doubt, a craving for perfection, as his autobiography reveals:

> *'There is something elevating, but at the same time, a something terrific in seeing one's thoughts spread so far, and among so many people; it is indeed, almost a fearful thing to belong to so many. The noble and the good in us becomes a blessing; but the bad, one's errors, shoot forth also, and involuntarily the thought forces itself from us: God! let me never write down a word of which I shall not be able to give an account to thee. A peculiar feeling, a mixture of joy and anxiety, fills my heart every time my good genius conveys my fictions to a foreign people.'*

Fear of oblivion is evident in the following diary entry, made on 5th March 1872 and prompted by the death of a friend: 'Is he now dust and ashes, dead, extinguished, put out like a flame which does not exist anymore? O God, my Lord! Can you let us disappear completely? I have a fear of that, and I have become too clever – and unhappy.'

George Borrow

George Borrow, author, explorer, linguist, animal lover and eccentric, gave some of the best accounts of obsessional disorder to be found anywhere. Borrow was born in 1803 in East Dereham, Norfolk, of a military family. He describes his birth as being premature and troubled. In his autobiographical classic *Lavengro*, Borrow describes himself as being 'born with excessive sensibility' and his life as characterized by 'wild imaginings and strange sensations'.[19] An outsider from conventional society, Borrow didn't fit into the school system, preferring to learn things in his own way. He suffered from fits and, as a child, was gloomy, introspective and withdrawn, liable to burst into tears. His strange behaviour and failure to conform to accepted standards was a source of great worry and incredulity to his parents. In his own words, he liked:

'. . . to look upon the heavens, and to bask in the rays of the sun, or to sit beneath hedgerows and listen to the chirping of the birds, indulging the while in musing and meditation.'

He was later to be described consistently as being of striking good looks and physical appearance, very tall, and of extraordinary courage and physical endurance. His memory was most impressive, and he was sentimental and extremely superstitious. He loved ghost stories.

Both as a child and as a grown-up, Borrow was an enigma, strongly egotistic, a natural 'show-off' and yet hypochondriacal, someone spending enormous lengths of time in secrecy. In later years he suffered from serious depression, and contemplated suicide. He was a man of firm opinions, either liking someone intensely or disliking them intensely. His irritability, pride and stubbornness offended many people and even frightened some.

Borrow's biographer, Michael Collie,[20] describes him as 'paranoid, secretive, uncommunicative and distrustful'. Even as a famous author, he was never at home in accepted and 'respectable' middle-class society, preferring instead the company of tramps, snake catchers, boxers, gypsies, criminals, down-and-outs and the assorted *marginal* individuals that he frequently encountered while trekking around the world.

Borrow exhibited an incredible talent for foreign languages, and was reckoned as one of the foremost linguists of his time. He acquired some languages by talking with gypsies, Irish peasants and other native speakers. Borrow's interest in Danish resulted from a fascination with wild and giant red-headed Vikings, aroused by seeing some Viking skulls. Borrow's learning technique stretched masochism to new lengths. He acquired a bible written in Danish, and literally night after night was spent systematically comparing the words with those of an English bible until he was fluent. By 18, he was said to have a good understanding of 12 languages, though the inevitable weaknesses of the self-taught were shown when he translated English into a foreign tongue. Borrow was acquainted with 42 languages.[21]

Borrow started his working life training to be a solicitor in Norwich, but abandoned this for the more exciting pastures of writing in London, printing bibles in Russia and selling them in Spain. His invitation for an interview at the London office of the Bible Society illustrates Borrow's boundless energy. Arriving first thing in the morning, he waited on the doorstep, having walked the 112 miles from Norwich to London in 27½ hours, and having spent fivepence-halfpenny on the way for one roll, two apples, a pint of ale and a glass of milk. Even more amazing is Borrow's well-documented experience in Russia. For an Englishman with no formal linguistic qualifications to teach himself Manchu in a few months would sound impressive. To then translate the Bible into Manchu sounds still more daunting. Finally, Borrow arranged in meticulous detail, and in spoken Russian, its printing by Russian workers.

Borrow's eloquence and persuasion were no less impressive than his linguistic skills and stamina. In Spain, he achieved what must be the salesman's ultimate accolade: by the conviction of his preaching, he got a number of customs officials who had been instructed to confiscate his illegal Bibles actually to purchase them from him. Later in the course of exploring the wilder regions of the Iberian peninsula, he came within a hair's breadth of public execution, but, by means of good luck and skill, managed to walk away a free man.

After a charmed life of audacity, unspeakable hardship and danger in various countries, sprinkled with the eccentric drama that he so loved, Borrow retired to the calm of East Anglia to write his autobiography. Not surprisingly, he found settling in the country to be somewhat lacking in adventure, and he yearned to be on the road again.

Michael Collie wrote of Borrow:[22]

'One part of the young Borrow was gregarious, inquisitive, outward-going. He went to prizefights, bear pits, taverns, galleries. He made many acquaintances, and *Lavengro* makes clear how much he enjoyed his first explorations in London. But another important part of this young man was essentially private, secretive, withdrawn, and these two parts of him were never reconciled, except in his books, creatively.'

In *Lavengro* Borrow writes:

'With respect to my mind and its qualities I shall be more explicit; for were I to maintain much reserve on this point, many things which appear in these memoirs would be highly mysterious to the reader, indeed incomprehensible. Perhaps no two individuals were ever more unlike in mind and disposition than my brother and myself: as light is opposed to darkness, so was that happy, brilliant, cheerful child to the sad and melancholy being who sprang from the same stock as himself, and was nurtured by the same milk.'

'A lover of nooks and retired corners, I was as a child in the habit of fleeing from society, and of sitting for hours together with my head on my breast. What I was thinking about it would be difficult to say at this distance of time; I remember perfectly well, however, being ever conscious of a peculiar heaviness within me, and at times of a strange sensation of fear, which occasionally amounted to horror, and for which I could assign no real cause whatever.'

As a young man, Borrow spent time in rumination about the meaning of existence and truth. His agonies, aroused by appreciation of the transient nature of existence, have been vividly recorded. In *Lavengro* he writes:

'Then there was myself; for what was I born? Are not all things to be forgotten? That's incomprehensible: yet is it not so? Those butterflies fall and are forgotten. In what is man better than a butterfly? All then is born to be forgotten. Ah! that was a pang indeed ...'

'In truth, it was a sore vexation of spirit to me when I saw, as the wise men saw of old, that whatever I could hope to perform must necessarily be of very temporary duration; and if so, why do it? I said to myself, whatever name I can acquire, will it endure for eternity? scarcely so.'

Later in *Lavengro* a specific rumination is described:

'My own peculiar ideas with respect to everything being a lying dream began also to revive. Sometimes at midnight, after having toiled for hours at my occupations, I would fling myself back on my chair, look about the poor apartment, dimly lighted by an unsnuffed candle, or upon the heaps of books and papers before me, and exclaim, – "Do I exist? Do these things, which I see about me exist, or do they not?"'

In an account that undoubtedly speaks from personal experience, Borrow beautifully describes an antagonism between thoughts of opposite polarity:

'No one is fortunate unless he is happy, and it is impossible for a being constructed like myself to be happy for an hour, or even enjoy peace and tranquillity; most of our pleasures and pains are the effects of imagination, and wherever the sensibility is great, the imagination is great also. No sooner has my imagination raised up an image of pleasure, than it is sure to conjure up one of distress and gloom; these two antagonistic ideas instantly commence a struggle in my mind, and the gloomy one generally, I may say, invariably, prevails.'

Thus, for example, Borrow was able to turn the pleasure of a gift into pain, by doubting the ownership of the gift. An obsessive-compulsive problem is described in *Lavengro*, where Borrow relates to the time when his mother was taken ill:

'. . . *the thought that I might possibly lose her now rushed into my mind for the first time; it was terrible, and caused me unspeakable misery, I may say horror.*

Suddenly I found myself doing that which even at the time struck me as being highly singular; I found myself touching particular objects that were near me, and to which my fingers seemed to be attracted by an irresistible impulse. It was now the table or the chair that I was compelled to touch; now the bell-rope; now the handle of the door; now I would touch the wall, and the next moment stooping down, I would place the point of my finger upon the floor: and so I continued to do day after day; frequently I would struggle to resist the impulse, but invariably in vain. I have even rushed away from the object, but I was sure to return, the impulse was too strong to be resisted: I quickly hurried back, compelled by the feeling within me to touch the object. Now I need not tell you that what impelled me to these actions was the desire to prevent my mother's death; whenever I touched any particular object, it was with a view to baffling the evil chance, as you would call it – in this instance my mother's death.'

Herbert Jenkins[23] quotes an observation made to him by a certain Mr Watts-Dunton:

'There was nothing that Borrow strove against with more energy than the curious impulse, which he seems to have shared with Dr Johnson, to touch objects along his path in order to save himself from the evil chance. He never conquered the superstition. In walking through Richmond Park he would step out of his way constantly to touch a tree, and he was offended if the friend he was with seemed to observe it.'

Another compulsive ritual that Borrow described in the context of avoiding evil happenings was to climb an elm tree next to his house and touch the top branch.

'. . . the difficulty and peril of such a feat startled me; I reasoned against the feeling, and strove more strenuously than I had ever done before; I even made a solemn vow not to give way to the temptation, but I believe nothing less than chains, and those strong ones, could have restrained me.'

Then Borrow gives such a beautiful account of the dilemma of the obsessional:

'Indeed, all the time that I was performing these strange feats, I knew them to be highly absurd, yet the impulse to perform them was irresistible – a mysterious dread hanging over me till I had given way to it; even at that early period I frequently used to reason within myself as to what could be the cause of my propensity to touch, but of course I could come to no satisfactory conclusion respecting it; being heartily ashamed of the practice, I never spoke of it to anyone, and was at all times highly solicitous that no one should observe my weakness.'

Agonies of perfectionism are richly described by Borrow in *Lavengro*. The reaction of an author following a good reception of his first published work form the subject in this case.

'. . . the reception which it met with was far beyond my wildest expectations. The public were delighted with it, but what were my feelings? Anything, alas! but those of delight. No sooner did the public express its satisfaction at the result of my endeavours, than my perverse imagination began to conceive a thousand chimerical doubts . . .'

'. . . I forthwith commenced touching the objects around me, in order to baffle the evil chance, as you call it; it was neither more nor less than a doubt of the legality of my claim to the thoughts, expressions, and situations contained in the book; that is to all that constituted the book.'

Later *Lavengro* describes the fear of death and what might follow it, in a way that would doubtless vividly 'ring true' for the sufferer from this type of obsessional rumination:

'*– and how long could I hope to live? perhaps fifty years; at the end of* *which I must go to my place; and then I would count the months and the days, nay even the hours which yet intervened between me and my doom. Sometimes I would comfort myself with the idea that a long time would elapse before my time would be out; but then again I thought that, however long the term might be, it must be out at last; and then I would fall into an agony, during which I would almost wish that the term were out, and that I were in my place; the horrors of which I thought could scarcely be worse than what I then endured.*[24]

Howard Hughes

Howard Hughes was a playboy, film producer and aircraft manufacturer. Handsome, dashing and daring were adjectives used to describe the young Hughes. He collected properties, aircraft and glamorous women with ruthless determination. If one is to believe the stories, [25] Hughes was devious, machiavellian in business dealing and employed the most suspect of methods for hunting females. However, despite his distance from the kind of 'philosophical obsessionality' with which we have been primarily concerned, Hughes presents a classical case of obsessional illness. The public image of Hughes as a devious eccentric conveys only an aspect of the truth; it is less widely known that he made a major contribution to the development of aeronautics.

Howard Robard Hughes was born on December 24th 1905 in Houston, Texas, the birth being a difficult one. His father had founded a successful business that made oil-drilling equipment. Hughes' mother, Allene, suffered from an intense cat-phobia (his grandmother was also strongly phobic). The young Howard was described as polite, shy, quiet and withdrawn, but also characterized by a determination to succeed at the tasks he undertook. Howard was fascinated by mechanical gadgets, inventing a novel form of motorcycle when he was 14 years of age.

In their excellent biography, Donald Barlett and James Steele[26] describe how the mother 'smothered Howard Jr. with care.' His physical condition was constantly monitored for the slightest sign of trouble and he was made to take mineral oil each night. They observe:

'*During Howard's childhood, Allene Hughes exerted an overpowering influence on his development. She was obsessed with her son's physical and emotional condition. If she was not worried about his digestion, feet, teeth, bowels, colour, cheeks, weight, or proximity to others with contagious diseases, she was anxious about what she called his "supersensitiveness", nervousness, and inability to make friends with other boys. If Howard had no inherent anxieties in those directions as a small boy, he certainly had them by the time he reached adolescence.*

His mother helped instill in him lifelong phobias about his physical and mental state. Howard also learned from her that the best way to attract attention or to escape unpleasant situations was to complain of illness. The slightest whimper from him would unleash a wave of smothering attention from Allene Hughes, and throughout his life he would pretend to be sick when he wanted to avoid responsibility or elicit sympathy.'

Howard was sent to an exclusive school in West Newton, Massachusetts. The records of his days there describe a shy and withdrawn boy, not much involved in the social life. However, he still tended to stand out on account of his height and good looks. Later he was enrolled at school in Ojai, California, where he again tended to avoid group activities, spending hours riding alone in the hills. While at Ojai, Howard learned of the death of his mother at the age of thirty-nine. He showed no open display of grief, but it might be significant that thereafter when in Houston he avoided the family home. Less than two years later, he suffered the loss of his father. His biographers believe that these two premature losses had a profound effect on consolidating Howard's own well-instilled fears for his own health. From this time onwards he was thrown into a panic by any mild irregularity in his physical condition. With the help of pills and other means, he started to protect himself from the dangers of the world.

At first, in spite of wealth and good looks, Hughes' social incompetence rendered him something of a flop with girls. He did manage to get married but the marriage was not a success; Hughes was too much of a workaholic to allow the necessary social life and sharing. He was able to combine his two great loves, films and aircraft, by producing movies about planes, in which he did some of the flying. Sometimes he would work for stretches of up to 36 hours and earned a reputation for extreme ambition and determination. In filming, he set perfectionist and 'impossible' goals, but managed to meet them.

In spite of a lack of social skills, fame brought with it the reward of a succession of glamorous women. However, he remained self-conscious and reticent, looking distinctly ill at ease at social gatherings. The contrast between the dashing, fearless test-pilot and the shy, 'highly-strung', self-effacing image that the public saw created an air of mystery around him.

In business life, Hughes earned a reputation for interfering, an inability to delegate. He demanded total control over all of his empire. Yet Hughes was unable to make decisions himself, engaging in lengthy and disastrous procrastination, unable to distinguish the trivial from the profound. Perfectionist traits were evident even in the relatively insignificant aspects of his work. His instructions were meticulous: for instance, visitors were even told in exact detail how they should park their cars and walk towards where Howard would meet them. In technical matters concerned with aircraft production, Hughes exhibited an astonishing, almost photographic, memory. Essentially a self-taught man, with very little formal education in aeronautical science, Hughes impressed a number of the country's foremost engineers with his understanding. His round-the-world flights were planned with the obsessional's capacity for thoroughness.

Even by Hollywood's liberal standards, Hughes was a distinct eccentric, a maverick, a loner who had a taste for the sensational and a love of being seen to be doing weird and wonderful things. In 1944, Hughes suffered his first mental breakdown.

In 1946 while on a test flight, he suffered a crash that left him injured. To overcome the pain, he was administered morphine, and then as a substitute, codeine. He developed a life-long addiction to codeine. Now Hughes' behaviour, always eccentric, was becoming bizarre in the extreme. Paranoia dictated that business meetings should be held either in cars parked in remote backstreets or in a bathroom with the tap turned on to mask the conversation. People were now seen as germ carriers, and elaborate schemes were put into force to protect Hughes.

Becoming a recluse, Hughes' whole lifestyle was dictated by the obsession with hidden germs. Curtains were permanently closed and windows and doors were sealed with masking tape. Everything became a potential menace, even the glance of a friend came to threaten contamination. Meticulous specifications were given to aides on how to protect him from germs; no threat seemed too bizarre to be considered. Earlier food fads were now accentuated, meals being taken only in the form of elaborate rituals. Another aspect of his obsession involved the abhorrence that part of his body might be wasted; hence Hughes' insistence that his urine should not be flushed down the toilet, but rather stored in bottles. His fear that his perspiration would be wasted prevented him from taking baths.

One of his aides, Bob Roberts, described 'The Old Man' sitting in a chair staring at the wall. The room was insulated to prevent germs entering in the air. Hughes was naked except for a napkin spread over his groin. He resembled an emaciated skeleton, like a survivor from a concentration camp. His hair was white and dirty, and it reached the middle of his back. The toenails and fingernails were some six inches in length. Hughes' doctor was allowed neither to touch him nor speak to him, having to communicate by writing notes on a pad. In the meantime, Hughes would himself struggle to cope with his haemorrhoids, using the fingers with the six-inch nails.

Donald Barlett and James Steele[27] write:

'If Howard Hughes had had a friend in the world in 1958, that person would now have encouraged or arranged psychiatric care for him before it was too late.'

In contrast, the highly-paid aides who surrounded Hughes did everything to cater for his every eccentric wish. This strengthened, rather than undermined, his conviction that both he and his second wife were under permanent threat from hidden germs. Also, by taking massive quantities of codeine by intravenous injection and Valium (28 times the recommended daily dose) orally, Hughes was poisoning his body. For the last 15 or so years of his life, Hughes never left his bedroom. Indeed, he hardly left his bed except to make visits to the toilet. Interminable hours were spent watching TV movies, whilst lying naked on dirty sheets and surrounded by piles of magazines.

Hughes died a 93-pound skeleton. He had never been able to enjoy the friendship of anyone and spent most of his married state living apart from his two wives. But in a sense, he died as he lived, an enigma, an eccentric, always in the gaze of publicity, an object of (now morbid) curiosity. As Donald Barlett and James Steele express it 'His shyness notwithstanding, the public spotlight was his oldest addiction.'

Hughes serves to illustrate that there is a grey area between obsessions and phobias.[28] He could probably equally well be described as having a germ phobia or an obsession about germs. Two possible extreme strategies are sometimes followed by a subject having a fear of germs: extensive washing rituals or withdrawal from possible contamination. These might be termed active and passive coping strategies, respectively. Hughes adopted a predominantly passive strategy. There are records of other patients, having fears similar to Hughes, who also switched from an active to a passive strategy. The irony is that either strategy taken to extremes actually brings the victims nearer to the feared object. Hands made raw by washing in detergent are presumably particularly vulnerable to infection. Similarly, by lying in filth, afraid to interact with an apparently hostile world, Hughes greatly increased his chances of infection with the hepatitis that he so dreaded.

Woody Allen

Perhaps the best-known and best-loved obsessional is Woody Allen, who manages to weave into his jokes and screen characters themes from his own ruminations and fear of death. This is brilliantly illustrated in such films as *Love and Death* and *Hannah and her Sisters*. In interviews, Allen conveys his anxiety:

'The fundamental thing behind *all* motivation and *all* activity is the constant struggle against annihilation and against death. It's absolutely stupefying in its terror, and it renders anyone's accomplishments meaningless.'

Allen expresses a terror at the prospect that the universe might one day not exist. What is the point of struggling for artistic perfection in the midst of such a precarious existence? Yet the same creative talent can give us:

'I do not believe in an afterlife, although I am bringing a change of underwear.'

and

'It's not that I'm afraid to die. I just don't want to be there when it happens.'

Studying Allen is not always easy. Though he undoubtedly incorporates features of his worst fears into his films, these works should not simply be taken as autobiographical. He shows a certain suspicion of interviews, books and articles that describe his life. However, there is sufficient reliable information,[29] some of it written by Allen himself, to give a fairly clear picture. Several well-written biographies exist and they show an impressive consensus of opinion.

He was born Alan Stewart Konigsberg on December 1st 1935 at Flatbush, a middle-class and then predominantly Jewish district in Brooklyn, New York City. Woody seems to have been reclusive as a child, spending most of his time hidden away in his room pursuing magic amongst other things. There appear to have been rather few friends. He didn't fit well into the school system and made little impression upon his teachers, being as he was essentially self-motivated. On his own, Woody showed enormous persistence at those tasks he chose to be interested in, particularly perfecting his music and conjuring tricks. There is some evidence that he was bullied by bigger boys at times; his small build, shortness and red hair might have contributed. He seems to have had little or no success regarding girlfriends. However, even at school, he was showing an unusual talent for writing gags and jokes, for which he was able to earn a considerable amount.

Allen dropped out of college and survived somewhat precarious-ly as a writer of humorous material for comedians, a very different career to that of doctor or lawyer, which a respectable Jewish mother would have wished for her son. Allen read a lot; Samuel Johnson, James Boswell, Sigmund Freud and Søren Kierkegaard were amongst his favourite writers. Fundamental issues of life, death and God, as depicted in the work of Kafka, Dostoevsky and the film director Ingmar Bergman held his fascination. By stages Allen was to develop into a film actor, writer and director, and to acquire the image known to millions, neurotic on screen as well as off, under psychoanalysis, inordinately fascinated by death, God and sex, chronically shy and prone to fads, and being *anhedonic*, that is tending to turn pleasure into sorrow. (The film title *Annie Hall* derives from the original intended title *Anhedonia*.)

Aspects of Allen's life reveal the obsessional's love of creating predictability and control, to be a creature of habit. For example, it is widely reported that while filming *What's New Pussycat?* in Paris, he ate the same meal for six months, *potage du jour* and sole. By all accounts Allen is extremely well disciplined and controlled. In addition, the real image is one characterized by scrupulous honesty, moral integrity and traits of extreme 'workaholism' and perfectionism. A 15-hour writing day is not uncommon.

Lee Guthrie's *Woody Allen A Biography*[30] reveals another aspect of Allen's make-up, that he tends to wish he were doing something other than what he is doing. This is a bizarre kind of extreme optimism shared with other obsessionals. 'I always think the next thing I do will be fun. Then when I do it I don't like it at all.' Guthrie also quotes Allen as describing himself as egotistical and vain.

Writing in *Time* magazine, film critic Richard Schickel[31] observes:

'The basic Woody persona has always been a well-loved figure, a projection of the modern urban Everyman's privately held fantasies and terrors.'

Allen is an (if not *the*) undisputed genius of American cinema, combining qualities of, on the one hand, Groucho Marx and Charlie Chaplin with, on the other, Samuel Johnson and Søren Kierkegaard. A more improbable blend of talents it would be difficult to imagine, but work it does, as millions of devoted followers testify. Vincent Canby,[32] a long-standing Woody fan and film critic of the *New York Times*, says of his hero:

'There's nobody else in American films who comes anywhere near him in originality and interest. One has to go back to Chaplin and Buster Keaton, people who were totally responsible for their own movies, to find anyone comparable.'

In her excellent biography[33] . . . *but we need the eggs – The Magic of Woody Allen*, Diane Jacobs makes the particularly apposite observation:

'. . . the obsessions that were with him in the nightclub acts are still with him today. These obsessions have mostly to do with the incongruity of things. Why can't the body perform what the mind can conceive – such as immortality? Why can't experience imitate the perfection of art? Why is the ideal always so much finer than the practice?'

In his peculiar ability for taking the utterly familiar, spotting its latent absurdity, its inherent incongruity, and being able to express this in a brilliant wit, Allen strongly reminds me of Johnson. There is something very Johnsonian in the style of expressing private fears in stories. In his rumination over moral dilemmas, such as the ethics of whether to kill Napoleon in the film *Love and Death*, Allen displays something of the talent of Kierkegaard.

Caryn James [34] notes that:

'Few artists of his stature admit to so many self doubts while displaying so much confidence; rarely is such an overwhelming need for control manifested in such a mild manner.'

James adds that:

'. . . his obsession with death is so strong it must be deflected through the skewed vision of comedy. In film, he has found his perfect vehicle.'

Indeed, Allen is quoted in *Time* magazine as having said that 'death is the big obsession behind all the things I've done.'

Allen has always held such a fear:[35]

'I was always obsessed with death, even as a child. It always used to frighten me. I have memories of being very young, probably six or eight, and being put to sleep at night and lying in the black, thinking "someday I will be dead", and really focusing vivid feelings on it, a vivid attempt to imagine the emptiness, the finality, the irrevocability of it.'

Although Allen's obsession is unwanted, it is not perceived as being at all illogical or senseless. On the contrary, Eric Lax in his biography *Woody Allen and his Comedy* notes that Allen will quote Tolstoy on the subject of death: 'any man over thirty-five with whom death is not the main consideration is a fool.'

17
Concluding remarks

Obsessional thoughts raise some profound questions about the nature of humans, thought and free will. To what extent do we have free will over our behaviour and pattern of thoughts? On closer examination, can we even couch this question in meaningful terms? Whatever answer is attempted to these questions needs to be qualified by the existence of subjects who are plagued by intrusive thoughts in spite of their attempts to get rid of them.

It would be nice to be able to draw together the various strands of this book into some clear-cut conclusions and suggestions for therapy. Unfortunately the investigation of obsessional thoughts remains something of an enigma. To state otherwise would be to deceive the reader. However, I believe that some pointers are now available, hints as to what might be going on, and there is every reason to believe that such hints will prove useful leads to further investigation. Behaviour therapy and clomipramine are very effective for some subjects.

Although the form of obsessionality might strike us as a puzzle, we should not be unduly surprised that behavioural systems 'go wrong'. TV sets and computers go wrong, so why not the infinitely more complex brain and behavioural systems? What is perhaps more surprising is that they normally work as well as they do. Obsessional problems probably seem all the more bizarre because the sufferers appear so 'very normal' in other respects. They seem rational, persistent and purposive in their lives. So why can't they cure themselves or be more receptive to therapy? When the sufferer happens to be a trained psychologist, the feeling that the solution should lie in one's own hands must seem all the more convincing. But this is not so, alas.

Caution is needed when we describe an individual as exhibiting obsessional personality traits, such as orderliness and perfection-ism. Without doubt, obsessionals tend to show such traits, but it should not be supposed that every aspect of their lives bears witness to meticulous planning and devotion to duty. After all, there are only 24 hours in a day and even obsessionals need to sleep. Thus extreme persistence and conscientiousness are likely to be shown in tasks that are given priority since they serve the individual's dominant goals. Tasks at odds with these goals or which take precious time away from them might assume a much lower place in the hierachy or even be treated with contempt. I can ruminate for long periods over the use of a 'which' rather than a 'that' in a piece of writing, in the midst of chaos, unpaid bills and uncashed cheques. This aspect of obsessionality is often overlooked; perfection might well be applied in only one or two areas of life.

In other words, I would argue that any perfectionism will be apparent in the contexts of the patient's overall goals. In the extreme, one part of the body can be the focus for washing rituals, while the rest of the body can remain filthy. Pierre Janet and Isaac Marks, amongst others, have reported visiting the homes of patients obsessed with cleanliness in, for example, the toilet, while the kitchen stinks of the rotten remains of food caked onto surfaces. One of Marks' patients, a man obsessed with cleaning away imaginary dog excrement, caught gonorrhoea from a prostitute.

From both my personal experience and academic viewpoint, I would emphasize the need to look closely at goal-direction in behaviour. Events that are in some way at odds with the dominant goals are particularly likely to cue fearful ruminations in me. Take a case of where I might plan to fly from London to New York. One might suppose that a certain level of anticipatory fear would be associated with such an event. In my case, the frequency and level of such fears would depend upon how the visit fitted my current concerns. If the woman of my dreams were to be waiting for me in the USA, there would be little or no fearful rumination in advance. If any were to appear, I could quickly dismiss it. If however this same woman were to be in Edinburgh, and I was flying half-heartedly to a New York conference that was not likely to be very valuable, the intrusions over flying would be frequent and more intense.

Another concept that emerges as being vital is that of *control*; the obsessional seems to have a greater need than normal to be able to exert control over her environment. This includes the physical and social environments. Thus the obsessional will seek relationships in which she can do the controlling rather than be the controlled. Interestingly, the need to exert control and *predictability* over the environment is now at the core of the study of animal welfare. The Dutch ethologist, Professor Piet Wiepkema, goes so far as to equate an absence of suffering and stress in farm animals with an ability to predict and control their environment. It would seem entirely reasonable that the obsessional human experiences a greater than normal need to possess these two capacities in a wider number of contexts. In a fascinating study entitled 'The obsessive's myth of control', Dr Allan Mallinger argues that at one level the obsessional can even convince himself that he has total control over his destiny. The similarities, in terms of loss of control, between depression, stress and obsessional disorders seem worthy of further analysis.

We must also be careful not to see ōbsessionals as too much of a homogeneous group. A number of common traits need to be exhibited, of course, for the term *personality type* to have any value, but beyond this we should expect rich variety amongst obsessionals. Indeed, in some ways it is difficult to imagine a greater difference than between, say, the promiscuous and empire-building Howard Hughes and the prudish Hans Christian Andersen, or between the timid character portrayed so vividly by Woody Allen and the giant and fearless George Borrow. The weeping and forever sentimental and nostalgic Andersen, the aggressive and morose Johnson, the passionate Borrow and the anxiety-ridden Allen do not lend themselves easily to the not-uncommon textbook image of the obsessional as being emotionally flat.

Now for a final word on a personal level, I would like to discuss some issues arising from the book. Have I learned anything about my life from a study of the personality type that I fit? Of course, I have learned a lot and have gained inspiration from knowing that others have suffered from the same condition. I feel that it is a bit like having a wooden leg or a tendency to epilepsy – life would be much better without the disorder but one can still make the best of it. I have lived a life rich in experiences with few fears that have actually stopped me doing things. I am not a pessimist and carrying out this study has not moved me in that direction. My life has had 'peak experiences': at Sussex, in Odense and Copenhagen, and later while on sabbatical in France and West Germany. These were experiences that I would not have missed, escaping completely from the troubles of life. Those things that have bothered me in life have done so intensely, but on the positive side very few things have, or do, bother me in the least. After the experience of mental breakdown, the content of so many concerns and worries of the affluent Western middle class can only seem to me to be of monumental triviality. This might sound arrogant but it is how I feel.

Suppose I had remained within the secure and predictable confines of my village in Cambridgeshire. Who can say what might have happened? I would have missed the stimulation of teaching Open University students and that is an experience that I would not have missed for anything.

When times seem bad, I get much inspiration from the words of George Borrow in *Lavengro*:

> '*Reader, amidst the difficulties and dangers of this life, should you ever be tempted to despair, call to mind these latter chapters of the life of Lavengro. There are few positions, however difficult, from which dogged resolution and perseverance may not liberate you.*'

References

Chapter 7

1. Heart rate is massively accelerated in the night terror; indeed it represents the highest acceleration known to medical science. At the time I had perhaps not fully appreciated just how bad the condition is. Only much later did I read the American psychoanalyst, Dr Jeanne Safer, who concluded a study by claiming that 'night terrors are among the most terrifying experiences human beings can endure' (in Kellerman, H. *The Nightmare*, Columbia University Press, New York, 1987). Even hardened psychiatric investigators have occasionally been frightened by observing them in the laboratory. In his book *The Nightmare*, Ernest Hartmann not only clearly distinguishes nightmares and night terrors, but correspondingly distinguishes the personality types that are most prone to them. Each phenomenon is perhaps most often associated with some more general disturbance in mental health. The obsessional is more likely to suffer from night terrors. However, although two distinct phenomena do exist, there are some subjects, such as myself, who at various times have suffered from both. Occasionally a given nocturnal experience would, as far as I remember, seem to incorporate features of both.

Chapter 9

1. Reed, G. F., *Obsessional Experience and Compulsive Behaviour – A Cognitive-Structural Approach*, (Academic Press, Orlando, 1985).

Chapter 10

1. Reed, G. F., *Obsessional Experience and Compulsive Behaviour – A Cognitive-Structural Approach*, (Academic Press, Orlando, 1985).
2. Lewis, A., 'The diagnosis and treatment of obsessional states', *The Practitioner* 1938; 141: 21–30
3. Rachman, S., de Silva, P., 'Abnormal and normal obsessions',

Behaviour Research and Therapy 1978; 16: 233–48.
4. Rapoport, J. L., *The Boy who Couldn't Stop Washing*, (E. P. Dutton, New York, 1989).
5. Skoog, G., 'Onset of anancastic conditions', *Acta Psychiatrica Scandinavica*, 1965; 41: Supplementum 184.
6. See 1
7. See 1
8. Marks, I. M., *Living with Fear*, (McGraw-Hill, New York, 1978).
9. Foa, E. B., 'Failure in treating obsessional-compulsives', *Behaviour Research and Therapy* 1979; 17: 160–76.
10. See 1

Chapter 11

1. Lewis, A., 'The diagnosis and treatment of obsessional states', *The Practitioner* 1938; 141: 21–30.
2. Guirdham, A., *Obsession*, (Neville Spearman, London, 1972).
3. Walker, V. J., 'Explanation in obsessional neurosis', *British Journal of Psychiatry* 1973; 123: 675–80.
4. See 3
5. Rapoport, J. L., *The Boy who Couldn't Stop Washing*, (E. P. Dutton, New York, 1989).
6. Rachman, S., 'Some similarities and differences between obsessional ruminations and morbid preoccupations', *Canadian Psychiatric Association Journal* 1973; 18: 71–4.
7. See 6
8. Rachman, S., Hodgson R., *Obsessions and Compulsions*, (Prentice Hall, New York, 1979).
9. Lewis, A. 'Problems of obsessional illness', *Proceedings of the Royal Society of Medicine* 1936; 29: 325–36.
10. Singer, J. L., *Daydreaming and Fantasy*, (Oxford University Press, Oxford, 1981).
11. Reed, G. F., *Obsessional Experience and Compulsive Behaviour – A Cognitive-Structural Approach*, (Academic Press, Orlando, 1985).
12. Guidano, V., Liotti, G., *Cognitive Processes and Emotional Disorders*, (The Guilford Press, New York, 1983).
13. Walkup, J. T., Leckman, J. F., Price, R. A., Hardin, M., Ort, S. I., Cohen, D. J., 'The relationship between obsessive-compulsive disorder and Tourette's syndrome: A twin study', *Psychopharmacology Bulletin* 1988; 24: 375–9;
    Robertson, M. M., Trimble, M. R., Lees, A. J., 'The psychopathology of the Gilles de la Tourette syndrome – A phenomenological analysis', *British Journal of Psychiatry* 1988; 152: 383–90;

Champion, L. M., Fulton, W. A., Shady, G. A., 'Tourette syndrome and social functioning in a Canadian population', *Neuroscience and Biobehavioural Reviews* 1988; 12: 255–7.

A high prevalence of obsessive-compulsive disorder has also been reported in patients suffering from Sydenham's chorea ('St Vitus' dance'): Swedo, S. E., Rapoport, J. L., Cheslow, D. L., Leonard, H. L., Ayoub, E. M., Hosier, D. M., and Wald, E. R., 'High prevalence of obsessive-compulsive symptoms in patients with Sydenham's chorea', *American Journal of Psychiatry* 1989; 146: 246–9.

14. See 5
15. See 12
16. Salzman, L., Thaler, F. H., 'Obsessive-compulsive disorders: A review of the literature', *American Journal of Psychiatry* 1981; 138: 286–96.
17. Orbach, S., *Hunger Strike*, (Faber, London, 1987).
18. The technical term is dysmorphophobia and is briefly mentioned (p.25) in Turner, S., Biedel, D. C., *Treating Obsessive-Compulsive Disorder*, (Pergamon Press, New York, 1988).
19. See also discussion in 5
20. See 2
21. See 3
22. See 11

Chapter 12

1. Akhtar, S., Wig, N. N., Varma, V. K., Pershad, D., Verma, S. K., 'A phenomenological analysis of symptoms in obsessive-compulsive neurosis', *British Journal of Psychiatry* 1975; 127: 342–8.
2. Lo, W. H. 'A follow-up study of obsessional neurotics in Hong Kong Chinese', *British Journal of Psychiatry* 1967; 113: 823–32.
3. De Silva, P., 'Early Buddhist and modern behavioural strategies for the control of unwanted intrusive cognitions', *The Psychological Record* 1985; 35: 437–43.
4. Reed, G. F., *Obsessional Experience and Compulsive Behaviour – A Cognitive-Structural Approach*, (Academic Press, Orlando, 1985).
5. Eysenck, H. J., Wilson, G., *Know Your Own Personality* (Penguin, Harmondsworth, 1975).
6. See 5
7. Mallinger, A. E., 'The obsessive's myth of control', *Journal of the American Academy of Psychoanalysis* 1984; 12: 147–65.
8. Mellet, P. G., 'The clinical problem', In: Beech, H. R., (ed.) *Obsessional States*, (Methuen, London, 1974) 55–94.

9. See 4

10. Eysenck, H. J., *You and Neurosis*, (Temple Smith, London, 1977).

11. See 4

12. Guirdham, A., *Obsession*, (Neville Spearman, London, 1972).

13. Adler, A., 'Compulsion neurosis', *International Journal of Individual Psychology* 1936; 2: 3–22.

14. Rowe, D., *Beyond Fear*, (Fontana, London 1987).

15. See 12

16. See 8

17. Rachman, S. J., 'An anatomy of obsessions', *Behaviour Analysis and Modification* 1978; 2: 253–78.

    Rachman, S., Hodgson, R., *Obsessions and Compulsions*. (Prentice Hall, New York, 1979).

18. See 4

19. See 4

20. Marks, I. M., *Living with Fear*, McGraw-Hill, New York, 1978).

21. Foa, E. B., Steketee, G., Grayson, J. B., Doppelt, H. G., 'Treatment of obsessive-compulsives: when do we fail?' in Foa, E. B. and Emmelkamp, P. M. G. (eds.), *Failures in Behaviour Therapy*. (Wiley, New York, 1983).

22. The literature describes a similar role of stress in accentuating the irritable colon syndrome as it does for obsessional disorder (Ruoff, M., 'The irritable colon syndrome', In: Lindner, A. E., (ed.) *Emotional Factors in Gastrointestinal Illness*, (Excerpta Medica, Amsterdam, 1973), pp.156–65.

    On an Eysenck Personality Inventory, sufferers from IBS (and those of obsessional personality) emerge as being more neurotic and introverted than controls (Palmer, R. L., Stonehill, E., Crisp, A. H., Waller, S., amd Misiewicz, J. J. 'Psychological characteristics of patients with the irritable bowel syndrome,' *Postgraduate Medical Journal* 1974; 50: 416–19). The psychological roots of this disorder are often missed by physicians (Young, S. J., Alpers, D. H., Norland, C. C., Woodruff, R. A., 'Psychiatric illness and the irritable bowel syndrome', *Gastroenterology*, 1976; 70: 162–6).

    There are reports that a large percentage of sufferers from ulcerative colitis display obsessional personality (Engel, G. L., 'Ulcerative colitis,' in: Lindner, A. E., (ed.) *Emotional Factors in Gastrointestinal Illness*, Excerpta Medica, Amsterdam, 1973), pp.99–112 and Engel, G. L., 'Studies of ulcerative colitis,' *American Journal of Medicine* 1955; 19: 231–56). Note though, that the converse, that a large percentage of those with obsessional personality can expect to suffer ulcerative colitis, does not follow from this.

23. Furlong, M., *Puritan's Progress – A Study of John Bunyan*, (Hodder and Stoughton, London, 1975).
24. Rachman, S., Hodgson, R., *Obsessions and Compulsions*, (Prentice Hall, New York, 1979).
25. Singer, J. L., *Daydreaming and Fantasy*, (Oxford University Press, Oxford, 1981).
26. See 4
27. See 24
28. Storr, A., *The Dynamics of Creation*, (Secker and Warburg, London, 1972).
29. Janet, P., *Les Obsessions et la Psychasthénie*, Vol. 1. (Alcan, Paris, 1903).
30. Rapoport, J. L., *The Boy who Couldn't Stop Washing*. (E. P. Dutton, New York, 1989).
31. See 28
32. Salzman, L., *The Obsessive Personality*. (Science House, New York, 1968).

Chapter 13

1. This analogy has been made by W. S. Agras
2. Marks, I. M., *Living with Fear*, (McGraw-Hill, New York, 1978).
3. See 2
4. Solyom, L., Garza-Perez, J., Ledwidge, B. L., Solyom, C., 'Paradoxical intention in the treatment of obsessive thoughts: A pilot study', *Comprehensive Psychiatry* 1972; 13: 291–7.
5. Lazarus, A., *Behaviour Therapy and Beyond*. (McGraw-Hill, New York, 1971).
6. Gerz, H. O., 'The treatment of the phobic and the obsessive-compulsive patient using paradoxical intention sec. Viktor E. Frankl', *Journal of Neuropsychiatry* 1962; 3:375–87.
7. Kocourek, K., Discussed in 8
8. Frankl, V., *The Unheard Cry for Meaning*, (Hodder and Stoughton, London, 1979).
9. Kora, T., 'A method of instruction in psychotherapy', *Jikei Medical Journal* 1968; 15: 315–25.
10. Beck, A. T., Emery, G., Greenberg, R. L., *Anxiety Disorders and Phobias – A Cognitive Perspective*, (Basic Books, New York, 1985).
11. Ellis, A., *Reason and Emotion in Psychotherapy*. (Lyle-Stuart, New York, 1962).
12. There are some provisional reports of successful treatment of obsessional disorder by cognitive therapy (Emmelkamp, P. M. G., Visser, S., Hoekstra, R. J., *Cognitive Therapy and Research* 1988; 12: 103–14). See also Savlovskis, P. M., 'Obsessional-compulsive problems: A cognitive-behavioural

analysis', *Behavioural Research and Therapy* 1985; 23: 571–83.

13. Frankl, V., *The Doctor and the Soul*, (Penguin, Harmondsworth, 1965).

14. Bunyan, J., *Grace Abounding to the Chief of Sinners*, (Clarendon Press, Oxford, 1962 edition).

15. Reed, G. F., *Obsessional Experience and Compulsive Behaviour – A Cognitive-Structural Approach*, (Academic Press, Orlando, 1985).

16. Emmelkamp, P. M. G., *Phobic and Obsessive-Compulsive Disorders*, (Plenum Press, New York, 1982).

17. See 16

18. See 15

19. Zohar, J., Insel, T. R., Zohar-Kadouch, R. C., Hill, J. L., Murphy, D. L., 'Serotonergic responsivity in obsessive-compulsive disorder', *Archives of General Psychiatry* 1988; 45: 167–72.

    Zak, J. P., Miller, J. A., Sheehan, D. V., Fanous, B. S. L., 'The potential role of serotonin reuptake inhibitors in the treatment of obsessive compulsive disorder', *Journal of Clinical Psychiatry* 1988; 49: 23–9.

20. Rapoport, J. L., *The Boy who Couldn't Stop Washing*, (E. P. Dutton, New York, 1989).

21. Goodman, W. K., Price, L. H., Rasmussen, S. A., Delgado, P. L., Heninger, G. R., Charney, D. S., 'Efficacy of fluvoxamine in obsessive-compulsive disorder', *Archives of General Psychiatry* 1989; 46: 36–44.

22. Insel, T. R., Murphy, D. L., Cohen, R. M., Alterman, I., Kilts, C., Linnoila, M., 'Obsessive-compulsive disorder: A double-blind trial of clomipramine and clorgyline,' *Archives of General Psychiatry* 1983; 40: 605–12.

23. See 20

24. See also Jenike, N. A., Baer, L. and Minichiello, W. E., *Obsessive-Compulsive Disorders – Theory and Management*. (PSG Publishing Company, Littleton, 1986).

25. Solyom, L., Turnbull, I. M., Wilensky, M. A., 'A case of self-inflicted leucotomy', *British Journal of Psychiatry* 1987; 151: 855–7.

Chapter 14

1. Reed, G. F., *Obsessional Experience and Compulsive Behaviour – A Cognitive-Structural Approach*, (Academic Press, Orlando, 1985).

2. Skinner, B. F., Vaughan, M. E., *How to Enjoy Your Old Age*, (Sheldon Press, London, 1983).

3. See 1

4. De Silva, P., 'Early Buddhist and modern behavioural strategies for the control of unwanted intrusive cognitions', *The Psychological Record* 1985; 35: 437–43.

5. Rapoport, J. L., *The Boy who Couldn't Stop Washing*, (E. P. Dutton, New York, 1989).

6. Scheffer, M., *Bach Flower Therapy*, (Thorsons Publishing Group, Wellingborough, 1986).

7. Pitman, R. K., 'Pierre Janet on obsessive-compulsive disorder (1903)', *Archives of General Psychiatry* 1987; 44: 226–32.

8. Lewis, A., 'The diagnosis and treatment of obsessional states', *The Practitioner* 1938; 141: 21–30.

9. Marks, I. M., *Living with Fear*, (McGraw-Hill, New York, 1978).

10. Frankl, V., *The Doctor and the Soul*, (Penguin, Harmondsworth, 1965).

11. There is some experimental evidence to suggest that simply trying by special effort to suppress thoughts might actually serve to strengthen them (Wegner, D. M., Schneider, D. J., Carter, S. R., White, T. L., 'Paradoxical effects of thought suppression', *Journal of Personality and Social Psychology* 1987; 53: 5–13). Some advice to the sufferer along these lines is to be found in *Psychology Today* June 1989, pp.64–66 and Wegner, D. M., *White Bears and Other Unwanted Thoughts: Suppression, Obsession and the Psychology of Mental Control*, (Viking, New York, 1989).

12. Bate, W. J., *Samuel Johnson*, (Chatto and Windus, London, 1978).

Chapter 15

1. Orford, J., *Excessive Appetites: A psychological view of addictions*, (Wiley, Chichester, 1985).

2. Rachman, S., Hodgson, R., *Obsessions and Compulsions*, (Prentice Hall, New York, 1979).

3. Wiepkema, P., 'Abnormal behaviours in farm animals: Ethological implications', *Netherlands Journal of Zoology* 1985; 35: 279–99.

4. Salzman, L., *The Obsessive Personality*, (Science House, New York, 1968).

5. Eysenck, H., 'The conditioning model of neurosis', *The Behavioural and Brain Sciences* 1979; 2: 155–99.

6. Beech, H. R., Perigault, J., 'Toward a theory of obsessional disorder', In: Beech, H. R., (ed.) *Obsessional States*, (Methuen, London, 1974), 113–41.

7. Skoog, G., 'Onset of anancastic conditions,' *Acta Psychiatrica Scandinavica*, 1965; 41: Supplementum 184.

8. Seligman, M. E. P., 'On the generality of the laws of learning', *Psychological Review*, 1970; 77: 406–18.

9. See 5

10. Skinner, B. F. A good account of Skinner's ideas is to be found in *The Behavioural and Brain Sciences* 1984; Vol. 7, No. 4.

11. Mellet, P. G., 'The clinical problem', In: Beech, H. R., (ed.) *Obsessional States*, (Methuen, London, 1974), 55–94 and Beech, H. R., Liddell, A., 'Decision-making, mood states and ritualistic behaviour among obsessional patients,' In: Beech, H. R., (ed.) *Obsessional States*, (Methuen, London, 1974), 143–60.

12. Mellett, P. G., 'The clinical problem,' In: Beech, H. R., (ed.) *Obsessional States*, (Methuen, London, 1974), 55–94.

13. Guirdham, A., *Obsession*, (Neville Spearman, London, 1972).

14. Capstick, N., Seldrup, J. 'A study in the relationship between abnormalities occurring at the time of birth and the subsequent development of obsessional symptoms', *Acta Psychiatrica Scandinavica* 1977; 56: 427–31.

15. See 13

16. Flor-Henry, P., Yeudall, L. T., Koles, Z. J., Howarth, B. G., 'Neuropsychological and power spectral EEG investigations of the obsessive-compulsive syndrome', *Biological Psychiatry* 1979; 14: 119–30. One group of researchers found the volume of a region of the brain, the caudate nucleus, to be significantly less in obsessional patients than in controls (Luxenberg, J. S., Swedo, S. E., Flament, M. F., Friedland, R. P., Rapoport, J., Rapoport, S. I., 'Neuroanatomical abnormalities in obsessive-compulsive disorder detected with quantitative X-ray computed tomography', *American Journal of Psychiatry* 1988; 145: 1089–93).

17. Hartmann, E., *Sleep and Dreaming*, (Little, Brown and Company, Boston, 1970).
Hartmann, E., *The Nightmare*, (Basic Books, New York, 1984).

18. Insel, T. R., Gillin, C., Moore, A., Mendelson, W. B., Loewenstein, R. J., Murphy, D. L., 'The sleep of patients with obsessive-compulsive disorder', *Archives of General Psychiatry* 1982; 39: 1372–7.

19. Zohar, J., Insel, T. R., Zohar-Kadouch, R. C., Hill, J. L., Murphy, D. L., 'Serotonergic responsivity in obsessive-compulsive disorder.' *Archives of General Psychiatry* 1988; 45: 167–72; Zak, J. P., Miller, J. A., Sheehan, D. V., Fanous, B. S. L., 'The potential role of serotonin reuptake inhibitors in the treatment of obsessive compulsive disorder', *Journal of Clinical Psychiatry* 1988; 49: 23–9.

20. Horowitz, M., 'Psychic Trauma', *Archives of General*

Psychiatry, 1969; 20: 552-559.

21. Parkinson, L., Rachman, S., 'Part III – Intrusive thoughts: The effects of an uncontrived stress', *Advances in Behaviour Research and Therapy* 1981; 3: 111-18.

22. Hartmann, E., *The Nightmare*, (Basic Books, New York, 1984).

23. Three authors simultaneously and independently and from different perspectives arrived at rather similar accounts. (1. Reed, G. F., *Obsessional Experience and Compulsive Behaviour – A Cognitive-Structural Approach*, (Academic Press, Orlando, 1985); 2. Pitman, R. K., 'A cybernetic model of obsessive-compulsive psychopathology', *Comprehensive Psychiatry* 1987; 28: 334–43; and 3. Gray, J. A., *The Psychology of Fear and Stress*, (Cambridge University Press, Cambridge, 1988).

24. Orbach, S., *Hunger Strike*, (Faber, London, 1987).

25. Reed, G. F., *Obsessional Experience and Compulsive Behaviour – A Cognitive-Structural Approach*, (Academic Press, Orlando, 1985).

26. Eysenck, H. J., *You and Neurosis*, (Temple Smith, London, 1977) and Eysenck, H. J., *Decline and Fall of the Freudian Empire*, (Penguin, Harmondsworth, 1985).

27. Pitman, R. K., 'A cybernetic model of obsessive-compulsive psychopathology', *Comprehensive Psychiatry* 1987; 28: 334–43.

28. Janet, P., *Les Obsessions et la Psychasthénie*, Vol. 1. (Alcan, Paris, 1903).

29. Hill, D. See Beech, H. R., (ed.) *Obsessional States*, Methuen, London, 1974).

30. Storr, A., *The Dynamics of Creation*, (Secker and Warburg, London, 1972).

Chapter 16

1. Bate, W. J., *Samuel Johnson*, (Chatto and Windus, London, 1978).

2. Wain, J., *Samuel Johnson*, (Macmillan, London, 1974).

3. Lewis, A., 'Problems of obsessional illness', *Proceedings of the Royal Society of Medicine* 1936; 29: 325–36.

4. See 1

5. Quoted in Boswell's *Life*.

6. See 5

7. Chase, P. P., 'The ailments and physicians of Dr Johnson', *Yale Journal of Biology and Medicine*, 1951; 23: 370-9.

8. In his diaries, Johnson reported his suffering from nocturnal flatulence and what he termed 'constrictions' and 'spasms in the stomach', these being so bad as to greatly disturb him over many years, as well as insomnia. His diaries record meticulous attention to his bowels and the quality of the stools that he

passed, though the full significance of this is perhaps lost on the present (non-Freudian) author. Some Johnsonian scholars have wondered why he apparently never questioned a possible association between his insomnia and the immense amounts of tea he took before retiring. He also suffered from asthma. At times, in order to obtain peace of mind and body, Johnson took opium in sufficient quantities to become comatose. Boswell also reported that: 'Such was the heat and irritability of his blood, that not only did he pare his nails to the quick; but scraped the joints of his fingers with a pen-knife, till they seemed quite red and raw.' Never, though, in spite of all Johnson's physical and mental suffering, was death viewed as a welcome escape from pain. Johnson held on to life tenaciously.

9. Thompson, J., *Kierkegaard*, (Victor Gollancz, London, 1974).
10. Andersen, H. C., *The True Story of my Life*, (George Routledge and Sons, London, 1926 edition).
11. See 10
12. Bredsdorff, E., *Hans Christian Andersen*, (Phaidon Press, London, 1975).
13. See 12
14. See 12
15. The irony is described by Lederer, W., *The Kiss of the Snow Queen*, (University of California Press, Berkeley, 1986).
16. See 15
17. See 12
18. See 12
19. Reading Borrow is a considerable challenge requiring some detective work since he manages to combine fact, fiction and fantasy into a uniquely confusing blend even in what appears to be autobiographical material. We can speculate that Borrow met some very articulate obsessionals in the course of his travels, or that he simply invented the characters and their problems, or, as seems much more likely, he wove his own obsessional experiences into the characters he describes. I would imagine there to be a relatively low probability of finding by chance 'out-of-the-closet' obsessional-compulsives in 19th-century rural England. Therefore the first possibility defies statistical expectation, even for someone meeting as many people as Borrow. The second is implausible in my view, since the accounts are far too good to be the product of invention and Borrow was not a noted inventor.
20. Collie, M., *George Borrow: Eccentric* (Cambridge University Press, Cambridge, 1982).
21. Jenkins, H., *The Life of George Borrow*, (John Murray, London, 1924).

22. See 20
23. See 21
24. In the second volume of his autobiography, entitled *The Romany Rye*, Borrow reveals more interesting information relevant to the present study, as well as extolling his own virtues at some length. He returns to consider the rich gentleman in *Lavengro* who has the touching compulsion, and asks if 'the kindness and providence of God' are not revealed in his case. 'This being has great gifts and many amiable qualities but does not everybody see that his besetting sin is selfishness?' The obsessional behaviour is seen as a way of curing the man of his egoism.
25. Maguglin, R., *Howard Hughes – His Achievements and Legacy*, (Wrather Port Properties, Long Beach, 1984); Mathison, R., *His Weird and Wanton Ways – The Secret Life of Howard Hughes*, (Robert Hale, London, 1977).
26. Barlett, D. L., Steele, J. B., *Empire – The Life, Legend and Madness of Howard Hughes*, (André Deutsch, London, 1979).
27. See 26
28. Brownstein, M., Solyom, L., 'The dilemma of Howard Hughes: Paradoxical behaviour in compulsive disorders', *Canadian Journal of Psychiatry* 1986; 31: 238-40.
29. Lax, E., *Woody Allen and his Comedy*, (Elm Tree Books, London, 1976); Guthrie, L., *Woody Allen – a Biography*, (Drake Publishers, New York, 1978); Jacobs, D., . . . *but we need the eggs – The Magic of Woody Allen*, (St. Martin's Press, New York, 1982).
30. Guthrie, L., *Woody Allen – a Biography*, (Drake Publishers, New York, 1978).
31. Schickel, R., 'Woody Allen comes of age', *Time* (April 30th 1979).
32. Cited by Caryn James. See 34
33. See 29
34. James, C., *The Times* (July 12th 1986).
35. Cited by C. James. See 34

Further Reading

Eysenck, H. J., *Decline and Fall of the Freudian Empire*, (Penguin, Harmondsworth, 1986).

Jacobs, D., . . . *but we need the eggs – The Magic of Woody Allen*, (St. Martin's Press, New York, 1982).

Jenike, M. A., Baer L., Minichiello, W. E., *Obsessive-Compulsive Disorders – Theory and Management*, (PSG Publishing Company, Littleton, Massachusetts, 1986).

Mallinger, A., 'The obsessive's myth of control', *Journal of the American Academy of Psychoanalysis* 1984; 12: 147–65.

Marks, I. M., *Fears, Phobias and Rituals*, (Oxford University Press, New York, 1987).

Mavissakalian, M., Turner, S. M., Michelson, L., *Obsessive-Compulsive Disorder*, (Plenum Press, New York, 1985).

Pollak, J., 'Relationship of obsessive-compulsive personality to obsessive compulsive disorder: A review of the literature', *The Journal of Psychology* 1987; 121: 137–48.

Rachman, S. J., 'An anatomy of obsessions', *Behaviour Analysis and Modification* 1978; 2: 253–78.

Rachman, S., Hodgson, R., *Obsessions and Compulsions*, (Prentice Hall, New York, 1979).

Rapoport, J. L., *The Boy who Couldn't Stop Washing* (E. P. Dutton, New York, 1989).

Reed, G. F., *Obsessional Experience and Compulsive Behaviour – A Cognitive-Structural Approach*, (Academic Press, Orlando, 1985).

Wegner, D. M., *White Bears and Other Unwanted Thoughts: Suppression, Obsession and the Psychology of Mental Control*, (Viking, New York, 1989).

Resources

A non-profit-making patient support organization exists in the United States and publishes a quarterly newsletter.

The OCD Foundation Inc.
P. O. Box 9573
New Haven
Connecticut 06535
Telephone (203) 772-0565
The foundation provide technical assistance in starting local self-help groups. Sufferers can be helped to come into contact with fellow-sufferers. Children can find penpals of a similar age who are also sufferers.

The Association for Advancement of Behaviour Therapy
15 West 36th Street
New York
NY 10018
Telephone (212) 279-7970

Information on Clomipramine (Anafranil):
Anafranil Information Hotline
c/o CIBA Geigy, Pharmaceutical Company
556 Morris Avenue
Summit
New Jersey 07901

Information on Fluvoxamine:
Kahli-Duphar
P. O. Box 29560
Columbus
Ohio 43229-1177

Australia:
Obsessive Compulsive Neurosis Support Group
Room 55, Epworth Building
33 Pirie Street
Adelaide SA 5000
Telephone 231 1588 or 362 6772

Index